Bravo!
Best of Bridge
Cookbook

Brand-New Volume
Brand-New Recipes

Robert
ROSE

Bravo! Best of Bridge Cookbook
Text copyright © 2009 by Sally Vaughan-Johnston and The Best of Bridge Publishing Ltd.
Photographs copyright © 2009 by Robert Rose Inc.
Cover and text design copyright © 2009 by Robert Rose Inc.

For complete cataloguing information, see page 337.

The recipes in this book have been carefully tested by our kitchen and our tasters. To the best of our knowledge, they are safe and nutritious for ordinary use and users. For those people with food or other allergies, or who have special food requirements or health issues, please read the suggested contents of each recipe carefully and determine whether or not they may create a problem for you. All recipes are used at the risk of the consumer.

We cannot be responsible for any hazards, loss or damage that may occur as a result of any recipe use.

For those with special needs, allergies, requirements or health problems, in the event of any doubt, please contact your medical adviser prior to the use of any recipe.

Cover design and page layout: PageWave Graphics, Inc.
Editor: Sue Sumeraj
Proofreader: Sheila Wawanash
Indexer: Gillian Watts
Photography: Colin Erricson
Food Styling: Kathryn Robertson
Prop Styling: Charlene Erricson

Cover image: Thai Chicken and Mango Stir-Fry (page 182)

We acknowledge the financial support of the Government of Canada through the Book Publishing Industry Development Program (BPIDP) for our publishing activities.

Published by Robert Rose Inc.
120 Eglinton Avenue East, Suite 800, Toronto, Ontario, Canada M4P 1E2
Tel: (416) 322-6552 Fax: (416) 322-6936

Printed in China

1 2 3 4 5 6 7 8 PPLS 16 15 14 13 12 11 10 09

CONTENTS

INTRODUCTION

IT'S BEEN FIVE YEARS SINCE WE LAST PUBLISHED A NEW BEST OF BRIDGE COOKBOOK. WE DECIDED IT WAS TIME TO RETIRE, CLOSE THE OFFICE AND HANG UP OUR APRONS — WHICH WE DID. BUT WE KEPT ON COOKING, TASTING AND SCRIBBLING KITCHEN NOTES. IN OUR "RETIREMENT," WE HAVE CONTINUED TO EXPAND OUR CULINARY REPERTOIRE THROUGH TRAVEL AND SHARING FOOD WITH FAMILY AND FRIENDS. WE THEN MET SALLY VAUGHAN-JOHNSTON, FOOD WRITER, COOKING PROFESSIONAL AND CULINARY WHIZ. NOT ONLY DID SHE SHARE OUR ENTHUSIASM FOR RETRO RECIPES AND NEW-FANGLED FOODS, BUT SHE HAD THE SAME IRREVERENT SENSE OF HUMOR. AND SO IT BEGAN, AND HERE WE ARE BACK WITH A BRAND-NEW VOLUME OF BRAND-NEW RECIPES.

SALLY SPURRED US ON TO TRY NEW HERBS AND SPICES AND A VARIETY OF OTHER INTERESTING INGREDIENTS THAT ARE NOW WIDELY AVAILABLE IN SUPERMARKETS (HELLO, CHIPOTLE PEPPERS AND FROZEN MANGO CUBES!). WE, IN TURN, AS THE "WISE WOMEN" WE'VE BECOME, GAVE SALLY THE BENEFIT OF OUR CONSIDERABLE ADVICE.

STILL, ONE THING HASN'T CHANGED. OUR MOTTO REMAINS "SIMPLE RECIPES WITH GOURMET RESULTS" AND, AS OUR LOYAL FANS HAVE COME TO EXPECT, THE RECIPES WORK AND THE ONE-LINERS WILL KEEP YOU SMILING IN THE KITCHEN. WE "LADIES" AND SALLY WISH YOU CONTINUED CULINARY SUCCESS AND KNOW YOU WILL ENJOY THIS NEW COLLECTION OF RECIPES.

BRUNCH AND LUNCH

SUNDAY OMELET

THIS HEARTY OMELET IS THE PERFECT BRUNCH FOR FOUR. SERVE WITH SLICES OF HOT, BUTTERY WHOLE WHEAT TOAST.

6	EGGS	6
1/4 CUP	CHOPPED FRESH PARSLEY	50 ML
	SALT AND FRESHLY GROUND BLACK PEPPER	
2	MILD OR HOT ITALIAN SAUSAGES, CASINGS REMOVED	2
1	RED BELL PEPPER, THINLY SLICED	1
1/2	RED ONION, THINLY SLICED	1/2
2	CLOVES GARLIC, MINCED	2
2 TBSP	OLIVE OIL, DIVIDED	25 ML
1 1/2 CUPS	FROZEN DICED OR SHREDDED HASH BROWN POTATOES	375 ML

IN A LARGE BOWL, WHISK EGGS WITH PARSLEY AND SALT AND PEPPER TO TASTE. SET ASIDE. IN A LARGE NONSTICK SKILLET, OVER MEDIUM-HIGH HEAT, COOK SAUSAGE, BREAKING UP WITH A SPATULA, FOR 8 TO 10 MINUTES OR UNTIL BROWNED. DRAIN ON A PAPER TOWEL AND TRANSFER TO A BOWL. DRAIN OFF ALL BUT 1 TBSP (15 ML) FAT FROM PAN. ADD RED PEPPER AND RED ONION; SAUTÉ, STIRRING OCCASIONALLY, FOR 5 MINUTES OR UNTIL SOFTENED AND STARTING TO BROWN. ADD GARLIC AND SAUTÉ FOR 15 SECONDS. TRANSFER TO BOWL WITH SAUSAGE. ADD 1 TBSP (15 ML) OF THE OIL TO PAN AND SAUTÉ POTATOES FOR 10 TO 12 MINUTES OR UNTIL BROWN AND TENDER. TRANSFER TO BOWL WITH SAUSAGE MIXTURE. STIR IN EGG MIXTURE. IN THE SKILLET, HEAT THE REMAINING OIL OVER MEDIUM HEAT.

ADD EGG MIXTURE AND COOK FOR ABOUT 10 SECONDS OR UNTIL EDGES START TO SET. USE A SPATULA TO LIFT EDGES OF OMELET TO ALLOW UNCOOKED EGG TO RUN ONTO THE PAN. WHEN BOTTOM IS SET BUT TOP IS STILL RUNNY, COVER, REDUCE HEAT TO LOW AND COOK FOR 3 TO 5 MINUTES. (OR, IF USING AN OVENPROOF SKILLET, PLACE UNDER A PREHEATED BROILER FOR 2 TO 3 MINUTES TO FINISH COOKING.) CUT INTO WEDGES AND SERVE. SERVES 4.

TIP: EGGS SHOULD ALWAYS BE STORED IN THE REFRIGERATOR IN THEIR ORIGINAL CARTON, WHICH PROTECTS THEM FROM ODORS AND DAMAGE. IF YOU ACCIDENTALLY CRACK AN EGGSHELL, REMOVE THE EGG FROM ITS SHELL, TRANSFER IT TO AN AIRTIGHT CONTAINER IN THE REFRIGERATOR AND USE WITHIN 4 DAYS.

IF YOU LEAVE ME, CAN I COME TOO?

BAKED EGGS-TASY

BAKING EGGS IN RAMEKINS IS AN EASY AND ATTRACTIVE WAY TO COOK BREAKFAST OR A LIGHT SUPPER. THE SIZE IS VERY APPEALING TO KIDS. THE FRENCH TERM FOR BAKED EGGS IS EN COCOTTE. WE SAY "EGG-CELLENT." SERVE WITH TOAST OR TOASTED MINI BAGELS.

2	SLICES BACON, CHOPPED	2
2	GREEN ONIONS, CHOPPED	2
1/2 CUP	FROZEN DICED HASH BROWN POTATOES	125 ML
	SALT AND FRESHLY GROUND BLACK PEPPER	
4	EGGS	4
4 TBSP	WHIPPING (35%) CREAM	60 ML
	BOILING WATER	

PREHEAT OVEN TO 375°F (190°C). BUTTER FOUR 3/4-CUP (175 ML) RAMEKINS OR OVENPROOF COFFEE CUPS. PLACE RAMEKINS IN A 9-INCH (2.5 L) METAL BAKING PAN. IN A MEDIUM SKILLET, OVER MEDIUM HEAT, FRY BACON UNTIL STARTING TO BROWN AND TURN CRISPY. ADD GREEN ONIONS, HASH BROWNS AND SALT AND PEPPER TO TASTE; COOK, STIRRING FREQUENTLY, FOR 5 MINUTES. DIVIDE BACON MIXTURE AMONG THE RAMEKINS (THEY WILL BE ONLY HALF FULL). CAREFULLY BREAK AN EGG INTO EACH RAMEKIN. SPRINKLE WITH SALT AND PEPPER. DRIZZLE 1 TBSP (15 ML) WHIPPING CREAM OVER EACH EGG. POUR ENOUGH BOILING WATER INTO THE BAKING PAN TO COME HALFWAY UP THE OUTSIDE OF THE RAMEKINS. COVER LOOSELY WITH FOIL AND BAKE FOR ABOUT 20 MINUTES OR UNTIL THE WHITE OF THE EGGS IS FIRM. SERVES 4.

BREAKFAST BAGEL

DON'T WAIT UNTIL MORNING. THESE ARE GREAT AT ANY TIME OF DAY.

4	SLICES BACON	4
2	EGGS	2
1/4 CUP	SHREDDED SHARP (OLD) CHEDDAR CHEESE	50 ML
2 TBSP	MILK	25 ML
1	GREEN ONION, CHOPPED	1
2 1/2 TBSP	BUTTER, SOFTENED, DIVIDED	32 ML
1 TBSP	DIJON MUSTARD	15 ML
2	BAGELS, HALVED AND TOASTED	2
2	SLICES TOMATO	2

IN A MEDIUM SKILLET, OVER MEDIUM-HIGH HEAT, FRY BACON UNTIL CRISP. DRAIN ON A PAPER TOWEL AND SET ASIDE. IN A SMALL BOWL, WHISK TOGETHER EGGS, CHEESE, MILK AND GREEN ONION. IN ANOTHER SMALL BOWL, COMBINE 2 TBSP (25 ML) OF THE BUTTER AND MUSTARD; SET ASIDE. IN A SMALL OMELET PAN, MELT THE REMAINING BUTTER OVER MEDIUM HEAT. ADD EGG MIXTURE, SWIRLING TO COVER BOTTOM OF PAN. COOK, LIFTING EDGES OF OMELET TO ALLOW UNCOOKED EGG TO RUN UNDER, FOR ABOUT 2 MINUTES OR UNTIL FIRM. GENTLY FOLD IN HALF AND, USING EDGE OF SPATULA, CUT INTO TWO WEDGES. SPREAD BAGELS WITH BUTTER-MUSTARD MIXTURE. PLACE A TOMATO SLICE ON THE BOTTOM HALF OF EACH BAGEL AND TOP WITH AN OMELET WEDGE, TWO BACON SLICES AND THE TOP HALF OF THE BAGEL. SERVES 2.

FAVORITE FRENCH TOAST

*HERE'S A GREAT WAY TO USE UP
LEFTOVER FRENCH BREAD.*

2	EGGS	2
2/3 CUP	MILK	150 ML
2 TBSP	GRANULATED SUGAR	25 ML
I TSP	GROUND CINNAMON	5 ML
I TSP	VANILLA EXTRACT	5 ML
4	THICK SLICES DAY-OLD FRENCH BREAD	4
2 TBSP	BUTTER OR VEGETABLE OIL	25 ML
	CONFECTIONER'S (ICING) SUGAR	
	MAPLE OR BERRY SYRUP	

IN A MEDIUM BOWL, WHISK TOGETHER EGGS, MILK, GRANULATED SUGAR, CINNAMON AND VANILLA. SOAK BREAD THOROUGHLY IN EGG MIXTURE. IN A LARGE SKILLET, MELT HALF THE BUTTER OVER MEDIUM HEAT. COOK SOAKED BREAD, TWO PIECES AT A TIME, FOR 3 TO 4 MINUTES PER SIDE OR UNTIL CRISP AND BROWNED, MELTING THE REMAINING BUTTER BEFORE THE SECOND BATCH. DUST WITH CONFECTIONER'S SUGAR AND SERVE WITH MAPLE SYRUP. SERVES 2.

TIP: FRENCH TOAST IS ALSO GOOD MADE WITH WHOLE WHEAT BREAD, RAISIN BREAD OR BRIOCHE, AN EGG BREAD THAT'S AVAILABLE IN MANY WELL-STOCKED GROCERY STORES.

OVERNIGHT RASPBERRY FRENCH TOAST

THE BEST EVER MAKE-AHEAD BREAKFAST.

8	SLICES WHITE BREAD, TORN INTO SMALL PIECES	8
1	PACKAGE (8 OZ/250 G) CREAM CHEESE, CUT INTO SMALL PIECES	1
1 CUP	FRESH OR FROZEN RASPBERRIES	250 ML
1/2 CUP	SLICED ALMONDS, TOASTED (SEE TIP, PAGE 61)	125 ML
6	EGGS	6
1/2 CUP	GRANULATED SUGAR, DIVIDED	125 ML
1/2 CUP	MILK	125 ML
1/2 CUP	HALF-AND-HALF (10%) CREAM	125 ML
1 TSP	GROUND CINNAMON	5 ML
	MAPLE OR FRUIT SYRUP	

GREASE AN 8-INCH (2 L) SQUARE GLASS BAKING DISH. SCATTER HALF THE BREAD PIECES IN DISH. ARRANGE CREAM CHEESE, RASPBERRIES AND ALMONDS ON TOP. FINISH WITH THE REMAINING BREAD PIECES. IN A LARGE BOWL, WHISK TOGETHER EGGS, 1/4 CUP (50 ML) OF THE SUGAR, MILK, CREAM AND CINNAMON. POUR OVER BREAD. SPRINKLE THE REMAINING SUGAR OVER TOP. COVER WITH FOIL AND REFRIGERATE OVERNIGHT.

PREHEAT OVEN TO 350°F (180°C). BAKE FRENCH TOAST, COVERED WITH FOIL, FOR 30 MINUTES. REMOVE FOIL AND BAKE FOR 30 MINUTES OR UNTIL PUFFY AND GOLDEN BROWN. SERVE WITH MAPLE SYRUP. SERVES 6.

TIP: IF YOU USE FROZEN RASPBERRIES, THERE'S NO NEED TO THAW THEM FIRST.

WHOLE WHEAT CINNAMON WAFFLES

IF YOU CAN MAKE PANCAKES, YOU CAN MAKE WAFFLES, BECAUSE THE BATTER IS MUCH THE SAME. ALTHOUGH THESE ARE HIGH IN FIBER, THEY ARE REMARKABLY LIGHT AND FLUFFY. SERVE WITH "MASSACRED" BERRIES (PAGE 311) AND WHIPPED CREAM FOR A SPECIAL BRUNCH.

2	EGGS	2
1 1/2 CUPS	BUTTERMILK (SEE TIP, OPPOSITE)	375 ML
1/4 CUP	VEGETABLE OIL	50 ML
1 TSP	VANILLA EXTRACT	5 ML
3/4 CUP	ALL-PURPOSE FLOUR	175 ML
1/2 CUP	WHOLE WHEAT FLOUR	125 ML
1/4 CUP	OAT BRAN	50 ML
2 TBSP	GRANULATED SUGAR	25 ML
1 TBSP	BAKING POWDER	15 ML
1 TSP	GROUND CINNAMON	5 ML
	VEGETABLE COOKING SPRAY	

PREHEAT AN ELECTRIC WAFFLE IRON. IN A MEDIUM BOWL, WHISK TOGETHER EGGS, BUTTERMILK, OIL AND VANILLA. IN ANOTHER BOWL, WHISK TOGETHER ALL-PURPOSE AND WHOLE WHEAT FLOURS, OAT BRAN, SUGAR, BAKING POWDER AND CINNAMON. ADD EGG MIXTURE TO FLOUR MIXTURE AND STIR UNTIL JUST COMBINED. GREASE THE WAFFLE IRON WITH COOKING SPRAY. SPOON ABOUT 1/3 CUP (75 ML) BATTER PER WAFFLE INTO IRON. CLOSE THE LID AND COOK UNTIL WAFFLES ARE GOLDEN BROWN AND STEAM STOPS COMING OUT THE SIDES. REPEAT WITH THE REMAINING BATTER. MAKES ABOUT 8 WAFFLES, DEPENDING ON SIZE OF WAFFLE IRON.

MAKE AHEAD: STORE WAFFLES IN AN AIRTIGHT CONTAINER IN THE REFRIGERATOR FOR UP TO 2 DAYS OR WRAP INDIVIDUALLY IN PLASTIC WRAP, PLACE IN AN AIRTIGHT CONTAINER AND FREEZE FOR UP TO 1 MONTH. REHEAT IN THE TOASTER.

TIP: IF YOU DON'T HAVE BUTTERMILK, STIR 1 TBSP (15 ML) VINEGAR OR LEMON JUICE INTO 1 CUP (250 ML) WHOLE, 2% OR SKIM MILK. LET IT SIT FOR A FEW MINUTES, UNTIL IT LOOKS LUMPY, THEN PROCEED WITH THE RECIPE.

VARIATION: USE $\frac{1}{4}$ CUP (50 ML) CORNMEAL IN PLACE OF THE OAT BRAN AND 1 TSP (5 ML) GRATED ORANGE ZEST INSTEAD OF THE CINNAMON.

I WOULD BE UNSTOPPABLE IF I COULD JUST GET STARTED!

CHOCOLATE CRÊPES
AND TOFFEE NUT BANANAS

A SWEET BREAKFAST TREAT FOR THE WHOLE FAMILY. THE CRÊPES AND THE TOFFEE NUT BANANAS CAN BE MADE AHEAD OF TIME. DON'T BE INTIMIDATED BY CRÊPES — THEY'RE JUST THIN PANCAKES WITH A FRENCH ATTITUDE, AND THEY'RE VERY EASY TO MAKE.

1 CUP	ALL-PURPOSE FLOUR	250 ML
2 TBSP	UNSWEETENED COCOA POWDER, SIFTED	25 ML
2 TBSP	GRANULATED SUGAR	25 ML
3	EGGS	3
1½ CUPS	MILK, DIVIDED	375 ML
2 TBSP	MELTED BUTTER, COOLED, OR VEGETABLE OIL	25 ML
	VEGETABLE OIL	
	TOFFEE NUT BANANAS (SEE RECIPE, OPPOSITE)	

IN A LARGE BOWL, WHISK TOGETHER FLOUR, COCOA AND SUGAR. MAKE A WELL IN THE CENTER AND ADD EGGS AND ½ CUP (50 ML) OF THE MILK; WHISK UNTIL SMOOTH. WHISK IN THE REMAINING MILK AND BUTTER. HEAT AN 8-INCH (20 CM) NONSTICK OMELET PAN OVER MEDIUM HEAT UNTIL DROPS OF WATER SKITTER ACROSS THE SURFACE. SWIRL ½ TSP (2 ML) OIL OVER BOTTOM OF PAN. POUR A SCANT ¼ CUP (50 ML) BATTER INTO THE PAN, TILTING BACK AND FORTH UNTIL BATTER COVERS THE BOTTOM. COOK FOR 10 SECONDS OR UNTIL THE BOTTOM IS STARTING TO BROWN. USING A SPATULA, FLIP THE CRÊPE OVER AND COOK FOR 10 SECONDS. SLIDE ONTO A PLATE. REPEAT WITH THE REMAINING BATTER, OILING PAN

LIGHTLY BETWEEN CRÊPES. TO SERVE, FOLD EACH CRÊPE INTO QUARTERS, MAKING A FAN SHAPE. PLACE TWO ON EACH PLATE AND SPOON TOFFEE NUT BANANAS OVER TOP. SERVES 6.

MAKE AHEAD: LAYER CRÊPES BETWEEN SHEETS OF WAXED PAPER IN AN AIRTIGHT CONTAINER AND REFRIGERATE FOR UP TO 3 DAYS OR FREEZE FOR UP 1 MONTH. REHEAT FROM FROZEN IN SMALL BATCHES IN THE MICROWAVE FOR 30 TO 40 SECONDS.

TOFFEE NUT BANANAS

½ CUP	BUTTER	125 ML
½ CUP	LIQUID HONEY	125 ML
½ CUP	CHOPPED WALNUTS OR PECANS	125 ML
½ CUP	WHIPPING (35%) CREAM	125 ML
2	BANANAS, SLICED INTO THICK COINS	2

IN A MEDIUM NONSTICK SKILLET, MELT BUTTER AND HONEY OVER MEDIUM HEAT; SIMMER FOR 3 TO 4 MINUTES OR UNTIL PALE GOLDEN. STIR IN WALNUTS AND SIMMER FOR 2 TO 3 MINUTES OR UNTIL SAUCE DARKENS AND THICKENS. REMOVE FROM HEAT AND GRADUALLY ADD WHIPPING CREAM. (BE VERY CAREFUL; IT WILL SPLATTER!) GENTLY STIR IN BANANAS. MAKES ABOUT 2 CUPS (500 ML).

MAKE AHEAD: TOFFEE NUT SAUCE, WITHOUT THE BANANAS, CAN BE STORED IN THE REFRIGERATOR FOR UP TO 5 DAYS. IT THICKENS WHEN COLD, SO WARM BEFORE ADDING THE BANANAS AND SERVING. IT'S ALSO AMAZING OVER ICE CREAM.

HAM AND MUSHROOM CRÊPE CASSEROLE

GOODY — A MAKE-AHEAD! WHEN THE COMPANY COMES IN THE DOOR, THE CASSEROLE GOES IN THE OVEN.

CRÊPES

I CUP	ALL-PURPOSE FLOUR	250 ML
3	EGGS	3
1 1/2 CUPS	MILK, DIVIDED	375 ML
2 TBSP	MELTED BUTTER, COOLED, OR VEGETABLE OIL	25 ML
	VEGETABLE OIL	

CHEESE SAUCE

2 1/2 TBSP	BUTTER	32 ML
3 TBSP	ALL-PURPOSE FLOUR	45 ML
2 CUPS	MILK, WARMED	500 ML
PINCH	GROUND NUTMEG	PINCH
2 TSP	DIJON MUSTARD	IO ML
I CUP	GRATED GRUYÈRE CHEESE	250 ML
1/2 CUP	FRESHLY GRATED PARMESAN CHEESE	I25 ML
	SALT AND FRESHLY GROUND BLACK PEPPER	

FILLING

I TBSP	VEGETABLE OIL	15 ML
3 CUPS	DICED MUSHROOMS	750 ML
1 1/2 CUPS	FINELY CHOPPED HAM	375 ML
2	GREEN ONIONS, CHOPPED	2
1/4 CUP	FRESHLY GRATED PARMESAN CHEESE	50 ML

CRÊPES: PLACE FLOUR IN A LARGE BOWL. MAKE A WELL IN THE CENTER AND ADD EGGS AND $\frac{1}{2}$ CUP (50 ML) OF THE MILK; WHISK UNTIL SMOOTH. WHISK IN THE REMAINING MILK AND BUTTER. HEAT AN 8-INCH (20 CM) NONSTICK OMELET PAN OVER MEDIUM HEAT UNTIL DROPS OF WATER SKITTER ACROSS THE SURFACE. SWIRL $\frac{1}{2}$ TSP (2 ML) OIL OVER BOTTOM OF PAN. POUR A SCANT $\frac{1}{4}$ CUP (50 ML) BATTER INTO THE PAN, TILTING BACK AND FORTH UNTIL BATTER COVERS THE BOTTOM. COOK FOR 10 SECONDS OR UNTIL THE BOTTOM IS STARTING TO BROWN. USING A SPATULA, FLIP THE CRÊPE OVER AND COOK FOR 10 SECONDS. SLIDE ONTO A PLATE. REPEAT WITH THE REMAINING BATTER, OILING PAN LIGHTLY BETWEEN CRÊPES.

CHEESE SAUCE: IN A LARGE SAUCEPAN, MELT BUTTER OVER MEDIUM HEAT. STIR IN FLOUR AND COOK FOR 2 TO 3 MINUTES OR UNTIL IT LOOKS SANDY. GRADUALLY WHISK IN MILK AND COOK, STIRRING CONSTANTLY, FOR 8 MINUTES OR UNTIL THICKENED. STIR IN NUTMEG AND MUSTARD. REMOVE FROM HEAT AND STIR IN GRUYÈRE AND THE $\frac{1}{2}$ CUP (125 ML) PARMESAN UNTIL MELTED. SEASON WITH SALT AND PEPPER TO TASTE.

FILLING: IN A LARGE SKILLET, HEAT OIL OVER MEDIUM HEAT. SAUTÉ MUSHROOMS FOR 5 TO 7 MINUTES OR UNTIL THEY BEGIN TO BROWN AND ANY LIQUID HAS EVAPORATED. STIR IN HAM, GREEN ONIONS AND ABOUT 2 TBSP (25 ML) OF THE CHEESE SAUCE.

CONTINUED ON NEXT PAGE...

HAM AND MUSHROOM CRÊPE CASSEROLE (CONTINUED)

PREHEAT OVEN TO 375°F (190°C). BUTTER A 13- BY 9-INCH (33 BY 23 CM) BAKING DISH. LAY CRÊPES OUT ON A CLEAN COUNTERTOP. SPOON ABOUT 3 TBSP (45 ML) FILLING DOWN THE CENTER OF EACH CRÊPE. FOLD EDGES OF CRÊPES OVER TO ENCLOSE THE FILLING. PLACE CRÊPES, SEAM SIDE DOWN, IN PREPARED BAKING DISH. SPOON CHEESE SAUCE OVER TOP AND SPRINKLE WITH THE 1/4 CUP (50 ML) PARMESAN. BAKE FOR ABOUT 25 MINUTES OR UNTIL SAUCE IS BUBBLING AND TOP IS BROWNED. SERVES 6 TO 8.

MAKE AHEAD: AFTER ASSEMBLING THE CRÊPES (BUT BEFORE BAKING), LET COOL, COVER AND REFRIGERATE FOR UP TO I DAY. INCREASE THE BAKING TIME TO ABOUT 35 MINUTES.

VARIATION: FRESHLY MADE CRÊPES ARE ALSO DELICIOUS SERVED WARM WITH NOTHING MORE THAN A SQUEEZE OF LEMON JUICE AND A LIGHT SPRINKLING OF SUGAR. TRY THEM IN PLACE OF PANCAKES AT BREAKFAST FOR A CHANGE.

I LIVE IN A WORLD OF MY OWN, BUT THAT'S OKAY — THEY KNOW ME HERE.

MUSHROOM AND HAM MINI PIZZAS

OKAY, IT'S TIME TO STOP BUYING THOSE EXPENSIVE FROZEN PIZZAS. YOU CAN DO THIS!

2 TBSP	VEGETABLE OIL	25 ML
4 CUPS	SLICED MUSHROOMS	1 L
2	CLOVES GARLIC, MINCED	2
2 TBSP	DRY WHITE WINE OR CHICKEN BROTH	25 ML
1 TSP	DRIED OREGANO	5 ML
	SALT AND FRESHLY GROUND BLACK PEPPER	
1 CUP	CHOPPED BOILED HAM	250 ML
1/4 CUP	CHOPPED FRESH PARSLEY	50 ML
4	GREEK-STYLE (NO POCKET) PITAS OR NAAN	4
	OLIVE OIL FOR BRUSHING	
1/4 CUP	FRESHLY GRATED PARMESAN CHEESE	50 ML
3 CUPS	SHREDDED MOZZARELLA CHEESE	750 ML

PREHEAT OVEN TO 375°F (190°C). IN A LARGE SKILLET, HEAT VEGETABLE OIL OVER MEDIUM HEAT. SAUTÉ MUSHROOMS FOR 5 TO 7 MINUTES OR UNTIL THEY BEGIN TO BROWN AND ANY LIQUID HAS EVAPORATED. ADD GARLIC, WINE, OREGANO AND SALT AND PEPPER TO TASTE; SAUTÉ FOR 2 MINUTES. STIR IN HAM AND PARSLEY. REMOVE FROM HEAT AND SET ASIDE. PLACE PITAS ON A LARGE BAKING SHEET. BRUSH TOPS WITH OLIVE OIL AND SPRINKLE WITH PARMESAN. SPREAD MUSHROOM MIXTURE OVER TOP OF PITAS, LEAVING A 1/2-INCH (1 CM) BORDER. SPRINKLE WITH MOZZARELLA. BAKE FOR 12 TO 15 MINUTES OR UNTIL CHEESE IS BUBBLING AND EDGES OF PIZZAS ARE BROWNED. CUT INTO QUARTERS AND SERVE IMMEDIATELY. SERVES 4.

DESPERATION ZUCCHINI QUICHE

HALLELUJAH — ANOTHER WAY TO DEAL WITH ALL THAT
ZUCCHINI. A FROZEN PIE SHELL CUTS THE WORK IN
HALF, AND NOW YOU HAVE BRUNCH, LUNCH OR DINNER
WITH A DIFFERENCE. SERVE WITH GREEN SALAD WITH
TOASTED PECANS AND CITRUS DRESSING (PAGE 70).

I	9-INCH (23 CM) FROZEN DEEP-DISH PIE SHELL	I
2	LARGE ZUCCHINI, GRATED	2
I TBSP	SALT	15 ML
I TBSP	BUTTER	15 ML
I	BUNCH GREEN ONIONS, THINLY SLICED (ABOUT $3/4$ CUP/175 ML)	I
4	EGGS	4
$2/3$ CUP	WHIPPING (35%) CREAM	150 ML
I CUP	CRUMBLED STILTON OR OTHER FIRM BLUE CHEESE (ABOUT 4 OZ/125 G)	250 ML
$1/3$ CUP	FRESHLY GRATED PARMESAN CHEESE	75 ML
	SALT AND FRESHLY GROUND BLACK PEPPER	

PREHEAT OVEN TO 375ºF (190ºC). REMOVE PIE SHELL FROM
FREEZER, PLACE ON A BAKING SHEET AND LET THAW FOR
15 MINUTES. PRICK BOTTOM AND SIDES WITH A FORK.
LOOSELY FIT PARCHMENT PAPER IN PIE SHELL AND FILL
WITH DRIED BEANS OR PIE WEIGHTS. BAKE FOR 8 MINUTES
OR UNTIL LIGHTLY BROWNED. REMOVE BEANS AND PAPER
AND LET PIE SHELL COOL. REDUCE OVEN TEMPERATURE TO
350ºF (180ºC).

MEANWHILE, PLACE ZUCCHINI IN A STRAINER, SPRINKLE
WITH SALT AND LET STAND FOR 30 MINUTES. RINSE
ZUCCHINI, PLACE IN A CLEAN TEA TOWEL AND WRING OUT

ALL MOISTURE. IN A LARGE SKILLET, MELT BUTTER OVER MEDIUM-HIGH HEAT. SAUTÉ ZUCCHINI AND GREEN ONIONS FOR 5 MINUTES OR UNTIL ANY LIQUID HAS EVAPORATED. REMOVE FROM HEAT AND LET COOL COMPLETELY.

IN A MEDIUM BOWL, WHISK TOGETHER EGGS, CREAM, STILTON, PARMESAN AND SALT AND PEPPER TO TASTE. SCATTER ZUCCHINI MIXTURE OVER BOTTOM OF PIE SHELL. POUR EGG MIXTURE OVER TOP. BAKE FOR 30 MINUTES OR UNTIL PUFFY AND SET. THE QUICHE WILL FALL SHORTLY AFTER IT COMES OUT OF THE OVEN. SERVES 6 TO 8.

MAKE AHEAD: AFTER COOLING, THE ZUCCHINI MIXTURE CAN BE STORED IN AN AIRTIGHT CONTAINER IN THE REFRIGERATOR FOR UP TO 1 DAY.

TIP: STILTON IS A RICH, CRUMBLY AND RELATIVELY MILD BLUE CHEESE THAT IS SUITABLE FOR MANY RECIPES. YOU MAY SUBSTITUTE OTHER BLUE-VEINED CHEESES, BUT KEEP IN MIND THAT ROQUEFORT, MADE FROM SHEEP'S MILK, AND GORGONZOLA ARE SOFTER AND CONSIDERABLY MORE PUNGENT. YOU MAY NEED TO USE SMALLER QUANTITIES OF THESE VARIETIES IN YOUR RECIPE.

IF YOU ARE GOOD, YOU WILL BE ASSIGNED ALL THE WORK. IF YOU ARE REALLY GOOD, YOU WILL GET OUT OF IT.

LEEK AND BACON QUICHE

SERVE WITH TOMATO HALVES THAT ARE SPRINKLED WITH PARMESAN CHEESE AND BAKED.

1	9-INCH (23 CM) FROZEN DEEP-DISH PIE SHELL	1
5	SLICES BACON, CHOPPED	5
1 TBSP	BUTTER	15 ML
1	LARGE LEEK, TRIMMED AND THINLY SLICED (SEE TIP, OPPOSITE)	1
4	EGGS	4
1 CUP	WHIPPING (35%) CREAM	250 ML
2 TBSP	DIJON MUSTARD, DIVIDED	25 ML
	SALT AND FRESHLY GROUND BLACK PEPPER	

PREHEAT OVEN TO 375°F (190°C). REMOVE PIE SHELL FROM FREEZER, PLACE ON A BAKING SHEET AND LET THAW FOR 15 MINUTES. PRICK BOTTOM AND SIDES WITH A FORK. LOOSELY FIT PARCHMENT PAPER IN PIE SHELL AND FILL WITH DRIED BEANS OR PIE WEIGHTS. BAKE FOR 8 MINUTES OR UNTIL LIGHTLY BROWNED. REMOVE BEANS AND PAPER AND LET PIE SHELL COOL. REDUCE OVEN TEMPERATURE TO 350°F (180°C).

MEANWHILE, IN A LARGE SKILLET, OVER MEDIUM-HIGH HEAT, SAUTÉ BACON UNTIL CRISP. DRAIN ON A PAPER TOWEL AND SET ASIDE. DRAIN FAT FROM PAN. ADD BUTTER TO PAN AND MELT OVER MEDIUM-HIGH HEAT. SAUTÉ LEEK FOR ABOUT 5 MINUTES OR UNTIL SOFTENED BUT NOT BROWNED. REMOVE FROM HEAT AND LET COOL COMPLETELY.

IN A MEDIUM BOWL, WHISK TOGETHER EGGS, CREAM, 1 TBSP (15 ML) OF THE MUSTARD AND SALT AND PEPPER TO TASTE. BRUSH THE REMAINING MUSTARD OVER BOTTOM OF COOLED PIE SHELL. SPOON BACON AND LEEKS INTO PIE SHELL. POUR EGG MIXTURE OVER TOP. BAKE FOR 30 MINUTES OR UNTIL PUFFY AND SET. THE QUICHE WILL FALL SHORTLY AFTER IT COMES OUT OF THE OVEN. SERVES 6 TO 8.

TIP: MANY RECIPES CALL FOR ONLY THE WHITE PART OF THE LEEK, BUT WE THINK THIS IS A WASTE. USE AS MUCH OF THE GREEN PART AS YOU WANT! LEEKS GENERALLY CONTAIN DIRT BETWEEN THEIR LAYERS. THE EASIEST WAY TO CLEAN THEM IS TO SWIRL CHOPPED OR SLICED LEEKS IN A LARGE BOWL OF WATER. LET THE DIRT FALL TO THE BOTTOM AND REMOVE LEEKS WITH A SLOTTED SPOON. REPEAT IF NECESSARY.

THE WORKERS AT THE FEDERAL MINT WENT ON STRIKE TODAY — THEY WANT TO MAKE LESS MONEY.

QUESADILLAS, FOUR WAYS

EACH OF THESE VARIATIONS MAKES ENOUGH FILLING FOR ONE LARGE FLOUR TORTILLA.

PEPPERY CHEESE QUESADILLAS

1	9-INCH (23 CM) SPINACH-FLAVORED FLOUR TORTILLA	1
1/2 CUP	SHREDDED JALAPEÑO MONTEREY JACK OR HAVARTI CHEESE	125 ML
1	PICKLED JALAPEÑO PEPPER, CHOPPED	1
2 TBSP	CHOPPED FRESH CILANTRO	25 ML
2 TSP	OLIVE OR VEGETABLE OIL	10 ML

LAY TORTILLA ON A WORK SURFACE. SPRINKLE CHEESE OVER HALF THE TORTILLA. TOP WITH JALAPEÑO AND CILANTRO. FOLD UNCOVERED HALF OVER FILLING AND BRUSH BOTH SIDES WITH OIL. HEAT A LARGE NONSTICK SKILLET OVER MEDIUM-HIGH HEAT. COOK QUESADILLA, PRESSING DOWN GENTLY WITH A SPATULA, FOR 3 TO 4 MINUTES PER SIDE OR UNTIL BROWNED AND CHEESE IS MELTED. TRANSFER TO A CUTTING BOARD AND CUT INTO 3 TRIANGLES. SERVES 1.

ITALIAN-STYLE QUESADILLAS

1	9-INCH (23 CM) TOMATO-BASIL-FLAVORED FLOUR TORTILLA	1
2	SLICES PROSCIUTTO	2
1/3 CUP	SHREDDED MOZZARELLA CHEESE	75 ML
3	LARGE BASIL LEAVES, SHREDDED	3
1/2	TOMATO, SEEDED AND CHOPPED	1/2
1 TBSP	FRESHLY GRATED PARMESAN CHEESE	15 ML
2 TSP	OLIVE OR VEGETABLE OIL	10 ML

LAY TORTILLA ON A WORK SURFACE. ARRANGE PROSCIUTTO OVER HALF THE TORTILLA. TOP WITH MOZZARELLA, BASIL, TOMATO AND PARMESAN. FOLD UNCOVERED HALF OVER FILLING AND BRUSH BOTH SIDES WITH OIL. HEAT A LARGE NONSTICK SKILLET OVER MEDIUM-HIGH HEAT. COOK QUESADILLA, PRESSING DOWN GENTLY WITH A SPATULA, FOR 3 TO 4 MINUTES PER SIDE OR UNTIL BROWNED AND CHEESE IS MELTED. TRANSFER TO A CUTTING BOARD AND CUT INTO 3 TRIANGLES. SERVES 1.

SPINACH AND FETA QUESADILLAS

1	9-INCH (23 CM) SUN-DRIED TOMATO–FLAVORED FLOUR TORTILLA	1
2 TBSP	SUN-DRIED TOMATO PESTO (SEE TIP, PAGE 53)	25 ML
1/4 CUP	SHREDDED MOZZARELLA CHEESE	50 ML
1/4 CUP	CRUMBLED FETA CHEESE	50 ML
8 TO 10	BABY SPINACH LEAVES	8 TO 10
1/2	TOMATO, SEEDED AND CHOPPED	1/2
2 TSP	OLIVE OR VEGETABLE OIL	10 ML

LAY TORTILLA ON A WORK SURFACE. SPREAD PESTO OVER HALF THE TORTILLA. TOP WITH MOZZARELLA, FETA, SPINACH AND TOMATO. FOLD UNCOVERED HALF OVER FILLING AND BRUSH BOTH SIDES WITH OIL. HEAT A LARGE NONSTICK SKILLET OVER MEDIUM-HIGH HEAT. COOK QUESADILLA, PRESSING DOWN GENTLY WITH A SPATULA, FOR 3 TO 4 MINUTES PER SIDE OR UNTIL BROWNED AND CHEESE IS MELTED. TRANSFER TO A CUTTING BOARD AND CUT INTO 3 TRIANGLES. SERVES 1.

CONTINUED ON NEXT PAGE...

SMOKED GOUDA, CHICKEN AND APPLE QUESADILLAS

1	9-INCH (23 CM) FLOUR TORTILLA	1
1 TBSP	PEACH OR APRICOT JAM	15 ML
1/4 CUP	SHREDDED MOZZARELLA CHEESE	50 ML
4 TO 5	THIN SLICES APPLE	4 TO 5
1	GREEN ONION, THINLY SLICED	1
1/4 CUP	CHOPPED COOKED CHICKEN	50 ML
1/4 CUP	SHREDDED SMOKED GOUDA CHEESE	50 ML
2 TSP	OLIVE OR VEGETABLE OIL	10 ML

LAY TORTILLA ON A WORK SURFACE. SPREAD JAM OVER HALF THE TORTILLA. SPRINKLE MOZZARELLA OVER THE JAM. TOP WITH APPLE, GREEN ONION, CHICKEN AND GOUDA. FOLD UNCOVERED HALF OVER FILLING AND BRUSH BOTH SIDES WITH OIL. HEAT A LARGE NONSTICK SKILLET OVER MEDIUM-HIGH HEAT. COOK QUESADILLA, PRESSING DOWN GENTLY WITH A SPATULA, FOR 3 TO 4 MINUTES PER SIDE OR UNTIL BROWNED AND CHEESE IS MELTED. TRANSFER TO A CUTTING BOARD AND CUT INTO 3 TRIANGLES. SERVES 1.

PLOUGHMAN'S LUNCH SANDWICH

GOOD-QUALITY AGED CHEDDAR CHEESE AND A FRESH CRUSTY BAGUETTE ARE ESSENTIAL TO THIS POPULAR ENGLISH LUNCH. SERVE WITH POTATO CHIPS AND BEER.

1/2 CUP	GRAINY DIJON MUSTARD	125 ML
1/2 CUP	MANGO CHUTNEY	125 ML
1	FRESH BAGUETTE, HALVED HORIZONTALLY	1
12 OZ	GOOD-QUALITY SHARP (OLD) CHEDDAR CHEESE, SLICED	375 G
2	CRISP APPLES (SUCH AS GOLDEN DELICIOUS), THINLY SLICED	2
1	RED ONION, VERY THINLY SLICED	1
2 CUPS	GREEN LEAF LETTUCE, TORN	500 ML

IN A BOWL, WHISK TOGETHER MUSTARD AND CHUTNEY. SPREAD MUSTARD MIXTURE ON BOTH HALVES OF BAGUETTE. ARRANGE CHEESE, APPLES, ONION AND LETTUCE ON BOTTOM HALF AND COVER WITH TOP HALF. CUT INTO 4 WEDGES. SERVES 4.

WHEN SOMEONE TELLS YOU NOTHING IS IMPOSSIBLE, ASK HIM TO DRIBBLE A FOOTBALL.

RUSTIC CHEDDAR AND HERB SCONES

THESE ARE THE CHEESIEST CHEESE SCONES YOU'VE EVER HAD. YOU MUST USE HIGH-QUALITY AGED CHEDDAR — YOU'RE WORTH IT. YUMMY WITH A BOWL OF SOUP.

2 2/3 CUPS	ALL-PURPOSE FLOUR	650 ML
1 TBSP	BAKING POWDER	15 ML
3/4 TSP	SALT	3 ML
PINCH	CAYENNE PEPPER	PINCH
1/2 CUP	UNSALTED BUTTER, CUT INTO SMALL CUBES	125 ML
3	EGGS	3
1/2 CUP	HALF-AND-HALF (10%) CREAM	125 ML
2 TBSP	DIJON MUSTARD	25 ML
2 CUPS	SHREDDED SHARP (OLD) CHEDDAR CHEESE	500 ML
1/2 CUP	FRESHLY GRATED PARMESAN CHEESE	125 ML
2 TBSP	CHOPPED FRESH DILL OR CHIVES	25 ML

PREHEAT OVEN TO 400°F (200°C). LINE A LARGE BAKING SHEET WITH PARCHMENT PAPER. SIFT FLOUR, BAKING POWDER, SALT AND CAYENNE INTO A LARGE BOWL. ADD BUTTER AND RUB FLOUR MIXTURE THROUGH YOUR FINGERTIPS UNTIL IT RESEMBLES COARSE BREAD CRUMBS (SEE TIP, OPPOSITE). IN ANOTHER BOWL, WHISK TOGETHER EGGS, CREAM AND MUSTARD. WHISK IN CHEDDAR, PARMESAN AND DILL, BREAKING UP CLUMPS OF CHEESE. ADD TO FLOUR MIXTURE AND GENTLY STIR WITH YOUR HANDS TO BRING THE DOUGH TOGETHER. (DON'T BE TEMPTED TO ADD EXTRA LIQUID. BE PATIENT; THE FLOUR

WILL GET INCORPORATED). DROP SCOOPS OF DOUGH IN ABOUT $\frac{1}{2}$ CUP (125 ML) AMOUNTS ON THE BAKING SHEET, LEAVING PLENTY OF SPACE BETWEEN SCONES. (FOR SMALLER SCONES, DO $\frac{1}{4}$ CUP/50 ML SCOOPS). BAKE FOR 20 TO 23 MINUTES OR UNTIL SCONES ARE WELL RISEN AND LIGHTLY BROWNED AND A TESTER INSERTED IN THE CENTER OF A SCONE COMES OUT CLEAN. SERVE WARM. MAKES 8 LARGE OR 16 SMALL SCONES.

TIP: FOR LIGHT AND FLAKY SCONES, IT'S IMPORTANT THAT YOU DON'T OVERWORK THE DOUGH. YOU MAY USE A FOOD PROCESSOR, RATHER THAN YOUR HANDS, TO WORK THE BUTTER INTO THE FLOUR, BUT MIX THE WET INGREDIENTS INTO THE DOUGH BY HAND.

VARIATION: OTHER SHARP-FLAVORED HARD CHEESES CAN BE USED IN PLACE OF THE OLD CHEDDAR, INCLUDING SMOKED GOUDA, GRUYÈRE AND PROVOLONE. YOU CAN ALSO REPLACE THE DILL OR CHIVES WITH OTHER FRESH HERBS, SUCH AS THYME, OREGANO OR ROSEMARY.

I HAD AMNESIA ONCE . . . OR TWICE.

DRIED CHERRY SCONES

JOLLY GOOD! ENJOY THESE SCONES THE ENGLISH WAY,
SPREAD WITH JAM AND A DOLLOP OF WHIPPED CREAM,
WASHED DOWN WITH A NICE HOT "CUPPA" TEA.

3 CUPS	ALL-PURPOSE FLOUR	750 ML
4 ~~TBSP~~ *TSP*	BAKING POWDER	~~20~~ ML
I TSP	SALT	5 ML
2 TBSP	GRANULATED SUGAR	25 ML
2/3 CUP	UNSALTED BUTTER, CUT INTO SMALL CUBES	150 ML
I CUP	SWEETENED DRIED TART CHERRIES (SEE TIP, OPPOSITE), ROUGHLY CHOPPED	250 ML
I	EGG	I
3/4 CUP	BUTTERMILK (SEE TIP, PAGE 13)	175 ML
	GRATED ZEST OF I ORANGE	
	BEATEN EGG	
	GRANULATED SUGAR	

PREHEAT OVEN TO 400°F (200°C). LINE A LARGE BAKING
SHEET WITH PARCHMENT PAPER. SIFT FLOUR, BAKING
POWDER AND SALT INTO A LARGE BOWL. STIR IN SUGAR.
ADD BUTTER AND RUB FLOUR MIXTURE THROUGH YOUR
FINGERTIPS UNTIL IT RESEMBLES COARSE BREAD CRUMBS
(SEE TIP, OPPOSITE). STIR IN CHERRIES. IN ANOTHER
BOWL, WHISK TOGETHER EGG, BUTTERMILK AND ORANGE
ZEST. ADD TO FLOUR MIXTURE AND GENTLY STIR WITH
YOUR HANDS TO BRING THE DOUGH TOGETHER. (DON'T BE
TEMPTED TO ADD EXTRA LIQUID. BE PATIENT; THE FLOUR
WILL GET INCORPORATED). TURN DOUGH OUT ONTO A
LIGHTLY FLOURED SURFACE AND LIGHTLY ROLL OUT TO
3/4-INCH (1.5 CM) THICKNESS. USE A COOKIE CUTTER (OR

THE RIM OF A GLASS) TO CUT INTO ABOUT 12 ROUNDS AND PLACE ON BAKING SHEET, LEAVING PLENTY OF SPACE BETWEEN SCONES. BRUSH TOPS WITH BEATEN EGG AND SPRINKLE WITH SUGAR. BAKE FOR 20 TO 23 MINUTES OR UNTIL WELL RISEN AND GOLDEN BROWN AND A TESTER INSERTED IN THE CENTER OF A SCONE COMES OUT CLEAN. BEST EATEN THE SAME DAY. MAKES 12 SCONES.

TIP: DRIED CHERRIES ARE AMONG THE GROWING VARIETY OF DRIED FRUITS — INCLUDING DRIED BLUEBERRIES, MANGO AND PAPAYA — THAT ARE NOW WIDELY AVAILABLE IN GROCERY STORES. FOR A TASTY TREAT, USE THEM IN PLACE OF RAISINS IN CEREAL, SALADS, MUFFINS, QUICK BREADS AND COOKIES.

TIP: FOR LIGHT AND FLAKY SCONES, IT'S IMPORTANT THAT YOU DON'T OVERWORK THE DOUGH. YOU MAY USE A FOOD PROCESSOR, RATHER THAN YOUR HANDS, TO WORK THE BUTTER INTO THE FLOUR, BUT MIX THE WET INGREDIENTS INTO THE DOUGH BY HAND.

ONE THING ABOUT EGOTISTS: THEY DON'T TALK ABOUT OTHER PEOPLE.

MARVELOUS MORNING MUFFINS

THESE HEARTY BRAN MUFFINS ARE LOADED WITH FRUIT AND NUTS — THE PERFECT START TO THE DAY.

1	EGG	1
3/4 CUP	PACKED BROWN SUGAR	175 ML
3/4 CUP	PLAIN YOGURT	175 ML
1/4 CUP	VEGETABLE OIL	50 ML
1 1/2 CUPS	WHEAT OR OAT BRAN	375 ML
1 CUP	ALL-PURPOSE FLOUR	250 ML
2 TSP	BAKING POWDER	10 ML
2 TSP	GROUND CINNAMON	10 ML
1/2 TSP	GROUND GINGER	2 ML
1/2 TSP	BAKING SODA	2 ML
1	APPLE (UNPEELED), GRATED	1
1/2 CUP	CHOPPED PECANS	125 ML
1/2 CUP	RAISINS	125 ML
1/4 CUP	FINELY CHOPPED CRYSTALLIZED GINGER (OPTIONAL)	50 ML

PREHEAT OVEN TO 375°F (190°C). GREASE A 12-CUP MUFFIN PAN OR LINE WITH PAPER LINERS. IN A LARGE BOWL, WHISK TOGETHER EGG, SUGAR, YOGURT AND OIL. STIR IN BRAN AND LET STAND FOR 10 MINUTES. IN ANOTHER BOWL, WHISK TOGETHER FLOUR, BAKING POWDER, CINNAMON, GROUND GINGER AND BAKING SODA. STIR APPLE INTO BRAN MIXTURE. POUR BRAN MIXTURE OVER FLOUR MIXTURE, SPRINKLE WITH PECANS, RAISINS AND CRYSTALLIZED GINGER AND STIR JUST UNTIL EVENLY COMBINED. SPOON INTO MUFFIN PAN. BAKE FOR 22 TO 25 MINUTES OR UNTIL A TESTER INSERTED IN THE CENTER OF A MUFFIN COMES OUT CLEAN. MAKES 12 MUFFINS.

Overnight Raspberry French Toast (page 11)

Rustic Cheddar and Herb Scones (page 28)

Caprese on a Stick (page 37)

Vodka Lemon Shrimp (page 42)

LEMONY ZUCCHINI FLAXSEED MUFFINS

WHEN YOUR GARDEN RUNNETH OVER WITH ZUCCHINI . . .

1 1/4 CUPS	ALL-PURPOSE FLOUR	300 ML
1/2 CUP	GROUND FLAXSEED	125 ML
1 TSP	BAKING POWDER	5 ML
1/2 TSP	GROUND CINNAMON	2 ML
1/4 TSP	BAKING SODA	1 ML
1/4 TSP	GROUND NUTMEG	1 ML
2	EGGS, LIGHTLY BEATEN	2
1 1/2 CUPS	GRATED ZUCCHINI	375 ML
3/4 CUP	DRIED CRANBERRIES	175 ML
3/4 CUP	GRANULATED SUGAR	175 ML
1/3 CUP	VEGETABLE OIL	75 ML
2 TBSP	GRATED LEMON ZEST	25 ML
2 TBSP	FRESHLY SQUEEZED LEMON JUICE	25 ML

PREHEAT OVEN TO 350°F (180°C). GREASE A 12-CUP MUFFIN PAN OR LINE WITH PAPER LINERS. IN A LARGE BOWL, WHISK TOGETHER FLOUR, FLAXSEED, BAKING POWDER, CINNAMON, BAKING SODA AND NUTMEG. IN ANOTHER BOWL, COMBINE EGGS, ZUCCHINI, CRANBERRIES, SUGAR, OIL, LEMON ZEST AND LEMON JUICE. POUR EGG MIXTURE OVER FLOUR MIXTURE AND STIR JUST UNTIL EVENLY COMBINED. SPOON INTO MUFFIN PAN. BAKE FOR ABOUT 20 MINUTES OR UNTIL A TESTER INSERTED IN THE CENTER OF A MUFFIN COMES OUT CLEAN. MAKES 12 MUFFINS.

TIP: WHEN MAKING THE BATTER FOR MUFFINS, STIR JUST ENOUGH TO COMBINE. IF YOU OVERMIX, YOU'LL GET TOUGH MUFFINS.

FRITTATA MUFFINS

1 TBSP	VEGETABLE OIL	15 ML
2 1/4 CUPS	SLICED MUSHROOMS	550 ML
1 1/2 CUPS	FROZEN DICED OR SHREDDED HASH BROWN POTATOES	375 ML
1	SMALL RED BELL PEPPER, CHOPPED	1
2 TO 3	CLOVES GARLIC, MINCED	2 TO 3
1 TSP	PAPRIKA	5 ML
	SALT AND FRESHLY GROUND BLACK PEPPER	
8	EGGS	8
1/3 CUP	2% OR WHOLE MILK	75 ML
1 TBSP	DIJON MUSTARD	15 ML
2	GREEN ONIONS, CHOPPED	2
1 CUP	SHREDDED SHARP (OLD) CHEDDAR CHEESE OR CRUMBLED FETA CHEESE	250 ML

PREHEAT OVEN TO 375°F (190°C). GREASE A 12-CUP MUFFIN PAN. IN A LARGE SKILLET, HEAT OIL OVER MEDIUM HEAT. ADD MUSHROOMS AND COOK, STIRRING OCCASIONALLY, FOR 5 TO 7 MINUTES OR UNTIL THEY BEGIN TO BROWN AND ANY LIQUID HAS EVAPORATED. STIR IN HASH BROWNS, RED PEPPER, GARLIC, PAPRIKA AND SALT AND PEPPER TO TASTE. REMOVE FROM HEAT AND LET COOL COMPLETELY.

IN A BOWL, WHISK TOGETHER EGGS, MILK AND MUSTARD. DIVIDE MUSHROOM MIXTURE AMONG MUFFIN CUPS. SPRINKLE WITH GREEN ONIONS AND CHEESE. POUR SOME EGG MIXTURE INTO EACH CUP AND LET IT SOAK IN. TOP UP EACH MUFFIN CUP WITH THE REMAINING EGG MIXTURE. BAKE FOR 20 TO 25 MINUTES OR UNTIL MUFFINS ARE SET IN THE CENTER. LET COOL IN PAN FOR 5 MINUTES, THEN TURN OUT ONTO A COOLING RACK. MAKES 12 MUFFINS.

APPETIZERS,
DIPS AND SAUCES

SPICED CASHEWS

GO NUTS!

1/2 CUP	PACKED BROWN SUGAR	125 ML
1 TBSP	WATER	15 ML
1 TSP	CHINESE FIVE-SPICE POWDER (SEE TIP, BELOW)	5 ML
1/2 TSP	HOT PEPPER FLAKES	2 ML
1/4 TSP	SALT	1 ML
2 CUPS	ROASTED UNSALTED CASHEWS	500 ML

IN A MEDIUM SAUCEPAN, OVER LOW HEAT, COMBINE BROWN SUGAR, WATER, FIVE-SPICE POWDER, HOT PEPPER FLAKES AND SALT; HEAT GENTLY UNTIL SUGAR DISSOLVES (DON'T BOIL OR IT WILL HARDEN). REMOVE FROM HEAT AND STIR IN CASHEWS UNTIL COMPLETELY COATED IN SUGAR MIXTURE. SPREAD NUTS IN A SINGLE LAYER ON A BAKING SHEET LINED WITH WAXED PAPER, USING THE TIP OF A KNIFE AND YOUR FINGERS TO SEPARATE NUTS THAT ARE STICKING TOGETHER. ALLOW TO AIR-DRY COMPLETELY, ABOUT 2 HOURS. MAKES ABOUT 2 CUPS (500 ML).

MAKE AHEAD: STORE IN AN AIRTIGHT CONTAINER AT ROOM TEMPERATURE FOR UP TO 2 WEEKS.

TIP: CHINESE FIVE-SPICE POWDER IS AN AROMATIC SEASONING BLEND THAT USUALLY INCLUDES CINNAMON, CLOVES, FENNEL SEEDS, STAR ANISE AND GINGER. IF YOU DON'T HAVE IT, SUBSTITUTE A PINCH EACH OF GROUND CINNAMON, CLOVES, GINGER AND FENNEL.

CAPRESE ON A STICK

CAPRESE IS A CLASSIC ITALIAN SALAD OF TOMATOES AND FRESH MOZZARELLA CHEESE. IN THIS MUNCHKIN VERSION, THE INGREDIENTS ARE THREADED ONTO TOOTHPICKS — AN ATTRACTIVE AND CONVENIENT PRESENTATION FOR A COCKTAIL PARTY.

2 CUPS	BALSAMIC VINEGAR	500 ML
24	CHERRY OR GRAPE TOMATOES	24
12	LARGE BASIL LEAVES, HALVED	12
24	PEARL BOCCONCINI (SEE TIP, BELOW)	24
24	TOOTHPICKS	24

IN A SMALL SAUCEPAN, OVER LOW HEAT, SIMMER BALSAMIC VINEGAR UNTIL IT IS REDUCED BY HALF AND IS THICK, SWEET AND SYRUPY. TRANSFER TO A SMALL BOWL AND SET ASIDE. THREAD 1 TOMATO, $1/2$ BASIL LEAF AND 1 BOCCONCINI ONTO EACH TOOTHPICK. ARRANGE ON A SERVING PLATE AND LIGHTLY DRIZZLE WITH BALSAMIC SYRUP. MAKES 24 APPETIZERS.

MAKE AHEAD: THE BALSAMIC SYRUP CAN BE STORED IN AN AIRTIGHT CONTAINER IN THE REFRIGERATOR FOR SEVERAL WEEKS. THE CAPRESE STICKS CAN BE PREPARED UP TO 3 HOURS AHEAD AND CHILLED IN THE REFRIGERATOR UNTIL YOU'RE READY TO SERVE.

TIP: PEARL BOCCONCINI ARE MARBLE-SIZE BALLS OF FRESH MOZZARELLA CHEESE SOLD IN TUBS IN THE DAIRY OR DELICATESSEN AISLES OF WELL-STOCKED GROCERY STORES.

CHEESE AND PECAN–STUFFED MUSHROOMS

MAKE THESE TASTY BITES AHEAD AND POP THEM IN THE OVEN A FEW MINUTES BEFORE SERVING.

16	WHITE MUSHROOMS (ABOUT 1 LB/500 G)	16
4 TBSP	BUTTER, DIVIDED	60 ML
1/4 CUP	FINELY CHOPPED ONION	50 ML
1/2 CUP	DRY BREAD CRUMBS	125 ML
1/4 CUP	FINELY CHOPPED PECANS	50 ML
2 TBSP	CHOPPED FRESH PARSLEY	25 ML
1	PACKAGE (5 OZ/142 G) BOURSIN GARLIC-AND-HERB-FLAVORED FRESH SOFT CHEESE (SEE TIP, OPPOSITE), CRUMBLED	1
	SALT AND FRESHLY GROUND BLACK PEPPER	

PREHEAT OVEN TO 375°F (190°C). WIPE MUSHROOMS CLEAN WITH A DAMP CLOTH. REMOVE STEMS AND SET CAPS ASIDE. FINELY CHOP STEMS. IN A MEDIUM SKILLET, MELT 1 TBSP (15 ML) OF THE BUTTER OVER MEDIUM HEAT. SAUTÉ MUSHROOM STEMS AND ONION UNTIL SOFTENED, ABOUT 5 MINUTES. STIR IN BREAD CRUMBS, PECANS AND PARSLEY. TRANSFER TO A LARGE BOWL, AND USING A SPATULA, EVENLY BLEND IN CHEESE. SEASON TO TASTE WITH SALT AND PEPPER. SPOON MIXTURE INTO MUSHROOM CAPS. MELT THE REMAINING BUTTER AND POUR HALF INTO A 13- BY 9-INCH (33 BY 23 CM) BAKING DISH, SWIRLING TO COVER BASE. ARRANGE MUSHROOMS IN DISH AND BRUSH TOPS WITH THE REMAINING MELTED BUTTER. BAKE FOR 15 TO 20 MINUTES OR UNTIL MUSHROOMS ARE TENDER, BUT STILL HOLD THEIR SHAPE, AND TOPS ARE BROWNED. MAKES 16 APPETIZERS.

MAKE AHEAD: AFTER ASSEMBLING THE MUSHROOM CAPS, PLACE IN A SINGLE LAYER IN AN AIRTIGHT CONTAINER AND REFRIGERATE FOR UP TO 4 HOURS. BRING TO ROOM TEMPERATURE BEFORE BAKING.

TIP: BOURSIN FRESH SOFT CHEESE, AVAILABLE IN SEVERAL FLAVORS, HAS THE TEXTURE OF WHIPPED BUTTER, WHICH MAKES IT PERFECT FOR MANY RECIPES. LOOK FOR IT IN THE DELI SECTION OF GROCERY STORES. IF YOU CAN'T FIND IT, SUBSTITUTE 5 OZ (142 G) HERBED CREAM CHEESE BLENDED WITH 2 TBSP (25 ML) SOFTENED BUTTER.

VARIATION: OMIT THE PECANS AND ADD 2 SLICES OF BACON, COOKED UNTIL CRISP AND CRUMBLED.

SHOW ME A MAN WITH BOTH FEET PLANTED FIRMLY ON THE GROUND AND I'LL SHOW YOU A MAN WHO CAN'T GET HIS PANTS OFF.

TINY SALMON CAKES AND LEMON CAPER MAYONNAISE

FRESHLY COOKED SALMON IS BEST FOR
THESE BITE-SIZE CAKES, BUT YOU CAN ALSO USE
LEFTOVER BAKED OR GRILLED SALMON.

LEMON CAPER MAYONNAISE

1/2 CUP	MAYONNAISE	125 ML
2 TBSP	FRESHLY SQUEEZED LEMON JUICE	25 ML
1 TBSP	DRAINED CAPERS	15 ML
1 TBSP	CHOPPED FRESH DILL (OR 1 TSP/5 ML DRIED)	15 ML
PINCH	CAYENNE PEPPER	PINCH

SALMON CAKES

1/4 CUP	COARSELY CHOPPED ONION	50 ML
1/4 CUP	PACKED FRESH PARSLEY LEAVES	50 ML
1	EGG	1
1 1/2 CUPS	FRESH BREAD CRUMBS	375 ML
1 TSP	GRATED LEMON ZEST	5 ML
2 TBSP	FRESHLY SQUEEZED LEMON JUICE	25 ML
2 TBSP	BUTTER, MELTED	25 ML
1 TBSP	DIJON MUSTARD	15 ML
1/2 TSP	HOT PEPPER SAUCE	2 ML
1 LB	SKINLESS SALMON FILLET, COOKED AND CHOPPED (ABOUT 2 1/2 CUPS/625 ML)	500 G
	SALT AND FRESHLY GROUND BLACK PEPPER	
1 1/2 CUPS	PANKO (SEE TIP, PAGE 133) OR DRY BREAD CRUMBS	375 ML
	VEGETABLE OIL	

LEMON CAPER MAYONNAISE: IN A SMALL BOWL, COMBINE
MAYONNAISE, LEMON JUICE, CAPERS, DILL AND CAYENNE.
COVER AND REFRIGERATE UNTIL READY TO SERVE.

SALMON CAKES: IN A FOOD PROCESSOR, PULSE ONIONS AND PARSLEY UNTIL FINELY CHOPPED. ADD EGG, FRESH BREAD CRUMBS, LEMON ZEST, LEMON JUICE, BUTTER, MUSTARD AND HOT PEPPER SAUCE; PULSE UNTIL WELL COMBINED. ADD SALMON AND PULSE TO COMBINE. TRANSFER TO A BOWL AND SEASON TO TASTE WITH SALT AND PEPPER. COVER AND REFRIGERATE FOR AT LEAST 2 HOURS OR OVERNIGHT.

SHAPE HEAPING TEASPOONFULS (5 ML) OF SALMON MIXTURE INTO SMALL PATTIES. PLACE PANKO IN A SHALLOW DISH AND ROLL SALMON PATTIES TO COAT. IN A LARGE SKILLET, HEAT OIL OVER MEDIUM-HIGH HEAT. WORKING IN BATCHES, FRY SALMON PATTIES FOR ABOUT 2 MINUTES PER SIDE OR UNTIL GOLDEN ON BOTH SIDES. TRANSFER TO A PLATE LINED WITH PAPER TOWELS TO REMOVE EXCESS OIL, THEN PLACE ON A BAKING SHEET AND KEEP WARM IN A LOW OVEN. REPEAT WITH THE REMAINING PATTIES, OILING SKILLET AS NECESSARY BETWEEN BATCHES. SERVE WITH LEMON CAPER MAYONNAISE ON THE SIDE. MAKES ABOUT 25 APPETIZERS.

MAKE AHEAD: PLACE UNCOOKED SALMON PATTIES IN A SINGLE LAYER ON A BAKING SHEET LINED WITH WAXED PAPER, COVER AND REFRIGERATE FOR UP TO 1 DAY. OR PLACE COOKED PATTIES ON A BAKING SHEET AND FREEZE. PACK FROZEN PATTIES INTO FREEZER BAGS AND STORE FOR UP TO 1 MONTH. REHEAT FROM FROZEN IN AN OVEN PREHEATED TO 375°F (190°C).

VODKA LEMON SHRIMP

YOUR GUESTS WILL BE DEMANDING A SECOND AND THIRD ROUND OF THESE INCREDIBLY TASTY SHRIMP.

VODKA LEMON SAUCE

3 TBSP	GRANULATED SUGAR	45 ML
I TBSP	GRATED LEMON ZEST	15 ML
1/3 CUP	FRESHLY SQUEEZED LEMON JUICE	75 ML
1/4 CUP	VODKA	50 ML
1/4 CUP	OLIVE OIL	50 ML
1 1/2 TSP	MINCED GINGERROOT	7 ML
I	CLOVE GARLIC, MINCED	I
1/4 TSP	SALT	I ML
1/4 TSP	FRESHLY GROUND BLACK PEPPER	I ML
30	MEDIUM OR LARGE SHRIMP, PEELED AND DEVEINED (ABOUT I LB/500 G)	30
1/2 TSP	CORNSTARCH	2 ML

SOAK 10 WOODEN SKEWERS IN COLD WATER FOR 30 MINUTES. PREHEAT BARBECUE GRILL TO MEDIUM-HIGH AND GREASE THE GRATES.

VODKA LEMON SAUCE: IN A SMALL SAUCEPAN, OVER LOW HEAT, COMBINE SUGAR, LEMON ZEST AND LEMON JUICE; HEAT GENTLY UNTIL SUGAR DISSOLVES, ABOUT 5 MINUTES. LET COOL, THEN STIR IN VODKA, OIL, GINGER, GARLIC, SALT AND PEPPER.

PLACE SHRIMP IN A DEEP BOWL AND SPOON 3 TBSP (45 ML) SAUCE OVER TOP; TOSS TO COMBINE. (DO THIS NO MORE THAN 30 MINUTES AHEAD OR THE LEMON JUICE WILL START TO TOUGHEN THE SHRIMP). SET THE

REMAINING SAUCE ASIDE IN THE SAUCEPAN. THREAD SHRIMP ONTO SKEWERS, LEAVING SPACE BETWEEN PIECES. GRILL, TURNING ONCE, FOR 5 MINUTES OR UNTIL PINK AND OPAQUE. ARRANGE SKEWERS ON A SERVING PLATE.

WHISK CORNSTARCH INTO THE REMAINING SAUCE AND BRING TO A BOIL; REDUCE HEAT AND SIMMER FOR 2 MINUTES OR UNTIL THICKENED AND GLOSSY. TRANSFER TO A BOWL AND PLACE NEXT TO THE SHRIMP SKEWERS, ALONG WITH SMALL COCKTAIL PLATES FOR YOUR GUESTS. MAKES 10 SKEWERS.

TIP: WHEN BUYING FRESH GINGERROOT, LOOK FOR FIRM PIECES. IF THE SKIN IS WRINKLY, IT'S PAST ITS BEST. TO PEEL GINGER, HOLD IT IN THE PALM OF YOUR HAND AND USE THE EDGE OF A TEASPOON TO SCRAPE AWAY THE SKIN, GETTING INTO ALL THE CREVICES AND AROUND THE KNOBBY BITS. BREAK THE PEELED GINGER INTO SMALLER PIECES AND WRAP TIGHTLY IN A DOUBLE LAYER OF PLASTIC WRAP. IT WILL KEEP IN THE FRIDGE FOR A COUPLE OF WEEKS AND IN THE FREEZER FOR SEVERAL MONTHS.

VARIATION: YOU CAN ALSO COOK THE MARINATED SHRIMP ON THE STOVETOP. HEAT A LARGE NONSTICK SKILLET OVER MEDIUM-HIGH HEAT. SAUTÉ SHRIMP, SHAKING PAN, FOR ABOUT 4 MINUTES OR UNTIL PINK AND OPAQUE.

I LIKE TO GIVE HOMEMADE GIFTS — WHICH ONE OF MY CHILDREN WOULD YOU LIKE?

SHRIMP IN THAI COCONUT SAUCE

THESE SHRIMP ARE PERFECT FOR SHARING WHEN YOU HAVE FRIENDS OVER FOR DRINKS. HAVE PLENTY OF NAPKINS ON HAND TO WIPE THE SAUCE OFF YOUR CHIN!

1½ TSP	CANOLA OR OLIVE OIL	7 ML
2	CLOVES GARLIC, MINCED	2
1 TBSP	MINCED GINGERROOT	15 ML
1 TSP	THAI RED CURRY PASTE	5 ML
2 CUPS	COCONUT MILK	500 ML
1 CUP	CHICKEN BROTH OR WATER	250 ML
2 TSP	PACKED BROWN SUGAR	10 ML
1 TSP	CORNSTARCH	5 ML
1 TBSP	FRESHLY SQUEEZED LIME JUICE	15 ML
2 TSP	SOY SAUCE	10 ML
30	LARGE SHRIMP, PEELED AND DEVEINED (ABOUT 1 LB/500 G)	30
1 TBSP	CHOPPED FRESH CILANTRO	15 ML
½ CUP	UNSWEETENED SHREDDED COCONUT, TOASTED (SEE TIP, PAGE 87)	125 ML

IN A LARGE NONSTICK SKILLET, HEAT OIL OVER MEDIUM-HIGH HEAT. SAUTÉ GARLIC, GINGER AND CURRY PASTE FOR 15 SECONDS. WHISK IN COCONUT MILK, CHICKEN BROTH, BROWN SUGAR, CORNSTARCH, LIME JUICE AND SOY SAUCE; SIMMER FOR 7 TO 10 MINUTES OR UNTIL SAUCE IS REDUCED AND SLIGHTLY THICKENED. ADD SHRIMP AND SIMMER, STIRRING OCCASIONALLY, FOR 3 TO 5 MINUTES OR UNTIL PINK AND OPAQUE. STIR IN CILANTRO. TRANSFER SHRIMP TO A SHALLOW SERVING DISH, SPREADING OUT IN A SINGLE LAYER. SPOON SAUCE OVER TOP AND SPRINKLE WITH TOASTED COCONUT. MAKES ABOUT 30 APPETIZERS.

VIETNAMESE CHICKEN BITES

SWEET AND SAVORY — ALWAYS A HIT.

1 LB	GROUND CHICKEN OR TURKEY	500 G
1/4 CUP	CHOPPED FRESH CILANTRO	50 ML
2	GREEN ONIONS, FINELY CHOPPED	2
2	CLOVES GARLIC, MINCED	2
1 TBSP	GRATED LEMON ZEST	15 ML
2 TSP	CORNSTARCH	10 ML
1 TSP	MINCED GINGERROOT	5 ML
3 TBSP	SOY SAUCE	45 ML
	GRANULATED SUGAR	
	SWEET ASIAN CHILI SAUCE	

PREHEAT OVEN TO 400°F (200°C). LINE A LARGE BAKING SHEET WITH FOIL AND SPRAY WITH COOKING SPRAY. IN A LARGE BOWL, COMBINE CHICKEN, CILANTRO, GREEN ONIONS, GARLIC, LEMON ZEST, CORNSTARCH, GINGER AND SOY SAUCE. FORM INTO 1-INCH (2.5 CM) BALLS. ROLL IN SUGAR AND PLACE ON PREPARED BAKING SHEET. BAKE FOR ABOUT 15 MINUTES, TURNING ONCE, UNTIL BROWNED AND GLAZED. TRANSFER TO A SERVING DISH AND SET A DISH OF TOOTHPICKS ON THE SIDE SO GUESTS CAN HELP THEMSELVES. SERVE WITH A BOWL OF CHILI SAUCE FOR DIPPING. MAKES ABOUT 30 MEATBALLS.

MAKE AHEAD: AFTER PLACING THE MEATBALLS ON THE BAKING SHEET, COVER AND REFRIGERATE FOR UP TO 4 HOURS BEFORE BAKING. INCREASE BAKING TIME TO 18 TO 20 MINUTES.

ROASTED RED PEPPER AND GOAT CHEESE TARTS

THESE DELICIOUS TARTS WILL DISAPPEAR RIGHT BEFORE YOUR EYES!

18	FROZEN UNSWEETENED MINI TART SHELLS	18
1/2 CUP	ROASTED RED BELL PEPPERS (SEE TIP, PAGE 117), DRAINED AND CHOPPED	125 ML
4 OZ	SOFT UNRIPENED GOAT CHEESE, CHOPPED, OR GOAT FETA CHEESE, CRUMBLED (ABOUT 1/2 CUP/125 ML)	125 G
3	EGGS	3
1 CUP	WHIPPING (35%) CREAM	250 ML
1/4 TSP	SALT	1 ML
1/4 TSP	FRESHLY GROUND BLACK PEPPER	1 ML

PREHEAT OVEN TO 375°F (190°C). PLACE TART SHELLS ON A BAKING SHEET. IN A BOWL, COMBINE ROASTED PEPPERS AND GOAT CHEESE. DIVIDE PEPPER MIXTURE EVENLY AMONG TART SHELLS. IN A BOWL, BEAT EGGS, WHIPPING CREAM, SALT AND PEPPER. POUR INTO TART SHELLS, FILLING JUST TO THE RIM. BAKE FOR 20 TO 25 MINUTES OR UNTIL PUFFY AND SET. THE FILLING WILL FALL AS IT COOLS. SERVE WARM OR AT ROOM TEMPERATURE. MAKES 18 TARTS.

MAKE AHEAD: COOL BAKED TARTS, PLACE BETWEEN LAYERS OF WAXED PAPER IN AN AIRTIGHT PLASTIC CONTAINER AND FREEZE FOR UP TO 1 MONTH. REHEAT FROM FROZEN IN A 375°F (190°C) OVEN FOR 15 MINUTES.

double the tart shells
or half the filling

ASPARAGUS BACON SWIRLS

MAKE A DOUBLE BATCH — THEY ARE THAT GOOD!

2 TSP	VEGETABLE OR OLIVE OIL	10 ML
1½ CUPS	THINLY SLICED ASPARAGUS	375 ML
1	SHALLOT, MINCED	1
1	PACKAGE (14 OZ/398 G) FROZEN PUFF PASTRY, THAWED	1
1½ CUPS	SHREDDED SHARP (OLD) CHEDDAR CHEESE	375 ML
8	SLICES BACON, COOKED CRISP AND CRUMBLED	8
	BEATEN EGG	

PREHEAT OVEN TO 375°F (190°C). LINE A BAKING SHEET WITH PARCHMENT PAPER. IN A MEDIUM SKILLET, HEAT OIL OVER MEDIUM HEAT. SAUTÉ ASPARAGUS AND SHALLOT UNTIL TENDER, ABOUT 5 MINUTES. ROLL PASTRY OUT TO A 16- BY 12-INCH (40 BY 30 CM) RECTANGLE. SPRINKLE ASPARAGUS MIXTURE, CHEESE AND BACON EVENLY OVER THE PASTRY. STARTING AT ONE LONG END, ROLL PASTRY UP TIGHTLY LIKE A JELLY ROLL. PLACE ON PREPARED BAKING SHEET AND FREEZE FOR 15 MINUTES. TRANSFER TO A CUTTING BOARD AND CUT INTO ½-INCH (1 CM) THICK SLICES. PLACE SLICES CUT SIDE UP ON BAKING SHEET AND BRUSH WITH EGG. BAKE FOR 15 TO 20 MINUTES OR UNTIL PUFFY AND GOLDEN. MAKES 32 APPETIZERS.

MAKE AHEAD: AFTER BAKING, LET COOL AND PLACE BETWEEN LAYERS OF WAXED PAPER IN AN AIRTIGHT CONTAINER. REFRIGERATE FOR UP TO 1 DAY OR FREEZE FOR UP TO 1 MONTH. REHEAT FROM FROZEN IN A 375°F (190°C) OVEN FOR ABOUT 15 MINUTES.

FLAKY PHYLLO SAUSAGE TRIANGLES

THE FLAVOR LIVES HERE!

4	HOT ITALIAN SAUSAGES, CASINGS REMOVED, CRUMBLED	4
1/2 CUP	FINELY CHOPPED RED BELL PEPPER	125 ML
6	GREEN ONIONS, CHOPPED	6
1 CUP	SHREDDED SHARP (OLD) CHEDDAR CHEESE	250 ML
8	SHEETS FROZEN PHYLLO PASTRY, THAWED	8
1/2 CUP	BUTTER, MELTED	125 ML
1	EGG, LIGHTLY BEATEN	1

IN A LARGE SKILLET, OVER MEDIUM-HIGH HEAT, SAUTÉ SAUSAGES, RED PEPPER AND GREEN ONIONS FOR 6 TO 8 MINUTES OR UNTIL SAUSAGE IS BROWNED. USING A SLOTTED SPOON, TRANSFER MIXTURE TO A PLATE LINED WITH PAPER TOWELS TO DRAIN FAT. TRANSFER TO A LARGE BOWL AND ADD CHEESE, PRESSING TO MAKE MIXTURE STICK TOGETHER SLIGHTLY. COVER AND REFRIGERATE FOR AT LEAST 30 MINUTES, UNTIL COOL, OR FOR UP TO 24 HOURS.

PREHEAT OVEN TO 375°F (190°C). LINE 2 LARGE BAKING SHEETS WITH PARCHMENT PAPER. CAREFULLY UNROLL PHYLLO PASTRY AND COVER WITH PLASTIC WRAP, THEN A DAMP CLOTH. PLACE ONE PHYLLO SHEET ON A WORK SURFACE AND BRUSH WITH MELTED BUTTER. REPEAT WITH ONE MORE LAYER OF PHYLLO. CUT LAYERED PHYLLO CROSSWISE INTO 8 STRIPS. PLACE 1 TSP (5 ML) SAUSAGE MIXTURE ABOUT 1/2 INCH (1 CM) FROM THE BOTTOM OF

EACH STRIP. FOLD ONE CORNER OF THE PHYLLO STRIP DIAGONALLY ACROSS TO THE OPPOSITE EDGE TO FORM A TRIANGLE, LIKE FOLDING A FLAG. CONTINUE TO FOLD IN THIS WAY TO THE END OF THE STRIP, ENSURING THAT THE FILLING IS SEALED IN. REPEAT WITH THE REMAINING PHYLLO AND FILLING. PLACE TRIANGLES, SEAM SIDE DOWN, ABOUT I INCH (2.5 CM) APART ON PREPARED BAKING SHEETS AND BRUSH WITH BEATEN EGG. BAKE FOR 15 TO 20 MINUTES OR UNTIL GOLDEN. MAKES 32 APPETIZERS.

MAKE AHEAD: AFTER ASSEMBLING THE TRIANGLES, PLACE BETWEEN LAYERS OF WAXED PAPER IN AIRTIGHT CONTAINERS AND REFRIGERATE FOR UP TO I DAY OR FREEZE FOR UP TO I MONTH. BAKE FROM FROZEN.

TIP: THAW PHYLLO OVERNIGHT IN THE REFRIGERATOR. DO NOT ATTEMPT TO DEFROST IT IN THE MICROWAVE, AS THIS WILL CAUSE IT TO STICK TOGETHER. BRUSHING THE PHYLLO WITH BUTTER PREVENTS THE EDGES FROM CRACKING. THE FILLING SHOULD BE COOL BEFORE YOU ASSEMBLE THE TRIANGLES.

I NEVER FINISH ANYTHI

SLIDERS

TWO-BITE BURGERS IN COCKTAIL BUNS WITH ALL THE FIXINS — EVERYONE LOVES THESE.

ALL-THE-FIXINS MAYONNAISE

1 CUP	MAYONNAISE	250 ML
1/4 CUP	KETCHUP	50 ML
2 TBSP	PREPARED YELLOW MUSTARD	25 ML
2 TBSP	SWEET GREEN RELISH	25 ML

BURGERS

2	SLICES BREAD, TORN INTO SMALL PIECES	2
1	EGG, LIGHTLY BEATEN	1
1/4 CUP	MILK	50 ML
2 TBSP	TOMATO-BASED CHILI SAUCE OR KETCHUP	25 ML
1 TSP	WORCESTERSHIRE SAUCE	5 ML
1 LB	LEAN GROUND BEEF	500 G
1	ONION, GRATED	1
	SALT AND FRESHLY GROUND BLACK PEPPER	

TO SERVE

12	COCKTAIL ROLLS (SEE TIP, OPPOSITE), TOASTED	12
	SHREDDED LETTUCE	
	SLICED TOMATO	
	BREAD-AND-BUTTER PICKLES	

ALL-THE-FIXINS MAYONNAISE: IN A BOWL, COMBINE MAYONNAISE, KETCHUP, MUSTARD AND RELISH. SET ASIDE.

BURGERS: IN ANOTHER BOWL, COMBINE BREAD PIECES, EGG, MILK, CHILI SAUCE AND WORCESTERSHIRE SAUCE. LET STAND UNTIL BREAD HAS ABSORBED LIQUID. IN A LARGE

BOWL, COMBINE BEEF AND ONION. ADD BREAD MIXTURE
AND SALT AND PEPPER TO TASTE; MIX THOROUGHLY.
FORM INTO 12 MINI PATTIES, ABOUT 2 INCHES (5 CM) WIDE
AND $\frac{1}{2}$ INCH (1 CM) THICK. GRILL OR PAN-FRY PATTIES
OVER MEDIUM-HIGH HEAT, TURNING ONCE, FOR 5 TO
7 MINUTES OR UNTIL NO LONGER PINK INSIDE.

TO SERVE: SPREAD MAYONNAISE ON TOASTED ROLLS.
LAYER LETTUCE, TOMATO AND PICKLES ON BOTTOM
HALVES OF ROLLS, TOP EACH WITH A BURGER AND COVER
WITH THE TOP HALVES OF ROLLS. IF SERVING ADULTS,
SECURE WITH COCKTAIL SKEWERS. MAKES 12 MINI
BURGERS.

MAKE AHEAD: PLACE UNCOOKED PATTIES BETWEEN
LAYERS OF WAXED PAPER IN AN AIRTIGHT CONTAINER AND
REFRIGERATE FOR UP TO 4 HOURS OR FREEZE FOR UP TO
2 WEEKS. COOK FROM FROZEN, INCREASING THE COOKING
TIME TO 12 TO 15 MINUTES

TIP: COCKTAIL ROLLS ARE LIKE SMALL DINNER ROLLS AND
ARE USUALLY AVAILABLE IN THE BAKERY SECTION OF THE
SUPERMARKET. ALTERNATIVELY, USE MINI PITA POCKETS.

VARIATION: BRUSH THE PATTIES WITH YOUR FAVORITE
BARBECUE SAUCE HALFWAY THROUGH THE COOKING TIME.

BACON-WRAPPED DATES

YOUR NEWEST FAVORITE APPETIZER!
YOU HAVE TO USE REAL MAPLE SYRUP.

12	SLICES MAPLE-SMOKED BACON, HALVED CROSSWISE	12
	CHILI POWDER AND CAYENNE PEPPER	
24	SOFT FRESH DATES, PITS REMOVED	24
1/2 CUP	PURE MAPLE SYRUP	125 ML
1/4 CUP	PACKED BROWN SUGAR	50 ML

PREHEAT OVEN TO 375°F (190°C). GREASE AN 8-INCH (2 L) SQUARE BAKING DISH. SPRINKLE ONE SIDE OF EACH PIECE OF BACON WITH CHILI POWDER AND CAYENNE TO TASTE. WRAP EACH DATE IN A PIECE OF BACON AND PACK CLOSELY IN BAKING DISH. DRIZZLE WITH MAPLE SYRUP AND SPRINKLE WITH BROWN SUGAR. BAKE FOR ABOUT 30 MINUTES OR UNTIL BACON LOOKS COOKED. DRAIN OFF EXCESS LIQUID. LET STAND FOR 15 MINUTES BEFORE SERVING. MAKES 24 APPETIZERS.

I HAVE REACHED THE LIMIT OF MY MAGNIFICENCE.

SUN-DRIED TOMATO PESTO FLATBREAD

A JAR OF STORE-BOUGHT PESTO IN THE PANTRY AND SOME FLATBREAD IN THE FREEZER — THE MAKINGS FOR FABULOUS FINGER FOOD.

4	GREEK-STYLE (NO POCKET) PITAS, NAAN OR MINI PIZZA SHELLS	4
1/2 CUP	SUN-DRIED TOMATO PESTO (SEE TIP, BELOW)	125 ML
2 CUPS	SHREDDED MOZZARELLA CHEESE	500 ML
16	CHERRY TOMATOES, EACH SLICED INTO 3 PIECES	16
1/3 CUP	TOASTED PINE NUTS (SEE TIP, PAGE 61)	75 ML
1/4 CUP	THINLY SLICED FRESH BASIL	50 ML

PREHEAT OVEN TO 375°F (190°C). PLACE PITAS ON 2 LARGE BAKING SHEETS. SPREAD ABOUT 2 TBSP (25 ML) PESTO OVER TOP OF EACH PITA. SPRINKLE WITH MOZZARELLA, THEN TOP WITH TOMATO SLICES. BAKE FOR ABOUT 15 MINUTES OR UNTIL CHEESE IS BUBBLING AND PITA IS BROWN AND CRISP AT THE EDGES. SPRINKLE WITH PINE NUTS AND BASIL AND LET COOL FOR 5 MINUTES. SLICE EACH PITA INTO 6 PIECES. MAKES 24 SLICES.

TIP: JARS OF READY-MADE SUN-DRIED TOMATO PESTO, AS WELL AS TRADITIONAL BASIL PESTO, ARE WIDELY AVAILABLE IN GROCERY STORES AND ARE WORTH HAVING ON HAND. PESTOS CAN BE SPREAD ON PIZZA, STIRRED INTO SOUP OR PASTA SAUCE OR MIXED WITH SOUR CREAM FOR A QUICK VEGETABLE DIP.

STILTON SHORTBREAD

TINY BITES OF A CHEESE LOVER'S DELIGHT.

1 CUP	STILTON CHEESE (ABOUT 4 OZ/125 G)	250 ML
3/4 CUP	UNSALTED BUTTER, AT ROOM TEMPERATURE	175 ML
1/4 TSP	SALT	1 ML
1 3/4 CUPS	ALL-PURPOSE FLOUR	425 ML
1	EGG, LIGHTLY BEATEN	1
1/2 CUP	FINELY CHOPPED WALNUTS OR PECANS	125 ML

PREHEAT OVEN TO 350°F (180°C). LINE 2 LARGE BAKING SHEETS WITH PARCHMENT PAPER. IN A LARGE BOWL, USING A FORK, COMBINE CHEESE AND BUTTER UNTIL BLENDED BUT STILL SLIGHTLY LUMPY. SPRINKLE WITH SALT AND GRADUALLY ADD FLOUR, STIRRING UNTIL THOROUGHLY MIXED. GATHER INTO A BALL. PINCH SMALL PIECES OF DOUGH AND ROLL INTO 1/4-INCH (0.5 CM) BALLS. PLACE ON PREPARED BAKING SHEETS AND USE THE BACK OF A SPOON TO FLATTEN TO ABOUT 1-INCH (2.5 CM) DIAMETER. (OR ROLL OUT DOUGH ON A FLOURED SURFACE TO 1/4-INCH/0.5 CM THICKNESS AND CUT WITH SMALL COOKIE CUTTER, THEN PLACE ON BAKING SHEETS.) BRUSH TOPS WITH BEATEN EGG AND SPRINKLE WITH NUTS. BAKE FOR 10 TO 12 MINUTES OR UNTIL GOLDEN. *MAKES ABOUT 6 DOZEN COOKIES.*

MAKE AHEAD: LET COOL, PLACE BETWEEN LAYERS OF WAXED PAPER IN AN AIRTIGHT PLASTIC CONTAINER AND FREEZE FOR UP TO 1 MONTH.

TIP: ALWAYS PLACE DOUGH ON A COOL BAKING SHEET, AS A WARM ONE WILL CAUSE DOUGH TO SOFTEN AND SPREAD.

CHEESE STRAWS

THESE ELEGANT PASTRY APPETIZERS LOOK VERY PROFESSIONAL, AND THEY WORK EVERY TIME.

1	PACKAGE (14 OZ/398 G) FROZEN PUFF PASTRY, THAWED	1
1	EGG, BEATEN	1
1 CUP	FRESHLY GRATED PARMESAN CHEESE	250 ML
2 TSP	PAPRIKA	10 ML
2 TSP	DRY MUSTARD	10 ML

LINE 2 LARGE BAKING SHEETS WITH PARCHMENT PAPER. CUT PUFF PASTRY IN HALF (IT IS USUALLY PARTIALLY PRECUT). ON A FLOURED SURFACE, ROLL OUT EACH HALF INTO A 10-INCH (25 CM) SQUARE. BRUSH THE SURFACE OF ONE SQUARE WITH BEATEN EGG. IN A SMALL BOWL, COMBINE PARMESAN, PAPRIKA AND MUSTARD. SPRINKLE HALF THE MIXTURE OVER PASTRY. PLACE THE SECOND SQUARE OF PASTRY ON TOP AND PRESS DOWN GENTLY WITH A ROLLING PIN TO SEAL EDGES. BRUSH THE SURFACE WITH BEATEN EGG AND SPRINKLE WITH THE REMAINING PARMESAN MIXTURE. FOLD PASTRY IN HALF FROM BOTTOM TO TOP, ENCLOSING CHEESE LIKE A SANDWICH. ROLL OUT AGAIN TO A ROUGHLY 17- BY 10-INCH (43 BY 25 CM) RECTANGLE. USING A SHARP KNIFE, CUT INTO 10- BY $1/2$-INCH (25 BY 1 CM) STRIPS. TWIST EACH STRIP THREE OR FOUR TIMES INTO A CORKSCREW SHAPE. PLACE ON PREPARED BAKING SHEETS. COVER AND REFRIGERATE FOR AT LEAST 1 HOUR, UNTIL CHILLED, OR FOR UP TO 1 DAY.

PREHEAT OVEN TO 375°F (190°C). BAKE CHEESE STRAWS UNTIL GOLDEN, ABOUT 20 MINUTES. MAKES 34 CHEESE STRAWS.

HOLIDAY BAKED BRIE

A DEE-LISHUS LAST-MINUTE APPETIZER.
KEEP A WHEEL OF BRIE IN THE REFRIGERATOR,
PISTACHIOS IN THE FREEZER AND DRIED CRANBERRIES
IN THE PANTRY, AND YOU'RE GOOD TO GO.

1	ROUND (8 OZ/250 G) BRIE CHEESE	1
1/2 CUP	CHOPPED PISTACHIOS, DIVIDED	125 ML

CRANBERRY SAUCE

1 CUP	FRESH OR FROZEN CRANBERRIES	250 ML
6 TBSP	PACKED BROWN SUGAR	90 ML
1 TSP	GRATED ORANGE ZEST, DIVIDED	5 ML
1 TBSP	FRESHLY SQUEEZED ORANGE JUICE	15 ML
1 TBSP	ORANGE-FLAVORED LIQUEUR	15 ML

PREHEAT OVEN TO 375°F (190°C). LINE A BAKING SHEET WITH PARCHMENT PAPER OR GREASED FOIL. SLICE BRIE HORIZONTALLY THROUGH THE MIDDLE AND SPRINKLE 1/4 CUP (50 ML) PISTACHIOS OVER BOTTOM HALF. REPLACE TOP HALF, PRESSING LIGHTLY TO SEAL EDGES. SET ASIDE.

CRANBERRY SAUCE: IN A MEDIUM SAUCEPAN, OVER MEDIUM HEAT, COMBINE CRANBERRIES, BROWN SUGAR, ORANGE JUICE AND LIQUEUR. SLOWLY BRING TO A BOIL, STIRRING. REDUCE HEAT AND SIMMER, STIRRING OCCASIONALLY, FOR 5 MINUTES OR UNTIL MIXTURE THICKENS AND CRANBERRIES SOFTEN. REMOVE FROM HEAT AND STIR IN 1/2 TSP (2 ML) ORANGE ZEST.

PLACE BRIE IN CENTER OF PREPARED BAKING SHEET AND SPOON CRANBERRY SAUCE OVER TOP. BAKE FOR 10 TO 12 MINUTES OR UNTIL CHEESE IS SOFTENED. SPRINKLE

WITH THE REMAINING PISTACHIOS AND ORANGE ZEST. SERVES 3 TO 4.

TIP: DOUBLE THE CRANBERRY SAUCE AND STORE IT IN AN AIRTIGHT CONTAINER IN THE REFRIGERATOR FOR UP TO 2 WEEKS. IT'S TERRIFIC ON TURKEY, BRIE AND CRANBERRY PANINI (SEE PAGE 190) OR WITH YOUR HOLIDAY TURKEY DINNER.

NO MATTER HOW MUCH YOU PUSH THE ENVELOPE, IT'LL STILL BE STATIONERY.

APPLE-CHEDDAR BRUSCHETTA

A CLASSIC COMBINATION.

I	BAGUETTE (FRENCH STICK)	I
2	RED-SKINNED APPLES, SLICED	2
24	THIN SLICES (2 BY I INCH/5 BY 2.5 CM) SHARP (OLD) WHITE CHEDDAR CHEESE	24
1/2 CUP	SWEET ASIAN CHILI SAUCE	125 ML
1/4 CUP	SNIPPED FRESH CHIVES	50 ML

PREHEAT OVEN TO 425°F (220°C). SLICE BAGUETTE DIAGONALLY INTO 24 SLICES AND PLACE ON A LARGE BAKING SHEET. TOP EACH SLICE WITH 2 APPLE SLICES AND I CHEESE SLICE. BAKE FOR 6 TO 8 MINUTES OR UNTIL CHEESE HAS MELTED AND EDGES OF TOASTS ARE BROWN. DRIZZLE WITH CHILI SAUCE AND SPRINKLE WITH CHIVES. MAKES 24 PIECES.

SUMMERTIME DIP

THE FLAVORS OF FRESH HERBS IN A LIGHT DIP.
SERVE WITH FRESH VEGGIES AND CRACKERS.

2	ANCHOVY FILLETS, CHOPPED	2
2	GREEN ONIONS, FINELY CHOPPED	2
1	CLOVE GARLIC, MINCED	1
1/2 CUP	MAYONNAISE	125 ML
1/2 CUP	SOUR CREAM	125 ML
1/4 CUP	SNIPPED FRESH CHIVES	50 ML
2 TBSP	CHOPPED FRESH PARSLEY	25 ML
2 TBSP	CHOPPED FRESH TARRAGON (OR 1 TSP/5 ML DRIED)	25 ML
2 TBSP	FRESHLY SQUEEZED LEMON JUICE	25 ML
1/4 TSP	SALT	1 ML
1/4 TSP	FRESHLY GROUND BLACK PEPPER	1 ML

IN A BLENDER OR FOOD PROCESSOR, PULSE ANCHOVIES,
GREEN ONIONS, GARLIC, MAYONNAISE, SOUR CREAM,
CHIVES, PARSLEY, TARRAGON, LEMON JUICE, SALT AND
PEPPER UNTIL COMBINED. TRANSFER TO AN AIRTIGHT
CONTAINER AND REFRIGERATE FOR AT LEAST 2 HOURS
OR FOR UP TO 1 DAY TO LET FLAVORS DEVELOP. TASTE
AND ADJUST SEASONING WITH MORE LEMON JUICE,
SALT AND/OR PEPPER AS DESIRED. *MAKES ABOUT
1 1/4 CUPS (300 ML).*

MEDITERRANEAN DIP

A TANGY, MAKE-AHEAD APPETIZER TO SERVE
WITH SMALL PITA POCKETS.

1 1/2 CUPS	CRUMBLED FETA CHEESE	375 ML
1	JAR (6 OZ/170 ML) MARINATED ARTICHOKES, DRAINED AND CHOPPED, MARINADE RESERVED	1
1/2 CUP	CHOPPED KALAMATA OLIVES (SEE TIP, BELOW)	125 ML
4 TSP	CHOPPED DRAINED OIL-PACKED SUN-DRIED TOMATOES, OIL RESERVED	20 ML
2 TSP	DRIED OREGANO	10 ML
3	CLOVES GARLIC, MINCED	3

IN A MEDIUM BOWL, COMBINE FETA, ARTICHOKES, OLIVES, TOMATOES, OREGANO AND GARLIC. STIR IN ENOUGH OF THE RESERVED ARTICHOKE MARINADE AND TOMATO OIL TO MAKE A SPREADABLE CONSISTENCY (YOU'LL LIKELY NEED BETWEEN 1/4 AND 1/2 CUP/50 AND 125 ML TOTAL LIQUID). TRANSFER TO A SERVING DISH, COVER AND REFRIGERATE FOR AT LEAST 1 HOUR, UNTIL CHILLED, OR FOR UP TO 3 DAYS. MAKES ABOUT 2 CUPS (500 ML).

TIP: FOR THE BEST-TASTING OLIVES, BUY FRESH ONES FROM THE DELI SECTION OR KALAMATA OLIVES IN JARS. NEVER BUY OLIVES IN CANS!

ROASTED RED PEPPER DIP

THIS CREAMY DIP CAN BE PREPARED IN ADVANCE AND POPPED IN THE OVEN JUST BEFORE GUESTS ARRIVE. SERVE WITH CHIPS, VEGETABLE STICKS OR PITA BREAD.

1	PACKAGE (8 OZ/250 G) CREAM CHEESE, SOFTENED	1
1 1/2 CUPS	SHREDDED SHARP (OLD) CHEDDAR CHEESE	375 ML
1 CUP	CHOPPED ROASTED RED BELL PEPPERS (SEE TIP, PAGE 117)	250 ML
3/4 CUP	MAYONNAISE	175 ML
2 TBSP	FINELY CHOPPED GREEN ONIONS	25 ML
2 TBSP	DIJON MUSTARD	25 ML
PINCH	HOT PEPPER FLAKES	PINCH
	SALT AND FRESHLY GROUND BLACK PEPPER	

PREHEAT OVEN TO 350°F (180°C). IN A BOWL, BEAT CREAM CHEESE, CHEDDAR, ROASTED PEPPERS, MAYONNAISE, GREEN ONIONS, MUSTARD AND HOT PEPPER FLAKES UNTIL SMOOTH. SEASON TO TASTE WITH SALT AND PEPPER. TRANSFER TO AN 8-INCH (20 CM) BAKING DISH. BAKE FOR 20 MINUTES OR UNTIL BUBBLY. MAKES ABOUT 2 CUPS (500 ML).

MAKE AHEAD: COVER BAKING DISH AND REFRIGERATE FOR UP TO 2 DAYS. INCREASE THE BAKING TIME TO ABOUT 25 MINUTES.

APPETIZER OF THE HOUR

LAST-MINUTE COMPANY? WHIP THIS UP WHEN THEY WALK THROUGH THE DOOR AND SERVE IT WITH COCKTAIL CRACKERS.

1	PACKAGE (8 OZ/250 G) CREAM CHEESE, SOFTENED	1
1/2 TSP	MADRAS CURRY POWDER	2 ML
1/4 CUP	JALAPEÑO JELLY	50 ML
1/4 CUP	MANGO CHUTNEY	50 ML
1/4 CUP	TOASTED PINE NUTS (SEE TIP, BELOW)	50 ML
1/4 CUP	DRIED CRANBERRIES OR RAISINS	50 ML
1/4 CUP	FINELY CHOPPED GREEN ONIONS	50 ML

IN A MEDIUM BOWL, BEAT CREAM CHEESE UNTIL SOFT. ADD CURRY POWDER AND MIX WELL. SPREAD INTO A SHALLOW GLASS SERVING DISH. TOP WITH JALAPEÑO JELLY AND CHUTNEY. SPRINKLE WITH PINE NUTS, CRANBERRIES AND GREEN ONIONS. MAKES ABOUT 1 CUP (250 ML).

TIP: TOASTING NUTS HELPS BRING OUT THEIR FLAVOR. THE QUICKEST METHOD IS ON THE STOVETOP. SPREAD NUTS OUT IN AN UNGREASED NONSTICK SKILLET AND PLACE OVER MEDIUM HEAT. SHAKE OR STIR FREQUENTLY, TO PREVENT BURNING, FOR 4 TO 5 MINUTES OR UNTIL FRAGRANT AND STARTING TO BROWN. TIP ONTO A COLD PLATE TO STOP THE COOKING PROCESS AND LET COOL COMPLETELY.

ROASTED RED PEPPER HUMMUS

THIS SMOOTH DIP IS ALWAYS A HIT, ESPECIALLY
WITH TEENAGERS. SERVE IT WITH VEGETABLE
STICKS, PITA BREAD OR CRACKERS.

1	CAN (14 TO 19 OZ/398 TO 540 ML) CHICKPEAS, DRAINED AND RINSED	1
2	CLOVES GARLIC, MINCED	2
1/2 CUP	CHOPPED ROASTED RED BELL PEPPERS (SEE TIP, PAGE 117)	125 ML
3 TBSP	FRESHLY SQUEEZED LEMON JUICE	45 ML
2 TBSP	PLAIN YOGURT	25 ML
2 TBSP	CHOPPED FRESH CILANTRO	25 ML
1 1/2 TBSP	TAHINI (SESAME PASTE)	22 ML
1 TSP	HOT PEPPER SAUCE	5 ML
1/2 TSP	GROUND CUMIN	2 ML
1/4 TSP	SALT	1 ML

IN A FOOD PROCESSOR, PURÉE CHICKPEAS, GARLIC,
ROASTED PEPPERS, LEMON JUICE, YOGURT, CILANTRO,
TAHINI, HOT PEPPER SAUCE, CUMIN AND SALT UNTIL
VERY SMOOTH. TASTE AND ADJUST SEASONING WITH
MORE LEMON JUICE, HOT PEPPER SAUCE AND/OR SALT
AS DESIRED. IF HUMMUS IS TOO THICK, STIR IN MORE
YOGURT. MAKES ABOUT 2 CUPS (500 ML).

TIP: FOR A SMOOTHER HUMMUS, REMOVE THE PAPERY
SKINS FROM THE CHICKPEAS. SPREAD THE DRAINED AND
RINSED CHICKPEAS ON ONE HALF OF A CLEAN TEA TOWEL.
PULL THE OTHER SIDE OF THE TOWEL OVER AND GENTLY
PRESS YOUR HANDS ON TOP, RUBBING AND ROLLING
THE CHICKPEAS TO LOOSEN THE SKINS. PICK OUT AND
DISCARD THE SKINS.

SMOKED SALMON SPREAD

A DELICIOUS ANYTIME SNACK. SERVE ON TOASTED
BAGELS, WHOLE WHEAT TOAST, CRACKERS OR ANY
OTHER FAVORITE CRUNCHY ACCOMPANIMENT.

1	PACKAGE (8 OZ/250 G) CREAM CHEESE, SOFTENED	1
5 OZ	SMOKED SALMON, CHOPPED	150 G
1/4 CUP	FINELY CHOPPED FRESH CHIVES	50 ML
3 TBSP	WHIPPING (35%) CREAM	45 ML
2 TBSP	FRESHLY SQUEEZED LEMON JUICE	25 ML
1 1/2 TSP	PREPARED HORSERADISH	7 ML
	HOT PEPPER SAUCE	
	SALT AND FRESHLY GROUND BLACK PEPPER	

IN A FOOD PROCESSOR, COMBINE CREAM CHEESE,
SALMON, CHIVES, WHIPPING CREAM, LEMON JUICE
AND HORSERADISH. TRANSFER TO A SERVING DISH AND
SEASON TO TASTE WITH HOT PEPPER SAUCE, SALT
AND PEPPER. COVER AND REFRIGERATE FOR AT LEAST
1 HOUR OR FOR UP TO 3 DAYS TO LET FLAVORS DEVELOP.
MAKES ABOUT 1 1/2 CUPS (375 ML).

ATHEISM IS A NON-PROPHET ORGANIZATION.

THREE FLAVORED BUTTERS

FLAVORED BUTTERS ADD ZIP TO GRILLED STEAK, FISH OR STEAMED VEGETABLES. THEY CAN BE MADE AHEAD AND KEPT IN THE FRIDGE OR FREEZER. JUST PLACE A DOLLOP OF THE BUTTER TO MELT ON TOP OF THE HOT FOOD. HERE ARE THREE FLAVORS TO GET YOU STARTED.

GARLIC HERB BUTTER

DELICIOUS WITH GRILLED STEAK.

$1/2$ CUP	UNSALTED BUTTER, SOFTENED	125 ML
3	CLOVES GARLIC, MINCED	3
I TBSP	SNIPPED FRESH CHIVES	15 ML
I TBSP	CHOPPED FRESH PARSLEY	15 ML
	SALT AND FRESHLY GROUND BLACK PEPPER	

IN A BOWL, BEAT BUTTER, GARLIC, CHIVES AND PARSLEY UNTIL SMOOTH AND CREAMY (OR USE A FOOD PROCESSOR TO COMBINE THE INGREDIENTS). SEASON TO TASTE WITH SALT AND PEPPER. MAKES ABOUT $1/2$ CUP (125 ML).

MAKE AHEAD: TRANSFER FLAVORED BUTTER TO AN AIRTIGHT CONTAINER (OR SEE TIP, BELOW) AND REFRIGERATE FOR UP TO 3 DAYS OR FREEZE FOR UP TO I MONTH.

TIP: FOR A FANCIER PRESENTATION, SPOON THE FLAVORED BUTTER ONTO A PIECE OF WAXED PAPER, ROLL INTO A LOG AND WRAP IN PLASTIC WRAP. IF FREEZING, WRAP IN ADDITIONAL FREEZER PLASTIC. TO SERVE, SLICE INTO COINS.

BLUE CHEESE BUTTER

SERVE WITH MEAT, FISH OR CHICKEN.

1/2 CUP	UNSALTED BUTTER, SOFTENED	125 ML
1/3 CUP	FIRM BLUE CHEESE, CRUMBLED	75 ML
1 TBSP	CHOPPED FRESH PARSLEY	15 ML
	SALT AND FRESHLY GROUND BLACK PEPPER	

IN A BOWL, BEAT BUTTER, BLUE CHEESE AND PARSLEY UNTIL SMOOTH AND CREAMY (OR USE A FOOD PROCESSOR TO COMBINE THE INGREDIENTS). SEASON TO TASTE WITH SALT AND PEPPER. MAKES ABOUT 3/4 CUP (175 ML).

MAKE AHEAD: SEE PAGE 64.

TANGY LIME BUTTER

EXCELLENT ON FISH OR SHRIMP.

1/2 CUP	UNSALTED BUTTER, SOFTENED	125 ML
2 TSP	GRATED LIME ZEST	10 ML
1 TBSP	FRESHLY SQUEEZED LIME JUICE	15 ML
1 TBSP	CHOPPED FRESH CILANTRO	15 ML
1/2 TSP	HOT PEPPER FLAKES	2 ML
	SALT AND FRESHLY GROUND BLACK PEPPER	

IN A BOWL, BEAT BUTTER, LIME ZEST, LIME JUICE, CILANTRO AND HOT PEPPER FLAKES UNTIL SMOOTH AND CREAMY (OR USE A FOOD PROCESSOR TO COMBINE THE INGREDIENTS). SEASON TO TASTE WITH SALT AND PEPPER. MAKES ABOUT 1/2 CUP (125 ML).

MAKE AHEAD: SEE PAGE 64.

MANGO CUCUMBER SALSA

FABULOUS WITH GRILLED FISH OR CHICKEN.

1	MANGO, PEELED AND CHOPPED (SEE TIP, BELOW)	1
½	ENGLISH CUCUMBER, CHOPPED	½
½ CUP	FINELY CHOPPED RED ONION	125 ML
2 TBSP	CHOPPED FRESH CILANTRO OR MINT	25 ML
2 TBSP	FRESHLY SQUEEZED LIME JUICE	25 ML
1 TBSP	LIQUID HONEY	15 ML
	SALT AND FRESHLY GROUND BLACK PEPPER	

IN A MEDIUM BOWL, COMBINE MANGO, CUCUMBER, RED ONION, CILANTRO, LIME JUICE AND HONEY. SEASON TO TASTE WITH SALT AND PEPPER. COVER AND REFRIGERATE FOR AT LEAST 1 HOUR, UNTIL CHILLED, OR FOR UP TO 3 HOURS. MAKES ABOUT 2 CUPS (500 ML).

TIP: MANGOS HAVE A LARGE PIT IN THE MIDDLE THAT CAN MAKE CHOPPING THE FRUIT A BIT TRICKY. THE FIRST STEP IS TO SELECT A MANGO THAT IS NOT OVERLY RIPE IF YOU DON'T WANT IT TO END UP AS MUSH! STAND THE MANGO STEM END DOWN ON A CUTTING BOARD. WITH A SHARP KNIFE, CUT AWAY THE PEEL, WORKING FROM TOP TO BOTTOM. THEN CUT A THICK SLICE OFF EACH SIDE OF THE PIT (THESE ARE KNOWN AS "CHEEKS"). SLICE OFF ANY REMAINING FLESH. CHOP THE PIECES AS DESIRED.

SALADS

CELERY ROOT AND APPLE COLESLAW

THIS COLESLAW, SIMILAR TO A WALDORF SALAD, GOES WELL WITH GRILLED CHICKEN, SALMON OR PORK CHOPS.

DRESSING

6 TBSP	MAYONNAISE	90 ML
2 TBSP	DIJON MUSTARD (NOT GRAINY)	25 ML
2 TSP	LIQUID HONEY (OR TO TASTE)	10 ML
	JUICE OF 1/2 LEMON	
	SALT AND FRESHLY GROUND BLACK PEPPER	

SALAD

6	GREEN ONIONS, THINLY SLICED	6
2	GOLDEN DELICIOUS OR GRANNY SMITH APPLES, CUT INTO MATCHSTICKS	2
1	CELERY ROOT (CELERIAC), CUT INTO MATCHSTICKS (SEE TIP, BELOW)	1
1/2 CUP	PECANS, TOASTED (SEE TIP, PAGE 61) AND CHOPPED	125 ML
1/4 CUP	CHOPPED FRESH PARSLEY	50 ML

DRESSING: IN A SMALL BOWL, WHISK TOGETHER MAYONNAISE, MUSTARD, HONEY AND LEMON JUICE. SEASON TO TASTE WITH SALT AND PEPPER. SET ASIDE.

SALAD: IN A LARGE BOWL, COMBINE GREEN ONIONS, APPLES, CELERY ROOT, PECANS AND PARSLEY. ADD DRESSING AND TOSS TO COAT. COVER AND REFRIGERATE FOR 1 HOUR TO LET FLAVORS DEVELOP. SERVES 8.

TIP: TO CUT CELERY ROOT INTO MATCHSTICKS, USE A SHARP KNIFE TO CUT OFF THE STUBBY END AND PEEL OFF THE BROWN, FIBROUS SKIN. CUT INTO THIN SLICES, THEN INTO MATCHSTICKS.

GREEN SALAD WITH ORANGE-WALNUT DRESSING

A GREEN SALAD IN A JIFFY.

1/2 CUP	WALNUT OIL (SEE TIP, BELOW)	125 ML
1/3 CUP	FRESHLY SQUEEZED ORANGE JUICE (ABOUT 1 ORANGE)	75 ML
3 TBSP	CIDER VINEGAR	45 ML
1 TBSP	LIQUID HONEY	15 ML
2 TSP	CHOPPED FRESH TARRAGON (OR 1 PINCH DRIED)	10 ML
1	SMALL SHALLOT, MINCED	1
	SALT AND FRESHLY GROUND BLACK PEPPER	
1	HEAD BUTTER LETTUCE, LEAVES SEPARATED	1
1/2	CAN (10 OZ/284 ML) MANDARIN ORANGES, DRAINED	1/2
1/2 CUP	PECANS, TOASTED (SEE TIP, PAGE 61) AND CHOPPED	125 ML

IN A BLENDER, PURÉE OIL, ORANGE JUICE, VINEGAR, HONEY, TARRAGON, SHALLOT AND SALT AND PEPPER TO TASTE UNTIL SMOOTH AND CREAMY-LOOKING. (YOU CAN ALSO WHISK IT IN A BOWL, BUT THE DRESSING WON'T BE AS THICK.) ARRANGE LETTUCE LEAVES ON INDIVIDUAL PLATES. ARRANGE MANDARIN ORANGE SEGMENTS ON THE LETTUCE, SPRINKLE WITH TOASTED PECANS AND DRIZZLE WITH DRESSING. SERVES 4.

MAKE AHEAD: THE DRESSING CAN BE STORED IN AN AIRTIGHT CONTAINER IN THE REFRIGERATOR FOR UP TO 1 WEEK. WHISK AGAIN BEFORE ADDING TO SALAD.

TIP: WALNUT OIL HAS A MILD, NUTTY FLAVOR THAT IS DELICIOUS IN SALADS. MOST SUPERMARKETS STOCK IT.

GREEN SALAD WITH TOASTED PECANS AND CITRUS DRESSING

THIS SIMPLE, VERSATILE GREEN SALAD GOES WELL WITH FISH, PORK AND CHICKEN.

CITRUS DRESSING

6 TBSP	GRAPESEED OIL, SAFFLOWER OIL OR OLIVE OIL	90 ML
4 TBSP	FRESHLY SQUEEZED ORANGE JUICE	60 ML
	GRATED ZEST OF 1 LIME	
2 TBSP	FRESHLY SQUEEZED LIME JUICE	25 ML
2 TSP	LIQUID HONEY	10 ML
1/2	SMALL SHALLOT, MINCED	1/2
	SALT AND FRESHLY GROUND BLACK PEPPER	

SALAD

6 CUPS	TORN MIXED GREENS OR ROMAINE LETTUCE	1.5 L
1/2 CUP	PECANS, TOASTED (SEE TIP, PAGE 61) AND CHOPPED	125 ML
1/2 CUP	DRIED CRANBERRIES (SWEETENED OR UNSWEETENED)	125 ML

CITRUS DRESSING: IN A SMALL BOWL, WHISK TOGETHER OIL, ORANGE JUICE, LIME ZEST, LIME JUICE, HONEY AND SHALLOT. SEASON TO TASTE WITH SALT AND PEPPER. SET ASIDE.

SALAD: PLACE GREENS IN A LARGE SALAD BOWL. ADD DRESSING AND TOSS TO COAT. SPRINKLE WITH PECANS AND CRANBERRIES. SERVES 4.

MAKE AHEAD: THE DRESSING CAN BE STORED IN AN AIRTIGHT CONTAINER IN THE REFRIGERATOR FOR UP TO 1 WEEK.

CREAMY BEET SALAD

THIS LOOKS AS GOOD AS IT TASTES. SERVE ON A BED OF MIXED GREENS.

5	BEETS, TRIMMED	5
1	SMALL RED ONION, THINLY SLICED	1
4 TBSP	RED WINE VINEGAR	60 ML
2 TBSP	OLIVE OIL	25 ML
1/2 CUP	SOUR CREAM	125 ML
1/2 CUP	CHOPPED PECANS	125 ML
	ROQUEFORT, STILTON OR OTHER BLUE CHEESE (SEE TIP, PAGE 21)	
	FRESHLY GROUND BLACK PEPPER	

IN A LARGE SAUCEPAN OF BOILING WATER, COOK BEETS FOR 45 TO 60 MINUTES OR UNTIL TENDER. DRAIN AND LET COOL. PEEL BEETS AND CUT INTO SLICES OR MATCHSTICKS. IN A LARGE BOWL, COMBINE BEETS AND ONION. ADD VINEGAR AND OIL; TOSS TO COAT. GENTLY STIR IN SOUR CREAM. SPRINKLE WITH PECANS AND CRUMBLE ROQUEFORT OVER TOP. SEASON TO TASTE WITH PEPPER. SERVES 6.

TIP: IT'S ALSO EASY TO ROAST BEETS, WHICH SAVES CLEANUP OF A MESSY SAUCEPAN. PREHEAT OVEN TO 450°F (230°C). SCRUB BEETS, WRAP IN FOIL AND ROAST UNTIL TENDER, ABOUT 40 MINUTES. PEEL AND SLICE. PROCEED WITH RECIPE.

FATTOUSH

A TASTE OF THE MIDDLE EAST — CRUNCHY AND BURSTING WITH FLAVORS.

DRESSING

4 TBSP	OLIVE OIL	60 ML
1 TSP	GRATED LEMON ZEST	5 ML
4 TBSP	FRESHLY SQUEEZED LEMON JUICE	60 ML
2	CLOVES GARLIC, MINCED	2
1/2 TSP	SALT	2 ML
	FRESHLY GROUND BLACK PEPPER	

SALAD

2	PITAS, OPENED	2
2	ROMAINE LETTUCE HEARTS (SEE TIP, OPPOSITE), CHOPPED	2
3	LARGE TOMATOES, CUT INTO LARGE PIECES	3
1	ENGLISH CUCUMBER, HALVED LENGTHWISE AND COARSELY CHOPPED	1
1	BUNCH RADISHES, TRIMMED AND QUARTERED (ABOUT 1 1/4 CUPS/300 ML)	1
1	RED BELL PEPPER, CHOPPED	1
1/2	LARGE RED ONION, VERY THINLY SLICED	1/2
1/2 CUP	CHOPPED FRESH PARSLEY	125 ML
2 TBSP	CHOPPED FRESH MINT	25 ML

DRESSING: IN A BOWL, WHISK TOGETHER OIL, LEMON ZEST, LEMON JUICE AND GARLIC. SEASON TO TASTE WITH SALT AND PEPPER. SET ASIDE.

SALAD: PREHEAT BROILER. BROIL PITAS, TURNING ONCE, FOR ABOUT 4 MINUTES OR UNTIL CRISP ON BOTH SIDES. LET COOL AND BREAK INTO BITE-SIZE PIECES. IN A LARGE

SALAD BOWL, COMBINE ROMAINE, TOMATOES, CUCUMBER, RADISHES, RED PEPPER, RED ONION, PARSLEY AND MINT. ADD DRESSING AND GENTLY TOSS TO COAT. SPRINKLE WITH TOASTED PITA PIECES. SERVES 6 TO 8.

MAKE AHEAD: THE DRESSING CAN BE STORED IN AN AIRTIGHT CONTAINER IN THE REFRIGERATOR FOR UP TO 3 DAYS.

TIP: HEARTS OF ROMAINE ARE PALE GREEN AND VERY CRISPY, PERFECT FOR THIS CRUNCHY SALAD. THEY ARE MORE EXPENSIVE THAN WHOLE ROMAINE LETTUCES, BUT BECAUSE THE OUTSIDE LEAVES HAVE BEEN REMOVED, THERE IS NO WASTE. LOOK FOR PACKS OF ROMAINE HEARTS IN THE PRODUCE AISLE.

VARIATION: USE 1 BUNCH OF GREEN ONIONS, CHOPPED, IN PLACE OF THE RED ONION. YOU CAN ALSO USE FRESH THYME OR OREGANO IN PLACE OF THE FRESH MINT.

SIGN ON THE LAWN OF A DRUG REHAB CENTER:
KEEP OFF THE GRASS.

FRUIT AND BROCCOLI BUFFET SALAD

ANOTHER GREAT SALAD FOR YOUR NEXT FAMILY BUN FIGHT!

POPPY SEED DRESSING

1/2 CUP	GRAPESEED OIL, SAFFLOWER OIL OR OLIVE OIL	125 ML
1/3 CUP	GRANULATED SUGAR	75 ML
3 TBSP	CIDER VINEGAR	45 ML
1 TSP	GRATED LIME ZEST	5 ML
2 TBSP	FRESHLY SQUEEZED LIME JUICE	25 ML
1	CLOVE GARLIC, MINCED	1
1/2 TSP	SALT	2 ML
1/2 TSP	POPPY SEEDS	2 ML
1/2 TSP	PAPRIKA	2 ML
1/2 TSP	DRY MUSTARD	2 ML

SALAD

2	ORANGES, PEELED, SEEDED AND SECTIONED	2
1	RED APPLE, CHOPPED	1
2 1/2 CUPS	BROCCOLI FLORETS, CUT INTO BITE-SIZE PIECES	625 ML
1 CUP	SEEDLESS RED OR GREEN GRAPES, HALVED	250 ML
1/2 CUP	PECANS, TOASTED (SEE TIP, OPPOSITE) AND CHOPPED	125 ML

DRESSING: IN A MEDIUM BOWL, WHISK TOGETHER OIL, SUGAR, VINEGAR, LIME ZEST, LIME JUICE, GARLIC, SALT, POPPY SEEDS, PAPRIKA AND MUSTARD. SET ASIDE.

SALAD: IN A LARGE BOWL, COMBINE ORANGES, APPLE, BROCCOLI AND GRAPES. ADD DRESSING AND GENTLY TOSS TO COAT. COVER AND REFRIGERATE FOR AT LEAST 2 HOURS, UNTIL CHILLED, OR FOR UP TO 6 HOURS. SPRINKLE WITH PECANS. SERVES 6.

MAKE AHEAD: THE DRESSING CAN BE STORED IN AN AIRTIGHT CONTAINER IN THE REFRIGERATOR FOR UP TO 3 DAYS.

TIP: TOASTING NUTS HELPS BRING OUT THEIR FLAVOR. THE QUICKEST METHOD IS ON THE STOVETOP. SPREAD NUTS OUT IN AN UNGREASED NONSTICK SKILLET AND PLACE OVER MEDIUM HEAT. SHAKE OR STIR FREQUENTLY, TO PREVENT BURNING, FOR 4 TO 5 MINUTES OR UNTIL FRAGRANT AND STARTING TO BROWN. TIP ONTO A COLD PLATE TO STOP THE COOKING PROCESS AND LET COOL COMPLETELY.

VARIATION: USE A CHOPPED RED-SKINNED PEAR IN PLACE OF THE APPLE AND TOASTED HAZELNUTS OR WALNUTS IN PLACE OF THE PECANS.

MY YOUNG GRANDSON CALLED THE OTHER DAY TO WISH ME A HAPPY BIRTHDAY. HE ASKED HOW OLD I WAS, AND I TOLD HIM, "62." HE WAS QUIET FOR A MOMENT AND THEN ASKED, "DID YOU START AT 1?"

FENNEL, ORANGE AND POMEGRANATE SALAD

THIS TRADITIONAL ITALIAN SALAD IS A DELIGHT IN CONTRASTS: CRUNCHY FENNEL, SWEET ORANGES AND JUICY POMEGRANATE SEEDS. FOR DRESSING, IT NEEDS ONLY A DRIZZLE OF FRESH ORANGE JUICE AND SOME GOOD OLIVE OIL (WE DON'T RECOMMEND USING EXTRA VIRGIN OLIVE OIL ON THIS SALAD, AS ITS DISTINCT, EARTHY FLAVOR MIGHT OVERPOWER THE FRESH FRUIT.) SERVE AS A REFRESHING STARTER OR AS AN ACCOMPANIMENT TO GRILLED CHICKEN, FISH OR PORK.

3	ORANGES	3
1	LARGE FENNEL BULB	1
	SEEDS FROM 1 FRESH POMEGRANATE (SEE TIP, OPPOSITE)	
3 TBSP	OLIVE OIL	45 ML
	SALT AND FRESHLY GROUND BLACK PEPPER	

IF THE FENNEL HAS THE FEATHERY STALKS ATTACHED, TRIM THEM OFF ABOUT 1 INCH (2.5 CM) ABOVE THE BULB. CUT BULB IN HALF VERTICALLY AND REMOVE THE WOODY CORE FROM EACH HALF. CUT EACH HALF INTO VERY THIN SLICES. REMOVE THE PEEL AND WHITE PITH FROM 2 OF THE ORANGES AND CUT THE FLESH CROSSWISE INTO THIN SLICES. CUT THE THIRD ORANGE IN HALF AND SET ASIDE. ARRANGE FENNEL AND ORANGE SLICES ON A PLATTER AND SCATTER WITH POMEGRANATE SEEDS. SQUEEZE THE JUICE FROM ONE OF THE RESERVED ORANGE HALVES OVER THE SALAD. (KEEP THE REMAINING HALF ORANGE TO EAT AS A SNACK LATER). DRIZZLE SALAD WITH OIL AND SEASON TO TASTE WITH SALT AND PEPPER. SERVE IMMEDIATELY.

SERVES 4.

TIP: HERE'S A SIMPLE WAY TO REMOVE POMEGRANATE SEEDS: SUBMERGE THE POMEGRANATE IN A LARGE BOWL OF COLD WATER AND REMOVE THE SKIN AND WHITE PITH. THE SEEDS WILL SINK TO THE BOTTOM AND THE PITH WILL FLOAT TO THE TOP. THIS METHOD PREVENTS THE JUICE FROM SQUIRTING ALL OVER YOUR FAVORITE WHITE BLOUSE.

HOMEMADE GARLIC CROUTONS

$\frac{1}{4}$ TO $\frac{1}{3}$ CUP	OLIVE OIL	50 TO 75 ML
2	CLOVES GARLIC, MINCED	2
1	LOAF BREAD (ANY KIND), CUT INTO 1-INCH (2.5 CM) CUBES	1
$\frac{1}{2}$ TSP	SALT	2 ML
	FRESHLY GROUND BLACK PEPPER	

PREHEAT OVEN TO 350°F (180°C). SPREAD OIL AND GARLIC OVER 1 OR 2 LARGE BAKING SHEETS. ADD BREAD CUBES AND TURN TO COAT IN OIL. SPRINKLE WITH SALT AND PEPPER TO TASTE. BAKE FOR 10 TO 15 MINUTES OR UNTIL CROUTONS ARE BROWN AND CRISPY. (CHECK THEM HALFWAY THROUGH, AS SOME TYPES OF BREAD BROWN FASTER THAN OTHERS.) LET COOL. MAKES ABOUT 8 CUPS (2 L).

MAKE AHEAD: STORE IN AN AIRTIGHT CONTAINER AT ROOM TEMPERATURE FOR UP TO 1 WEEK.

VARIATION: SPRINKLE BREAD CUBES WITH $\frac{1}{3}$ CUP (75 ML) FRESHLY GRATED PARMESAN CHEESE BEFORE BAKING.

MANGO AND ASPARAGUS CURRIED SALAD

THIS SALAD WORKS WELL FOR A BUFFET
BECAUSE IT HOLDS ITS CRUNCH.

1 CUP	MAYONNAISE	250 ML
2 TBSP	MADRAS CURRY POWDER	25 ML
2 TBSP	LIQUID HONEY	25 ML
	GRATED ZEST AND JUICE OF 1 LIME	
	SALT AND FRESHLY GROUND BLACK PEPPER	
1	BUNCH ASPARAGUS (ABOUT 24 SPEARS), ENDS TRIMMED	1
1	MANGO, PEELED AND SLICED (SEE TIP, PAGE 66)	1
1	ORANGE, PEELED AND SLICED	1
1	CAN (8 OZ/227 ML) SLICED WATER CHESTNUTS, DRAINED	1
2 CUPS	BEAN SPROUTS, RINSED AND DRAINED	500 ML
1½ CUPS	CHOPPED CELERY	375 ML
1 CUP	ROASTED UNSALTED CASHEWS	250 ML

IN A BOWL, WHISK TOGETHER MAYONNAISE, CURRY POWDER, HONEY, LIME ZEST AND LIME JUICE. SEASON TO TASTE WITH SALT AND PEPPER. COVER AND REFRIGERATE FOR 30 MINUTES, UNTIL CHILLED, OR FOR UP TO 1 DAY.

IN A LARGE POT OF BOILING WATER, BLANCH ASPARAGUS FOR 1 MINUTE. DRAIN AND PLUNGE INTO A BOWL OF ICE WATER. DRAIN AGAIN AND CUT INTO 1-INCH (2.5 CM) PIECES. IN A LARGE SALAD BOWL, COMBINE ASPARAGUS, MANGO, ORANGE, WATER CHESTNUTS, BEAN SPROUTS, CELERY AND CASHEWS. JUST BEFORE SERVING, ADD DRESSING AND TOSS TO COAT. *SERVES 6 TO 8.*

WATERMELON, RADISH AND FETA SALAD

WITH THE SALTY FLAVOR OF FETA CHEESE AND THE PEPPERY TASTE OF RADISHES, THIS REFRESHING SALAD NEEDS BARELY ANY DRESSING. SERVE AS A REFRESHING SUMMER STARTER OR AS AN ACCOMPANIMENT TO GRILLED CHICKEN OR LAMB.

4 CUPS	WATERMELON CHUNKS	1 L
1 CUP	DICED FETA CHEESE	250 ML
1 CUP	THINLY SLICED RADISHES	250 ML
3 TBSP	THINLY SLICED FRESH MINT OR BASIL	45 ML
3 TBSP	FRESHLY SQUEEZED LIME JUICE	45 ML
	FRESHLY GROUND BLACK PEPPER (OPTIONAL)	

IN A LARGE BOWL, GENTLY COMBINE WATERMELON, FETA, RADISHES, MINT AND LIME JUICE, BEING CAREFUL TO KEEP THE WATERMELON CHUNKS INTACT. SEASON TO TASTE WITH PEPPER, IF USING. COVER AND REFRIGERATE FOR 1 HOUR TO LET FLAVORS DEVELOP. SERVES 4.

A SMALL BOY SWALLOWED SOME COINS AND WAS TAKEN TO THE HOSPITAL. WHEN HIS GRANDMOTHER PHONED TO ASK HOW HE WAS, A NURSE SAID, "NO CHANGE YET."

GRILLED PEACH AND BLUE CHEESE SALAD

THE UNLIKELY COMBINATION OF FLAVORS IN THIS SALAD CREATES A DELIGHTFUL TASTE SENSATION. ARRANGE IT ON INDIVIDUAL PLATES AS A STARTER, OR HEAP IT ON A PLATTER AND LET EVERYONE HELP THEMSELVES. IT GOES WELL WITH GRILLED PORK OR CHICKEN.

I	CAN (14 OZ/398 ML) PEACH HALVES IN JUICE, DRAINED, OR 3 FRESH PEACHES, PEELED AND HALVED (SEE TIP, OPPOSITE)	I
2 TBSP	PURE MAPLE SYRUP OR LIQUID HONEY	25 ML
1/4 CUP	OLIVE OIL	50 ML
2 TBSP	CIDER VINEGAR	25 ML
I TSP	HONEY MUSTARD	5 ML
	SALT AND FRESHLY GROUND BLACK PEPPER	
4 CUPS	MIXED SALAD GREENS	I L
I CUP	CRUMBLED STILTON OR OTHER BLUE CHEESE (SEE TIP, PAGE 21)	250 ML
1/2 CUP	PECANS, TOASTED (SEE TIP, PAGE 75) AND CHOPPED	125 ML

PREHEAT BROILER. LINE A BAKING SHEET WITH FOIL AND GREASE FOIL. IN A LARGE BOWL, GENTLY TOSS PEACH HALVES WITH MAPLE SYRUP. TRANSFER TO BAKING SHEET AND BROIL FOR 5 TO 7 MINUTES, TURNING ONCE, UNTIL PEACHES ARE STARTING TO BROWN AND SYRUP IS BUBBLING. LET COOL SLIGHTLY. CUT EACH PEACH HALF INTO FOUR SLICES AND SET ASIDE. IN A LARGE BOWL, WHISK TOGETHER OIL, VINEGAR AND MUSTARD. SEASON TO TASTE WITH SALT AND PEPPER. ADD SALAD GREENS AND TOSS TO COAT. ARRANGE GREENS ON INDIVIDUAL

PLATES OR ON A PLATTER. ARRANGE PEACHES ON GREENS. SPRINKLE WITH STILTON AND PECANS. SERVES 4.

TIP: BUY A QUALITY BRAND OF CANNED PEACHES — THE CHEAPER VARIETIES ARE SOMETIMES MUSHY. IF YOU DECIDE TO USE FRESH PEACHES, YOU'LL NEED TO PEEL THEM FIRST. LIGHTLY SCORE THE SKIN WITH THE POINT OF A PARING KNIFE. PLUNGE INTO BOILING WATER FOR 15 SECONDS. DRAIN AND PLUNGE INTO A BOWL OF ICE WATER. ONCE COOL ENOUGH TO HANDLE, PEEL AWAY SKIN AND CUT PEACHES IN HALF.

VARIATION: IF YOU'RE SHORT ON TIME, DON'T BOTHER TO BROIL THE PEACHES. SIMPLY TOSS THEM IN THE MAPLE SYRUP AND ADD TO THE SALAD. IT'LL STILL TASTE WONDERFUL.

THE ROUNDEST KNIGHT AT KING ARTHUR'S ROUND TABLE WAS SIR CUMFERENCE. HE ACQUIRED HIS SIZE FROM TOO MUCH PI.

NIÇOISE SALAD

THIS TRADITIONAL MAKE-AHEAD SALAD (SOUNDS LIKE "KNEE-SWAHZ") FEATURES THE LOCAL PRODUCE OF NICE — PERFECT FOR A SUMMER'S LUNCH. PRESENT IT ON A LARGE PLATTER AND LET YOUR GUESTS SERVE THEMSELVES. VERY FRENCH AND TRÈS DELICIEUX!

DRESSING

³⁄₄ CUP	EXTRA VIRGIN OLIVE OIL (SEE TIP, OPPOSITE)	175 ML
6 TBSP	RED WINE VINEGAR	90 ML
2 TBSP	CHOPPED FRESH PARSLEY	25 ML
4 TSP	DIJON MUSTARD	20 ML
1 TBSP	FINELY CHOPPED SHALLOTS	15 ML
¹⁄₂ TSP	DRIED TARRAGON	2 ML
	SALT AND FRESHLY GROUND BLACK PEPPER	

SALAD

5	EGGS	5
12	TINY RED POTATOES	12
1 LB	GREEN BEANS, TRIMMED	500 G
1	HEAD BUTTER LETTUCE, LEAVES SEPARATED	1
6	SMALL TOMATOES, CUT INTO WEDGES	6
1	CAN (6 OZ/170 G) SOLID WHITE TUNA IN WATER, DRAINED	1
¹⁄₂ CUP	NIÇOISE OR KALAMATA OLIVES	125 ML
2 TBSP	DRAINED CAPERS	25 ML
4	ANCHOVY FILLETS, DRAINED AND PATTED DRY (OPTIONAL)	4

DRESSING: IN A SMALL BOWL, WHISK TOGETHER OIL, VINEGAR, PARSLEY, MUSTARD, SHALLOTS AND TARRAGON. SEASON TO TASTE WITH SALT AND PEPPER. SET ASIDE.

SALAD: HARD-BOIL EGGS, COVER AND REFRIGERATE (SEE TIP, PAGE 89). IN A POT OF BOILING SALTED WATER, COOK POTATOES UNTIL TENDER, ABOUT 20 MINUTES. DRAIN AND LET COOL. CUT POTATOES IN HALF AND PLACE IN A MEDIUM BOWL. IN A POT OF BOILING WATER, BLANCH BEANS FOR 2 TO 3 MINUTES OR UNTIL TENDER-CRISP. DRAIN AND PLUNGE INTO A BOWL OF ICE WATER. PAT DRY AND ADD TO POTATOES. DRIZZLE WITH A SMALL AMOUNT OF DRESSING AND TOSS TO COAT. COVER POTATO MIXTURE AND THE REMAINING DRESSING AND REFRIGERATE OVERNIGHT.

PEEL EGGS AND CUT INTO WEDGES. LINE A PLATTER WITH LETTUCE LEAVES AND ARRANGE POTATO MIXTURE, TOMATOES AND EGGS ON LETTUCE. PILE BITE-SIZE CHUNKS OF TUNA IN THE CENTER AND GARNISH WITH OLIVES, CAPERS AND ANCHOVIES. JUST BEFORE SERVING, DRIZZLE WITH DRESSING, TAKING CARE NOT TO ADD TOO MUCH. SERVE THE REMAINING DRESSING ON THE SIDE. SERVES 6.

TIP: WE DON'T GENERALLY USE EXTRA VIRGIN OLIVE OIL IN SALAD DRESSINGS BECAUSE ITS EARTHINESS CAN BE OVERPOWERING. WE PREFER THE MILDER FLAVOR OF GRAPESEED OIL, SAFFLOWER OIL OR REGULAR OLIVE OIL. HOWEVER, IN THIS DISH, WE FEEL THAT THE HEARTINESS OF EXTRA VIRGIN OLIVE OIL WORKS WELL WITH THE OTHER BOLD-FLAVORED INGREDIENTS. OF COURSE, IT'S ALL A QUESTION OF PERSONAL TASTE, SO BE DARING AND EXPERIMENT WITH THE VARIOUS OILS TO FIND THE ONE YOU LIKE BEST!

SUMMERY SHRIMP SALAD WITH RASPBERRY VINAIGRETTE

THE VIVID PINK COLOR OF THIS RASPBERRY VINAIGRETTE IS UNUSUAL, BUT IT'S 100% NATURAL! ARRANGE THE SALAD ON FOUR INDIVIDUAL PLATES AND SERVE AS AN ELEGANT LUNCH OR DINNER STARTER.

RASPBERRY VINAIGRETTE

1/2 CUP	GRAPESEED OIL, SAFFLOWER OIL OR OLIVE OIL	125 ML
1/4 CUP	FRESH OR THAWED FROZEN RASPBERRIES	50 ML
3 TBSP	RASPBERRY-FLAVORED OR RED WINE VINEGAR	45 ML
2 TO 3 TBSP	LIQUID HONEY	25 TO 45 ML
I TBSP	DIJON MUSTARD	15 ML
2 TSP	MINCED SHALLOT	10 ML
2 TSP	FRESHLY SQUEEZED LIME JUICE (APPROX.)	10 ML
	SALT AND FRESHLY GROUND BLACK PEPPER	

SALAD

I	HEAD BUTTER LETTUCE, LEAVES SEPARATED	I
2	AVOCADOS, PEELED AND SLICED	2
2 CUPS	CHOPPED PAPAYA (ABOUT I MEDIUM)	500 ML
2 TBSP	FRESHLY SQUEEZED LIME JUICE	25 ML
	SALT AND FRESHLY GROUND BLACK PEPPER	
20	LARGE SHRIMP (ABOUT 12 OZ/375 G), COOKED	20
1/2 CUP	SLICED ALMONDS, TOASTED (SEE TIP, PAGE 75)	125 ML

RASPBERRY VINAIGRETTE: IN A BLENDER, PURÉE OIL, RASPBERRIES, VINEGAR, 2 TBSP (25 ML) HONEY, MUSTARD, SHALLOT AND LIME JUICE UNTIL THICK AND CREAMY-LOOKING. STRAIN INTO A SMALL BOWL (TO REMOVE THE RASPBERRY SEEDS) AND SEASON TO TASTE WITH SALT AND PEPPER. TASTE AND ADD MORE HONEY OR LIME JUICE TO GET DESIRED TANGINESS (IT WILL DEPEND ON THE SWEETNESS OF THE RASPBERRIES). SET ASIDE.

SALAD: ARRANGE LETTUCE ON INDIVIDUAL PLATES. IN A LARGE BOWL, COMBINE AVOCADOS AND PAPAYA. DRIZZLE WITH LIME JUICE AND SEASON TO TASTE WITH SALT AND PEPPER; GENTLY STIR TO COAT. ARRANGE FRUIT MIXTURE ON TOP OF THE LETTUCE, DIVIDING EVENLY. ARRANGE 5 SHRIMP ON EACH PLATE. DRIZZLE WITH RASPBERRY VINAIGRETTE AND SPRINKLE WITH TOASTED ALMONDS. SERVE IMMEDIATELY. SERVES 4.

MAKE AHEAD: THE DRESSING CAN BE STORED IN AN AIRTIGHT CONTAINER IN THE REFRIGERATOR FOR UP TO 3 DAYS.

CHUTNEY CHICKEN SALAD

A LIGHT AND FRESH-TASTING SALAD THAT'S PERFECT FOR A BUFFET LUNCH.

DRESSING

I CUP	MAYONNAISE	250 ML
I CUP	SOUR CREAM OR PLAIN YOGURT	250 ML
1/4 CUP	MANGO CHUTNEY	50 ML
I TBSP	SOY SAUCE	15 ML
I TSP	MADRAS CURRY POWDER	5 ML

SALAD

5 CUPS	CHOPPED COOKED CHICKEN BREAST (BITE-SIZE PIECES)	1.25 L
2 CUPS	SEEDLESS RED GRAPES, HALVED	500 ML
2 CUPS	FRESH OR DRAINED CANNED PINEAPPLE CHUNKS	500 ML
2 CUPS	CRUNCHY CHOW MEIN NOODLES	500 ML
I CUP	CHOPPED CELERY	250 ML
I CUP	RAISINS	250 ML
1/2 CUP	SLICED ALMONDS, TOASTED (SEE TIP, PAGE 75)	125 ML
2	CANS (EACH 8 OZ/227 G) SLICED WATER CHESTNUTS, DRAINED	2
I CUP	UNSWEETENED SHREDDED COCONUT, TOASTED (SEE TIP, OPPOSITE)	250 ML

DRESSING: IN A MEDIUM BOWL, WHISK TOGETHER MAYONNAISE, SOUR CREAM, CHUTNEY, SOY SAUCE AND CURRY POWDER. REFRIGERATE FOR AT LEAST I HOUR OR FOR UP TO I DAY TO LET FLAVORS DEVELOP.

SALAD: IN A LARGE SALAD BOWL, COMBINE CHICKEN, GRAPES, PINEAPPLE, NOODLES, CELERY, RAISINS, ALMONDS

AND WATER CHESTNUTS. ADD DRESSING AND GENTLY TOSS TO COAT. SERVE WITH COCONUT ON THE SIDE. SERVES 8.

TIP: TOASTING COCONUT GIVES IT A NICE CARAMELIZED FLAVOR AND A CRISP TEXTURE. THE QUICKEST METHOD IS ON THE STOVETOP. SPREAD COCONUT OUT IN AN UNGREASED NONSTICK SKILLET AND PLACE OVER MEDIUM HEAT. SHAKE OR STIR FREQUENTLY FOR ABOUT 5 MINUTES OR UNTIL MOSTLY GOLDEN BROWN. TIP ONTO A COLD PLATE TO STOP THE COOKING PROCESS AND LET COOL COMPLETELY. ALTERNATIVELY, SPREAD ON A BAKING SHEET AND TOAST IN A 325°F (160°C) OVEN, STIRRING FREQUENTLY, UNTIL EVENLY BROWNED. CHECK COCONUT OFTEN, AS IT CAN BURN QUICKLY.

"I HAD A ROSE NAMED AFTER ME AND I WAS VERY FLATTERED. BUT I WAS NOT PLEASED TO READ THE DESCRIPTION IN THE CATALOG: 'NO GOOD IN A BED, BUT FINE AGAINST A WALL.'"
— ELEANOR ROOSEVELT

COBB SALAD

THIS LEGENDARY SALAD WAS REPORTEDLY CREATED IN THE 1920S BY BOB COBB AT HIS BROWN DERBY RESTAURANT IN LOS ANGELES. IT REALLY DOES STAND THE TEST OF TIME. SERVE FOR LUNCH OR AS A LIGHT SUMMER DINNER.

DRESSING

4 TBSP	OLIVE OIL	60 ML
4 TBSP	CANOLA OIL	60 ML
3 TBSP	RED WINE VINEGAR	45 ML
1 TBSP	FRESHLY SQUEEZED LEMON JUICE	15 ML
2 TSP	LIQUID HONEY	10 ML
1/2 TSP	DRY MUSTARD	2 ML
1	CLOVE GARLIC, MINCED	1
	SALT AND FRESHLY GROUND BLACK PEPPER	

SALAD

4 CUPS	CHOPPED ROMAINE LETTUCE	1 L
1 1/2 CUPS	DICED COOKED CHICKEN OR TURKEY BREAST	375 ML
12	GRAPE OR CHERRY TOMATOES	12
2	EGGS, HARD-BOILED (SEE TIP, OPPOSITE), PEELED AND CHOPPED	2
1	AVOCADO, DICED	1
1/2 CUP	CRUMBLED FIRM BLUE CHEESE (SEE TIP, PAGE 21)	125 ML
4	SLICES BACON, COOKED CRISP AND CRUMBLED	4
4	GREEN ONIONS, THINLY SLICED	4

DRESSING: IN A MEDIUM BOWL, WHISK TOGETHER OLIVE OIL, CANOLA OIL, VINEGAR, LEMON JUICE, HONEY,

MUSTARD AND GARLIC. SEASON TO TASTE WITH SALT AND PEPPER. SET ASIDE.

SALAD: LINE A PLATTER WITH ROMAINE AND ARRANGE CHICKEN, TOMATOES, EGGS AND AVOCADO ON TOP IN ATTRACTIVE ROWS. SPRINKLE WITH BLUE CHEESE, BACON AND GREEN ONIONS. DRIZZLE WITH DRESSING AND SERVE IMMEDIATELY. SERVES 3 TO 4.

MAKE AHEAD: THE DRESSING CAN BE STORED IN AN AIRTIGHT CONTAINER IN THE REFRIGERATOR FOR UP TO 3 DAYS.

TIP: TO HARD-BOIL EGGS, PLACE EGGS IN A SAUCEPAN AND COVER WITH COLD WATER. BRING WATER TO A BOIL, COVER AND IMMEDIATELY REMOVE PAN FROM HEAT. LET STAND FOR 20 MINUTES. CAREFULLY TRANSFER HARD-BOILED EGGS TO A STRAINER (YOU DON'T WANT TO CRACK THE SHELLS) AND PLACE UNDER COLD RUNNING WATER UNTIL COOLED. WITHOUT REMOVING SHELLS, PLACE EGGS IN AN AIRTIGHT CONTAINER AND REFRIGERATE FOR UP TO 1 WEEK.

VARIATION: DON'T BOTHER TO MAKE OUR DRESSING — JUST BUY YOUR FAVORITE BOTTLED BLUE CHEESE DRESSING AND ADJUST THE AMOUNT OF CRUMBLED BLUE CHEESE TO SUIT YOUR TASTE.

"LAST WEEK, I STATED THIS WOMAN WAS THE UGLIEST WOMAN I HAD EVER SEEN. I HAVE SINCE BEEN VISITED BY HER SISTER AND NOW I WISH TO WITHDRAW THAT STATEMENT."
— MARK TWAIN

— WARM CHICKEN TACO SALAD —

A TEX-MEX FAVE. THE REDUCED-FAT CREAMY DRESSING TAMES THE FIERINESS OF THE CHIPOTLE PEPPERS.

DRESSING

1/2 CUP	LIGHT SOUR CREAM	125 ML
1/2 CUP	LIGHT MAYONNAISE	125 ML
1/4 CUP	CHOPPED FRESH CILANTRO	50 ML
2 TBSP	FRESHLY SQUEEZED LIME JUICE	25 ML
1 TO 2 TSP	PURÉED CANNED CHIPOTLE PEPPER (SEE TIP, PAGE 153)	5 TO 10 ML
1 TSP	GROUND CUMIN	5 ML
2	CLOVES GARLIC, MINCED	2
	SALT	

CHICKEN

1 TSP	PAPRIKA	5 ML
1 TSP	PACKED BROWN SUGAR	5 ML
1/2 TSP	SALT	2 ML
	GRATED ZEST OF 1 LIME	
4	BONELESS SKINLESS CHICKEN BREASTS	4
	OLIVE OIL	

SALAD

6 CUPS	TORN ROMAINE LETTUCE	1.5 L
2 CUPS	CHERRY TOMATOES, HALVED	500 ML
2 CUPS	LIGHTLY CRUSHED CORN TORTILLA CHIPS	500 ML
1	ENGLISH CUCUMBER, CHOPPED	1
1	BUNCH GREEN ONIONS, CHOPPED (ABOUT 3/4 CUP/175 ML)	1
1	RED BELL PEPPER, CHOPPED	1
1/2	CAN (12 OZ/340 ML) CORN KERNELS, DRAINED AND RINSED	1/2

DRESSING: IN A MEDIUM BOWL, WHISK TOGETHER SOUR CREAM, MAYONNAISE, CILANTRO, LIME JUICE, CHIPOTLE PEPPER, CUMIN AND GARLIC. SEASON TO TASTE WITH SALT. REFRIGERATE FOR AT LEAST I HOUR OR FOR UP TO I DAY TO LET FLAVORS DEVELOP.

CHICKEN: PREHEAT OVEN TO 375°F (190°C) OR BARBECUE GRILL TO MEDIUM-HIGH. IN A SMALL BOWL, COMBINE PAPRIKA, BROWN SUGAR, SALT AND LIME ZEST. RUB OVER BOTH SIDES OF CHICKEN BREASTS. BRUSH CHICKEN LIGHTLY WITH OIL. IF BAKING, PLACE ON A GREASED BAKING SHEET. BAKE OR GRILL FOR ABOUT 15 MINUTES, TURNING ONCE, UNTIL NO LONGER PINK INSIDE. REMOVE FROM HEAT AND KEEP WARM.

SALAD: IN A LARGE SALAD BOWL, COMBINE LETTUCE, TOMATOES, TORTILLA CHIPS, CUCUMBER, GREEN ONIONS, RED PEPPER AND CORN. ADD DRESSING AND TOSS GENTLY TO COAT. TRANSFER CHICKEN TO A CUTTING BOARD AND SLICE DIAGONALLY INTO THIN STRIPS. ARRANGE ON TOP OF SALAD. SERVES 4.

MAKE AHEAD: THE CHICKEN CAN BE SEASONED WITH THE PAPRIKA MIXTURE, COVERED AND REFRIGERATED FOR UP TO 4 HOURS BEFORE BAKING OR GRILLING.

VARIATIONS: ADD A PEELED, SLICED AVOCADO OR MANGO, OR 2 CUPS (500 ML) DRAINED AND RINSED CANNED BLACK BEANS OR KIDNEY BEANS. YOU COULD ALSO USE GRILLED SHRIMP IN PLACE OF THE CHICKEN.

WEST COAST STEAK SALAD

*AN EXCELLENT ENTRÉE SALAD FOR A
WARM SUMMER DAY.*

3/4 CUP	SOY SAUCE	175 ML
1 TBSP	MINCED GINGERROOT	15 ML
2	CLOVES GARLIC, MINCED	2
1 LB	THICK BEEF STRIP LOIN OR OTHER GRILLING STEAK	500 G
1/2 CUP	GRANULATED SUGAR	125 ML
1/2 CUP	TOMATO-BASED CHILI SAUCE	125 ML
1/2 CUP	RICE VINEGAR	125 ML
4 TBSP	VEGETABLE OIL	60 ML
6 CUPS	BABY SPINACH LEAVES	1.5 L
2 CUPS	BEAN SPROUTS, RINSED AND DRAINED	500 ML
12	CHERRY TOMATOES	12
2 TBSP	TOASTED SESAME SEEDS (SEE TIP, OPPOSITE)	25 ML

IN A SMALL BOWL, COMBINE SOY SAUCE, GINGER AND
GARLIC. RESERVE 4 TBSP (60 ML) FOR THE DRESSING.
PLACE STEAK IN A SHALLOW BOWL AND POUR IN THE
REMAINING MARINADE, TURNING STEAK TO COAT EVENLY.
COVER AND REFRIGERATE FOR AT LEAST 3 HOURS OR
OVERNIGHT.

IN A MEDIUM SAUCEPAN, COMBINE SUGAR, CHILI SAUCE,
VINEGAR, OIL AND RESERVED MARINADE; BRING TO A BOIL
OVER MEDIUM-HIGH HEAT. REDUCE HEAT AND SIMMER FOR
3 TO 4 MINUTES OR UNTIL SLIGHTLY THICKENED. REMOVE
FROM HEAT AND KEEP WARM.

PREHEAT BARBECUE GRILL TO MEDIUM-HIGH. REMOVE STEAK FROM MARINADE, DISCARDING MARINADE. GRILL STEAK FOR 5 MINUTES PER SIDE FOR MEDIUM-RARE, OR UNTIL DESIRED DONENESS. TRANSFER TO A PLATE, COVER LOOSELY WITH FOIL AND LET STAND FOR 5 MINUTES.

MEANWHILE, ARRANGE SPINACH ON A LARGE PLATTER. TOP WITH BEAN SPROUTS AND TOMATOES. CUT STEAK INTO THIN SLICES AND ARRANGE ON TOP OF SALAD. DRIZZLE WITH WARM DRESSING AND SPRINKLE WITH SESAME SEEDS. SERVES 3 TO 4.

TIP: TOASTED SESAME SEEDS ADD A NICE NUTTY FLAVOR TO DISHES. TOAST A BATCH AND FREEZE 'EM UNTIL YOU NEED 'EM. SIMPLY SPREAD SESAME SEEDS IN THE BOTTOM OF A LARGE NONSTICK SKILLET. TOAST SEEDS OVER MEDIUM-HIGH HEAT, GENTLY SHAKING THE SKILLET, FOR ABOUT 5 MINUTES OR UNTIL SEEDS START TO BROWN AND GIVE OFF A NUTTY AROMA. TRANSFER TO A COLD PLATE. WHEN COOL, PLACE IN AN AIRTIGHT CONTAINER AND FREEZE FOR UP TO 3 MONTHS.

PESTO AND CHERRY TOMATO PASTA SALAD

READY-MADE SUN-DRIED TOMATO PESTO FROM THE GROCERY STORE GIVES THIS SPEEDY PASTA SALAD A WALLOP OF FLAVOR. SERVE IT AT YOUR NEXT BARBECUE OR FAMILY GET-TOGETHER.

DRESSING

1/2 CUP	FRESHLY GRATED PARMESAN CHEESE	125 ML
1/2 CUP	SUN-DRIED TOMATO PESTO	125 ML
4 TBSP	RED WINE VINEGAR	60 ML
4 TBSP	EXTRA VIRGIN OLIVE OIL (SEE TIP, PAGE 83)	60 ML
3	CLOVES GARLIC, MINCED	3

SALAD

6 CUPS	FARFALLE (BOWTIE) PASTA (ABOUT 12 OZ/375 G)	1.5 L
24	CHERRY TOMATOES, HALVED	24
1	RED BELL PEPPER, CHOPPED	1
1 CUP	KALAMATA OLIVES (NOT CANNED), HALVED	250 ML
	SALT AND FRESHLY GROUND BLACK PEPPER (OPTIONAL)	
1/2 CUP	TOASTED PINE NUTS (SEE TIP, PAGE 75)	125 ML
1/4 CUP	THINLY SLICED FRESH BASIL (SEE TIP, OPPOSITE)	50 ML

DRESSING: IN A LARGE BOWL, WHISK TOGETHER PARMESAN, PESTO, VINEGAR, OIL AND GARLIC. SET ASIDE.

SALAD: COOK PASTA ACCORDING TO PACKAGE INSTRUCTIONS. DRAIN AND RINSE UNDER COLD RUNNING WATER. IN A LARGE BOWL, COMBINE PASTA, TOMATOES,

RED PEPPER AND OLIVES. ADD DRESSING AND TOSS TO COAT. COVER AND REFRIGERATE FOR 1 HOUR TO LET FLAVORS DEVELOP. JUST BEFORE SERVING, TASTE THE SALAD FOR SEASONING (THE PARMESAN, PESTO AND OLIVES ARE QUITE SALTY). IF DESIRED, SEASON TO TASTE WITH SALT AND PEPPER. STIR IN PINE NUTS AND BASIL. SERVES 6 TO 8.

TIP: TO SHRED OR THINLY SLICE BASIL, FIRST REMOVE THE LEAVES FROM THE STALK. STACK BASIL LEAVES ABOUT 6 DEEP AND GENTLY ROLL THEM INTO A TIGHT CIGAR SHAPE. USING A SHARP KNIFE, SLICE VERY THINLY. THE CHEF'S TERM FOR THIS IS "CHIFFONADE." OH-LA-LA!

VARIATION: USE BASIL PESTO IN PLACE OF THE SUN-DRIED TOMATO PESTO.

"THE SECRET OF A GOOD SERMON IS TO HAVE A GOOD BEGINNING AND A GOOD ENDING, AND TO HAVE THE TWO AS CLOSE TOGETHER AS POSSIBLE."
— GEORGE BURNS

TWO-RICE SALAD WITH FRUIT AND NUTS

THIS DISH IS MADE WITH A MIXTURE OF BROWN AND WHITE BASMATI RICE, STUDDED WITH DRIED FRUIT AND NUTS. THE SWEET TASTE AND LIGHT, NUTTY TEXTURE MAKE IT THE PERFECT ACCOMPANIMENT FOR GRILLED MEATS OR BAKED HAM.

DRESSING

3 TBSP	CIDER VINEGAR	45 ML
2 TBSP	GRAPESEED OIL (SEE TIP, OPPOSITE) OR SAFFLOWER OIL	25 ML
2 TBSP	FRESHLY SQUEEZED ORANGE JUICE	25 ML
I TBSP	LIQUID HONEY	15 ML
2 TSP	DIJON MUSTARD	10 ML
2	CLOVES GARLIC, MINCED	2
	SALT AND FRESHLY GROUND BLACK PEPPER	

SALAD

I CUP	BROWN BASMATI RICE	250 ML
1/2 CUP	WHITE BASMATI RICE	125 ML
4 CUPS	BOILING WATER	I L
1/2 CUP	DRIED SWEETENED CRANBERRIES	125 ML
1/2 CUP	DRIED CHERRIES OR APRICOTS, CHOPPED	125 ML
1/2 CUP	PISTACHIOS, CHOPPED	125 ML
I	ORANGE, CHOPPED	I
4	GREEN ONIONS, THINLY SLICED	4
1/4 CUP	CHOPPED FRESH PARSLEY	50 ML

CONTINUED ON PAGE 97...

Fruit and Broccoli Buffet Salad (page 74)

West Coast Steak Salad (page 92)

Asian Spicy Shrimp and Noodle Soup (page 106)

Roasted Winter Vegetable and Orange Soup (page 114)

DRESSING: IN A MEDIUM BOWL, WHISK TOGETHER VINEGAR, OIL, ORANGE JUICE, HONEY, MUSTARD AND GARLIC. SEASON TO TASTE WITH SALT AND PEPPER. SET ASIDE.

SALAD: IN A LARGE SAUCEPAN, COMBINE BROWN AND WHITE RICE. ADD ENOUGH COLD WATER TO COVER AND LET SOAK FOR 30 MINUTES. DRAIN, RETURN TO SAUCEPAN, ADD BOILING WATER AND BRING BACK TO A BOIL. REDUCE HEAT, COVER AND SIMMER FOR ABOUT 25 MINUTES OR UNTIL RICE IS TENDER AND WATER IS ABSORBED. (BROWN RICE IS A BIT UNPREDICTABLE, SO PEEK UNDER THE LID A COUPLE OF TIMES AND ADD MORE BOILING WATER IF IT GETS TOO DRY.) TRANSFER TO A LARGE BOWL AND LET COOL. STIR IN CRANBERRIES, CHERRIES, PISTACHIOS AND DRESSING. JUST BEFORE SERVING, STIR IN ORANGE, GREEN ONIONS AND PARSLEY. TASTE AND ADJUST SEASONING WITH SALT AND PEPPER, IF DESIRED. SERVES 6 TO 8.

MAKE AHEAD: AFTER DRESSING THE SALAD, COVER AND REFRIGERATE FOR UP TO 1 DAY.

TIP: GRAPESEED OIL HAS A VERY MILD FLAVOR AND, UNLIKE EXTRA VIRGIN OLIVE OIL, DOESN'T DOMINATE IN A SALAD DRESSING. SAFFLOWER OIL, REGULAR OLIVE OIL OR EVEN CANOLA OIL CAN BE USED IN PLACE OF GRAPESEED OIL.

LEMON COUSCOUS SALAD

SO EASY TO ASSEMBLE, THIS SALAD IS
BOUND TO BECOME A FAVORITE. IT'S A GREAT
ACCOMPANIMENT FOR GRILLED CHICKEN. OR TUCK
A CONTAINER OF IT INTO YOUR LUNCH BAG.

1 CUP	COUSCOUS	250 ML
6	GREEN ONIONS, CHOPPED	6
1/2	ENGLISH CUCUMBER, DICED	1/2
1 CUP	RINSED DRAINED CANNED CHICKPEAS (GARBANZO BEANS)	250 ML
1/4 CUP	CHOPPED FRESH PARSLEY	50 ML
2 TBSP	CHOPPED FRESH DILL OR MINT	25 ML
2 TBSP	OLIVE OIL	25 ML
	GRATED ZEST AND JUICE OF 1 LEMON	
	SALT AND FRESHLY GROUND BLACK PEPPER	
1/3 CUP	HAZELNUTS, TOASTED (SEE TIP, PAGE 75) AND CHOPPED	75 ML

IN A MEDIUM SAUCEPAN, BRING 2 CUPS (500 ML) WATER
TO A BOIL. STIR IN COUSCOUS AND IMMEDIATELY REMOVE
FROM HEAT. COVER AND LET STAND UNTIL WATER IS
ABSORBED, ABOUT 8 MINUTES. FLUFF WITH A FORK AND
TRANSFER TO A LARGE BOWL. STIR IN GREEN ONIONS,
CUCUMBER, CHICKPEAS, PARSLEY, DILL, OIL, LEMON ZEST
AND LEMON JUICE. SEASON TO TASTE WITH SALT AND
PEPPER. COVER AND REFRIGERATE OVERNIGHT TO LET
FLAVORS DEVELOP. SERVE TOPPED WITH HAZELNUTS.
SERVES 4.

SOUPS

CREAMY SEAFOOD CHOWDER

A HEARTY BOWL OF CHOWDER, A CRUSTY ROLL . . . AND MAYBE A LITTLE WINE!

1/4 CUP	BUTTER	50 ML
3	STALKS CELERY, DICED	3
1	SMALL ONION, FINELY CHOPPED	1
2 CUPS	DICED RED POTATOES	500 ML
1 CUP	DICED CARROTS	250 ML
1	RED BELL PEPPER, FINELY CHOPPED	1
1	CAN (7 OZ/200 ML) CORN KERNELS, DRAINED	1
1 1/2 CUPS	WATER	375 ML
1	BAY LEAF	1
1 LB	FIRM WHITE FISH (SUCH AS COD, HALIBUT OR SNAPPER), CUT INTO BITE-SIZE CHUNKS	500 G
6 OZ	SCALLOPS, CUT INTO BITE-SIZE PIECES	175 G
6 OZ	SMALL SHRIMP, PEELED AND DEVEINED	175 G
6 OZ	CRABMEAT OR MOCK CRABMEAT, FLAKED	175 G
3 CUPS	WHOLE MILK (SEE TIP, OPPOSITE)	750 ML
1/4 TSP	DRIED THYME	1 ML
1/4 TSP	HOT PEPPER FLAKES OR CAYENNE PEPPER	1 ML
	SALT AND FRESHLY GROUND BLACK PEPPER	
	CHOPPED FRESH PARSLEY	

IN A LARGE SAUCEPAN OR DUTCH OVEN, MELT BUTTER OVER MEDIUM HEAT. SAUTÉ CELERY AND ONION FOR 5 TO 7 MINUTES OR UNTIL SOFTENED. ADD POTATOES, CARROTS, RED PEPPER, CORN, WATER AND BAY LEAF; BRING TO A BOIL. REDUCE HEAT AND SIMMER FOR ABOUT 10 MINUTES OR UNTIL POTATOES ARE FORK-TENDER.

ADD FISH AND SIMMER FOR 5 MINUTES OR UNTIL OPAQUE.
ADD SCALLOPS, SHRIMP, CRABMEAT, MILK, THYME, HOT
PEPPER FLAKES AND SALT AND BLACK PEPPER TO TASTE.
INCREASE HEAT TO MEDIUM AND SIMMER FOR 3 TO
4 MINUTES OR UNTIL SHRIMP ARE PINK AND OPAQUE. DO
NOT LET BOIL OR THE SEAFOOD WILL TOUGHEN. DISCARD
BAY LEAF. TASTE AND ADJUST SEASONING WITH HOT
PEPPER FLAKES, SALT AND BLACK PEPPER, IF DESIRED.
SERVE SPRINKLED WITH PARSLEY. SERVES 4 TO 6.

TIP: WHOLE MILK GIVES THIS CHOWDER A SMOOTH
TEXTURE AND CREAMY FLAVOR. YOU CAN SUBSTITUTE
2% MILK IN A PINCH, BUT DON'T USE SKIM MILK, AS
THIS WILL RESULT IN A WATERY SOUP.

"SANTA CLAUS HAS THE RIGHT IDEA.
VISIT PEOPLE ONLY ONCE A YEAR."
— VICTOR BORGE

SEAFOOD AND TOMATO CHOWDER

TOMATO-BASED SEAFOOD CHOWDERS ARE
LIGHTER THAN THEIR CREAMY COUSINS
BUT EVERY BIT AS TASTY.

1 TBSP	BUTTER	15 ML
1 TBSP	VEGETABLE OIL	15 ML
2	CARROTS, FINELY CHOPPED	2
2	STALKS CELERY, FINELY CHOPPED	2
1	LARGE ONION, FINELY CHOPPED	1
2	CLOVES GARLIC, MINCED	2
1 TSP	DRIED OREGANO	5 ML
PINCH	HOT PEPPER FLAKES (OPTIONAL)	PINCH
1	CAN (28 OZ/796 ML) WHOLE TOMATOES WITH JUICE (SEE TIP, OPPOSITE), CHOPPED	1
1	LARGE POTATO, PEELED AND DICED	1
3 CUPS	CHICKEN BROTH	750 ML
2	BAY LEAVES	2
1/2 TSP	WORCESTERSHIRE SAUCE	2 ML
1 1/2 LBS	FIRM WHITE FISH (SUCH AS COD, SNAPPER, OCEAN PERCH OR HALIBUT, OR ANY COMBINATION), CUT INTO BITE-SIZE PIECES	750 G
15	MEDIUM SHRIMP, PEELED AND DEVEINED	15
1/4 CUP	CHOPPED FRESH PARSLEY	50 ML
	SALT AND FRESHLY GROUND BLACK PEPPER	
2 TBSP	DRY SHERRY (OPTIONAL)	25 ML

IN A LARGE SAUCEPAN OR DUTCH OVEN, HEAT BUTTER
AND OIL OVER MEDIUM-HIGH HEAT. SAUTÉ CARROTS,
CELERY AND ONION FOR 5 TO 7 MINUTES OR UNTIL
SOFTENED. ADD GARLIC, OREGANO AND HOT PEPPER

FLAKES; SAUTÉ UNTIL FRAGRANT, ABOUT 15 SECONDS. ADD TOMATOES, POTATO, CHICKEN BROTH, BAY LEAVES AND WORCESTERSHIRE SAUCE; BRING TO A BOIL. REDUCE HEAT AND SIMMER FOR 15 TO 20 MINUTES OR UNTIL POTATO IS TENDER BUT NOT MUSHY. GENTLY STIR IN FISH, SHRIMP, PARSLEY AND SALT AND PEPPER TO TASTE; SIMMER FOR ABOUT 5 MINUTES OR UNTIL SHRIMP ARE PINK AND OPAQUE AND FISH IS OPAQUE AND FLAKES EASILY WITH A FORK. DISCARD BAY LEAVES AND STIR IN SHERRY (IF USING). SERVE IMMEDIATELY. SERVES 6 TO 8.

TIP: WHEN COOKING WITH CANNED TOMATOES, WE PREFER TO USE WHOLE TOMATOES PACKED IN JUICE, WITH NO ADDED SALT OR SEASONINGS. THEY ARE CLOSEST TO FRESH TOMATOES IN TASTE AND TEXTURE, AND WE LIKE TO ADD OUR OWN SALT AND OTHER SEASONINGS. DICED, CRUSHED OR STEWED TOMATOES MAY HAVE ADDED WATER, ACID AND FLAVORINGS, WHICH CAN AFFECT THE OUTCOME OF A RECIPE. IF YOU DON'T HAVE WHOLE CANNED TOMATOES, YOU CAN SUBSTITUTE DICED OR CRUSHED TOMATOES, BUT TASTE THE DISH AS YOU COOK IT TO ADJUST THE SEASONINGS ACCORDINGLY. IF YOU HAVE WHOLE TOMATOES PACKED IN WATER, DRAIN OFF THE WATER AND USE EXTRA TOMATOES TO GET THE AMOUNT CALLED FOR IN THE RECIPE.

THAI CORN AND SHRIMP CHOWDER

A SPECIAL SOUP FOR SKIERS, SKATERS AND ROMANTIC DINNER DATERS.

1 TBSP	BUTTER	15 ML
1	SMALL ONION, FINELY CHOPPED	1
1	YELLOW OR RED BELL PEPPER, FINELY CHOPPED	1
1	POTATO, PEELED AND DICED	1
½ TSP	THAI RED CURRY PASTE (OR TO TASTE)	2 ML
2 CUPS	FROZEN CORN KERNELS	500 ML
2 CUPS	CHICKEN OR VEGETABLE BROTH	500 ML
1	CAN (14 OZ/400 ML) COCONUT MILK	1
1 TSP	PACKED BROWN SUGAR	5 ML
¼ TSP	SALT	1 ML
24	MEDIUM SHRIMP, PEELED AND DEVEINED	24
1 TBSP	CHOPPED FRESH CILANTRO	15 ML
1 TBSP	FRESHLY SQUEEZED LIME JUICE	15 ML
	CHOPPED GREEN ONIONS	
1	LIME, CUT INTO WEDGES	1

IN A LARGE SAUCEPAN, MELT BUTTER OVER MEDIUM HEAT. SAUTÉ ONION, YELLOW PEPPER AND POTATO FOR 5 TO 7 MINUTES OR UNTIL ONION AND PEPPER ARE SOFTENED. ADD CURRY PASTE AND SAUTÉ FOR 15 SECONDS. ADD CORN, CHICKEN BROTH, COCONUT MILK, BROWN SUGAR AND SALT; BRING TO A BOIL. REDUCE HEAT AND SIMMER FOR ABOUT 15 MINUTES OR UNTIL POTATO IS TENDER BUT NOT MUSHY. ADD SHRIMP AND SIMMER FOR 3 TO 4 MINUTES OR UNTIL SHRIMP ARE PINK AND OPAQUE. STIR IN CILANTRO AND LIME JUICE. TASTE AND ADJUST

SEASONING WITH BROWN SUGAR, SALT AND LIME JUICE, IF DESIRED. SERVE IMMEDIATELY, GARNISHED WITH GREEN ONIONS AND A LIME WEDGE. SERVES 4.

TIP: CANNED COCONUT MILK ADDS A RICH, CREAMY FLAVOR TO SOUPS, SAUCES AND CAKES. IN THAI COOKING, IT HELPS TO MELLOW THE HEAT FROM CHILES AND OTHER CURRY SPICES. COCONUT MILK IS WIDELY AVAILABLE IN GROCERY STORES, IN REGULAR AND REDUCED-FAT VERSIONS. THE TWO TYPES CAN BE USED INTERCHANGEABLY IN THIS RECIPE. LOOK FOR COCONUT MILK IN EITHER THE ASIAN FOOD AISLE OR NEAR EVAPORATED AND CONDENSED MILKS. LEFTOVER COCONUT MILK MAY BE FROZEN FOR FUTURE USE.

VARIATION: IF YOU LIKE A THICKER SOUP, BEFORE ADDING THE SHRIMP, TRANSFER ABOUT ONE-THIRD OF THE SOUP TO A FOOD PROCESSOR OR BLENDER, PURÉE UNTIL SMOOTH AND RETURN TO THE PAN. YOU CAN ALSO USE AN IMMERSION BLENDER TO PARTIALLY BLEND THE SOUP: JUST PULSE THE SOUP IN 2 OR 3 QUICK SPURTS.

*"I HAVE NEVER HATED A MAN ENOUGH
TO GIVE HIS DIAMONDS BACK."
– ZSA ZSA GABOR*

ASIAN SPICY SHRIMP AND NOODLE SOUP

THIS FRAGRANT AND HEALTHY SOUP IS READY IN ABOUT 30 MINUTES, SO DON'T BE PUT OFF BY THE LONG LIST OF INGREDIENTS. EAT THE NOODLES WITH CHOPSTICKS AND SLURP THE BROTH STRAIGHT FROM THE BOWL FOR AN AUTHENTIC ASIAN EXPERIENCE.

4 CUPS	CHICKEN BROTH	1 L
2 CUPS	WATER	500 ML
4	CLOVES GARLIC, SLIGHTLY CRUSHED	4
2 TBSP	SOY SAUCE	25 ML
1 TBSP	GRANULATED SUGAR	15 ML
1½ TSP	GRATED GINGERROOT	7 ML
½ TSP	HOT PEPPER FLAKES (OR TO TASTE)	2 ML
½ TSP	CHINESE FIVE-SPICE POWDER (SEE TIP, OPPOSITE)	2 ML
2 CUPS	SLICED WHITE MUSHROOMS	500 ML
4 CUPS	SPINACH, TRIMMED	1 L
16	LARGE SHRIMP, PEELED AND DEVEINED	16
5 CUPS	STEAMED CHINESE NOODLES (ABOUT HALF OF A 1-LB/500 G PACKAGE)	1.25 L
1 TBSP	CHOPPED FRESH CILANTRO OR BASIL	15 ML
2	GREEN ONIONS, THINLY SLICED	2

BRING A LARGE SAUCEPAN OF WATER TO A BOIL, REDUCE HEAT AND LET SIMMER UNTIL YOU ARE READY TO COOK THE NOODLES. IN ANOTHER LARGE SAUCEPAN, COMBINE CHICKEN BROTH, WATER, GARLIC, SOY SAUCE, SUGAR, GINGER, HOT PEPPER FLAKES AND FIVE-SPICE POWDER; BRING TO A BOIL. REDUCE HEAT AND SIMMER FOR 15 MINUTES TO BLEND THE FLAVORS. REMOVE AND DISCARD

GARLIC. ADD MUSHROOMS AND SIMMER FOR 5 MINUTES OR UNTIL TENDER. ADD SPINACH AND SHRIMP; SIMMER FOR 3 TO 4 MINUTES OR UNTIL SPINACH WILTS AND SHRIMP ARE PINK AND OPAQUE. MEANWHILE, DROP NOODLES INTO THE PAN OF SIMMERING WATER AND COOK FOR ABOUT 30 SECONDS OR UNTIL JUST TENDER. DRAIN AND DIVIDE NOODLES AMONG FOUR LARGE SOUP BOWLS. STIR CILANTRO INTO SOUP AND SPOON SOUP OVER NOODLES. SPRINKLE WITH GREEN ONIONS. SERVES 4.

TIP: CHINESE FIVE-SPICE POWDER IS AN AROMATIC SEASONING BLEND THAT USUALLY INCLUDES CINNAMON, CLOVES, FENNEL SEEDS, STAR ANISE AND GINGER. IF YOU DON'T HAVE IT, SUBSTITUTE A PINCH EACH OF GROUND CINNAMON, CLOVES, GINGER AND FENNEL.

VARIATION: OMIT THE SHRIMP AND ADD 2 CUPS (500 ML) THINLY SLICED COOKED CHICKEN, PORK OR BEEF TO SOUP 5 MINUTES BEFORE SERVING, ALLOWING MEAT TO HEAT THROUGH.

"ONLY IRISH COFFEE PROVIDES IN A SINGLE GLASS ALL FOUR ESSENTIAL FOOD GROUPS: ALCOHOL, CAFFEINE, SUGAR AND FAT."
– ALEX LEVINE

MULLIGATAWNY SOUP

BABY, IT'S COLD OUTSIDE, BUT HERE'S DINNER.
THIS ANGLO-INDIAN SOUP IS SPICY BUT DOESN'T
BURN YOUR MOUTH. THAT'S RIGHT — THERE'S A
BANANA IN THE SOUP, A NOD TO CARIBBEAN COOKING.
IT LENDS A SUBTLE SWEETNESS.

4 CUPS	CHICKEN BROTH (APPROX.)	1 L
1/2 CUP	GROUND ALMONDS	125 ML
1 TBSP	ALL-PURPOSE FLOUR	15 ML
1 TBSP	BUTTER	15 ML
1	ONION, FINELY CHOPPED	1
1	CARROT, FINELY CHOPPED	1
2	CLOVES GARLIC, MINCED	2
2 TBSP	GRATED GINGERROOT	25 ML
1 TBSP	MADRAS CURRY POWDER	15 ML
1 TSP	GROUND CUMIN	5 ML
1	BANANA, BROKEN INTO PIECES	1
1	SKINLESS BONE-IN CHICKEN BREAST (SEE TIP, OPPOSITE)	1
	SALT AND FRESHLY GROUND BLACK PEPPER	
1 CUP	COOKED BASMATI OR LONG-GRAIN WHITE RICE	250 ML
2 TBSP	FRESHLY SQUEEZED LIME JUICE	25 ML
	TOASTED SLICED ALMONDS, TOASTED UNSWEETENED SHREDDED COCONUT OR CHOPPED FRESH CILANTRO	

IN A BOWL, WHISK TOGETHER CHICKEN BROTH, ALMONDS
AND FLOUR; SET ASIDE. IN A LARGE SAUCEPAN, MELT
BUTTER OVER MEDIUM HEAT. SAUTÉ ONION AND CARROT
FOR 5 TO 7 MINUTES OR UNTIL SOFTENED. ADD GARLIC,

GINGER, CURRY POWDER AND CUMIN; SAUTÉ UNTIL
FRAGRANT, ABOUT 15 SECONDS. ADD BROTH MIXTURE,
BANANA AND CHICKEN; BRING TO A BOIL. REDUCE HEAT
AND SIMMER FOR ABOUT 25 MINUTES OR UNTIL CHICKEN
IS NO LONGER PINK IN THE CENTER. USING TONGS,
TRANSFER CHICKEN TO A PLATE AND LET COOL. USING
AN IMMERSION BLENDER, OR IN A FOOD PROCESSOR OR
BLENDER IN BATCHES, PURÉE SOUP UNTIL VERY SMOOTH.
RETURN TO PAN, IF NECESSARY, AND SEASON TO TASTE
WITH SALT AND PEPPER. ADD RICE AND LIME JUICE. SHRED
CHICKEN, DISCARDING BONE, AND RETURN TO SOUP. IF
SOUP SEEMS TOO THICK, ADD A LITTLE MORE CHICKEN
BROTH. SERVE GARNISHED WITH ALMONDS, COCONUT
OR CILANTRO. SERVES 4.

MAKE AHEAD: LET SOUP COOL, TRANSFER TO AN AIRTIGHT
CONTAINER AND REFRIGERATE FOR UP TO 1 DAY OR FREEZE
FOR UP TO 1 MONTH. THAW AND REHEAT TO SERVE.

TIP: USING A BONE-IN CHICKEN BREAST ADDS FLAVOR
TO THE SOUP. IF YOU SUBSTITUTE A BONELESS CHICKEN
BREAST, REDUCE THE COOKING TIME FOR THE CHICKEN
TO 15 TO 20 MINUTES.

BAJA BEAN SOUP

SERVE THIS DINNER-IN-A-BOWL WITH CRUSTY BREAD. OLE.

2	SLICES BACON, CHOPPED	2
I	CHORIZO SAUSAGE (SEE TIP, OPPOSITE), SLICED	I
I	ONION, CHOPPED	I
I	CARROT, CHOPPED	I
I	STALK CELERY, CHOPPED	I
I	RED OR GREEN BELL PEPPER, CHOPPED	I
2	CLOVES GARLIC, MINCED	2
I TSP	GROUND CUMIN	5 ML
I	CAN (28 OZ/796 ML) WHOLE TOMATOES WITH JUICE (SEE TIP, PAGE 103)	I
3 CUPS	CHICKEN BROTH OR WATER	750 ML
I CUP	FROZEN CORN KERNELS	250 ML
I	CAN (14 TO 19 OZ/398 TO 540 ML) BLACK BEANS, DRAINED AND RINSED	I
2 TBSP	CHOPPED FRESH CILANTRO	25 ML
I TSP	HOT PEPPER SAUCE	5 ML
	SALT AND FRESHLY GROUND BLACK PEPPER	
	SOUR CREAM	

IN A LARGE SAUCEPAN OR DUTCH OVEN, OVER MEDIUM-HIGH HEAT, SAUTÉ BACON AND SAUSAGE FOR 6 TO 8 MINUTES OR UNTIL BROWNED. USING A SLOTTED SPOON, TRANSFER TO A PLATE LINED WITH PAPER TOWELS TO DRAIN FAT. DRAIN OFF ALL BUT I TBSP (15 ML) OF THE FAT FROM THE PAN. SAUTÉ ONION, CARROT, CELERY AND RED PEPPER FOR 5 TO 7 MINUTES OR UNTIL SOFTENED. ADD GARLIC AND CUMIN; SAUTÉ UNTIL FRAGRANT, ABOUT

15 SECONDS. STIR IN TOMATOES, BREAKING THEM UP WITH A SPOON AND SCRAPING UP BROWN BITS FROM BOTTOM OF PAN. ADD CHICKEN BROTH, CORN, BEANS AND RESERVED BACON AND SAUSAGE; BRING TO A BOIL. REDUCE HEAT AND SIMMER FOR 20 MINUTES OR UNTIL VEGETABLES ARE TENDER. STIR IN CILANTRO AND HOT PEPPER SAUCE. SEASON TO TASTE WITH SALT AND PEPPER. SERVE DOLLOPED WITH SOUR CREAM. SERVES 6.

MAKE AHEAD: LET SOUP COOL, TRANSFER TO AN AIRTIGHT CONTAINER AND REFRIGERATE FOR UP TO 1 DAY OR FREEZE FOR UP TO 1 MONTH. THAW AND REHEAT TO SERVE.

TIP: CHORIZO IS A SPICY AND VERY FLAVORFUL SAUSAGE THAT IS WIDELY AVAILABLE IN SUPERMARKETS, EITHER FRESH OR CURED LIKE A SALAMI. FOR THIS RECIPE, WE SUGGEST USING FRESH. IF YOU CAN'T FIND CHORIZO, SUBSTITUTE HOT ITALIAN SAUSAGE.

"BY THE TIME A MAN IS OLD ENOUGH TO WATCH HIS STEP,
HE'S TOO OLD TO GO ANYWHERE."
— BILLY CRYSTAL

MINESTRONE

HERE'S OUR VERSION OF THE CLASSIC ITALIAN SOUP. CHECK OUT THE VARIATIONS AND CREATE YOUR OWN DESIGNER SOUP. FOR A COMPLETE MEAL, SERVE WITH SUN-DRIED TOMATO PESTO FLATBREAD (PAGE 53).

I TBSP	OLIVE OIL	15 ML
2	ONIONS, FINELY CHOPPED	2
2	CARROTS, FINELY CHOPPED	2
2	STALKS CELERY, FINELY CHOPPED	2
4 CUPS	CHICKEN BROTH	I L
2 CUPS	SHREDDED GREEN CABBAGE	500 ML
I	ZUCCHINI, FINELY CHOPPED	I
I	CAN (28 OZ/796 ML) WHOLE TOMATOES WITH JUICE (SEE TIP, PAGE 103), CHOPPED	I
2	BAY LEAVES	2
I TSP	DRIED OREGANO	5 ML
I TSP	DRIED BASIL	5 ML
I TSP	SALT	5 ML
1/4 TSP	FRESHLY GROUND BLACK PEPPER	I ML
PINCH	HOT PEPPER FLAKES	PINCH
I	CAN (14 TO 19 OZ/398 TO 540 ML) WHITE KIDNEY OR CANNELLINI BEANS, DRAINED AND RINSED	I
2 TBSP	BASIL PESTO	25 ML
	FRESHLY GRATED PARMESAN CHEESE	

IN A LARGE SAUCEPAN OR DUTCH OVEN, HEAT OIL OVER MEDIUM HEAT. SAUTÉ ONIONS, CARROTS AND CELERY UNTIL SOFTENED, 5 TO 7 MINUTES. ADD CHICKEN BROTH, CABBAGE, ZUCCHINI, TOMATOES, BAY LEAVES, OREGANO, BASIL, SALT, BLACK PEPPER AND HOT PEPPER FLAKES; BRING TO A BOIL. REDUCE HEAT, COVER, LEAVING

LID AJAR, AND SIMMER FOR ABOUT 30 MINUTES OR UNTIL VEGETABLES ARE TENDER BUT NOT MUSHY. ADD BEANS AND BRING BACK TO A SIMMER, UNCOVERED, FOR 5 MINUTES. STIR IN PESTO. TASTE AND ADJUST SEASONING WITH SALT, BLACK PEPPER AND HOT PEPPER FLAKES, IF DESIRED. SERVE WITH A BOWL OF PARMESAN ON THE SIDE. SERVES 8.

TIP: KEEP A BLOCK OF FRESH PARMESAN CHEESE IN THE REFRIGERATOR AND GRATE IT AS NEEDED. IT'S A BIT MORE EXPENSIVE THAN THE STUFF IN BOXES, BUT IT TASTES SO MUCH BETTER!

VARIATIONS: BEFORE ADDING THE VEGETABLES, COOK 2 CHOPPED BACON SLICES IN THE OIL UNTIL CRISP. DRAIN OFF EXCESS FAT AND PROCEED WITH THE RECIPE. OR REPLACE THE CABBAGE WITH SWISS CHARD OR SPINACH AND THE ZUCCHINI WITH 1 CUP (250 ML) GREEN BEANS. OR ADD 2 CUPS (500 ML) COOKED SMALL PASTA, SUCH AS MACARONI, A FEW MINUTES BEFORE SERVING.

THE CARDIOLOGIST'S DIET:
IF IT TASTES GOOD, SPIT IT OUT.

ROASTED WINTER VEGETABLE AND ORANGE SOUP

*WHEN THE COLD WINDS BLOW, WARM UP
WITH THIS SOULFUL SOUP.*

I	LARGE ONION, COARSELY CHOPPED	I
2	SMALL PARSNIPS, PEELED AND COARSELY CHOPPED	2
2 CUPS	COARSELY CHOPPED PEELED SWEET POTATO (ABOUT I MEDIUM)	500 ML
2 CUPS	COARSELY CHOPPED PEELED BUTTERNUT SQUASH (ABOUT I SMALL)	500 ML
3 TBSP	VEGETABLE OIL, DIVIDED	45 ML
I TBSP	CHOPPED GINGERROOT	15 ML
I TSP	GROUND CORIANDER	5 ML
4 CUPS	CHICKEN BROTH	I L
I TSP	LIQUID HONEY	5 ML
	JUICE OF I ORANGE	
	SALT AND FRESHLY GROUND BLACK PEPPER	
	CHOPPED FRESH CILANTRO OR PARSLEY	
	SLICED ALMONDS, TOASTED (SEE TIP, PAGE 149)	

PREHEAT OVEN TO 375°F (190°C). IN A LARGE BOWL, TOSS
ONION, PARSNIPS, SWEET POTATO AND SQUASH WITH
2 TBSP (25 ML) OF THE OIL. SPREAD IN A SINGLE LAYER
ON A LARGE RIMMED BAKING SHEET AND ROAST, TURNING
ONCE, FOR 45 TO 50 MINUTES OR UNTIL SOFTENED AND
BROWNED. IN A LARGE SAUCEPAN, HEAT THE REMAINING
OIL OVER MEDIUM HEAT. SAUTÉ GINGER AND CORIANDER
UNTIL FRAGRANT, ABOUT 15 SECONDS. ADD ROASTED
VEGETABLES, CHICKEN BROTH AND HONEY; BRING TO A
BOIL. REDUCE HEAT AND SIMMER FOR 15 MINUTES OR UNTIL

SLIGHTLY THICKENED. USING AN IMMERSION BLENDER, OR IN A FOOD PROCESSOR OR BLENDER IN BATCHES, PURÉE SOUP UNTIL SMOOTH. RETURN TO PAN, IF NECESSARY. STIR IN ORANGE JUICE AND REHEAT OVER MEDIUM HEAT, STIRRING OFTEN AND ADDING A LITTLE WATER IF SOUP IS TOO THICK, UNTIL STEAMING. SEASON TO TASTE WITH SALT AND PEPPER. SERVE GARNISHED WITH CILANTRO AND ALMONDS. SERVES 6.

MAKE AHEAD: LET SOUP COOL, TRANSFER TO AN AIRTIGHT CONTAINER AND REFRIGERATE FOR UP TO 1 DAY OR FREEZE FOR UP TO 1 MONTH. THAW AND REHEAT TO SERVE.

TIP: ROASTING THE VEGETABLES TAKES AWHILE, BUT IT CARAMELIZES THEIR NATURAL SUGARS, MAKING THEM SWEET AND DELICIOUS.

VARIATION: USE CARROTS, TURNIPS, PUMPKIN OR REGULAR POTATOES IN PLACE OR ONE OR TWO OF THE VEGETABLES IN THIS RECIPE. JUST BE SURE TO INCLUDE ONE ORANGE VEGETABLE FOR AN APPEALING AND COLORFUL SOUP.

A PENNY SAVED IS A GOVERNMENT OVERSIGHT.

ROASTED RED PEPPER AND TOMATO SOUP

RED SOUP! A DELICIOUS BLEND OF ROASTED RED PEPPERS AND TOMATOES DOUBLES AS A SPAGHETTI SAUCE. SERVE WITH RUSTIC CHEDDAR AND HERB SCONES (PAGE 28).

1 TBSP	BUTTER	15 ML
2	CARROTS, CHOPPED	2
1	LARGE ONION, CHOPPED	1
1	CAN (28 OZ/796 ML) WHOLE TOMATOES WITH JUICE (SEE TIP, PAGE 103)	1
1¼ CUPS	CHOPPED ROASTED RED BELL PEPPERS (SEE TIP, OPPOSITE)	300 ML
2 CUPS	CHICKEN BROTH	500 ML
2 TBSP	GRANULATED SUGAR	25 ML
1 TSP	SALT	5 ML
½ TSP	DRIED BASIL	2 ML
¼ TSP	FRESHLY GROUND BLACK PEPPER	1 ML
½ CUP	WHIPPING (35%) CREAM, WARMED (OPTIONAL)	125 ML
2 TBSP	SLICED FRESH BASIL (OPTIONAL)	25 ML

IN A LARGE SAUCEPAN, MELT BUTTER OVER MEDIUM-HIGH HEAT. SAUTÉ CARROTS AND ONION UNTIL SOFTENED, ABOUT 5 MINUTES. ADD TOMATOES, ROASTED PEPPERS, CHICKEN BROTH, SUGAR, SALT, DRIED BASIL AND PEPPER; BRING TO A BOIL. REDUCE HEAT AND SIMMER FOR 20 MINUTES OR UNTIL SLIGHTLY REDUCED AND THICKENED. USING AN IMMERSION BLENDER, OR IN A FOOD PROCESSOR OR BLENDER IN BATCHES, PURÉE SOUP UNTIL SMOOTH. RETURN TO PAN, IF NECESSARY. STIR IN CREAM (IF USING) AND REHEAT OVER MEDIUM HEAT, STIRRING OFTEN, UNTIL

STEAMING. IF USING CREAM, DO NOT LET BOIL OR CREAM MAY CURDLE. TASTE AND ADJUST SEASONING WITH SALT AND PEPPER, IF DESIRED. SERVE GARNISHED WITH FRESH BASIL, IF DESIRED. SERVES 6 TO 8.

MAKE AHEAD: AFTER PURÉEING THE SOUP, LET COOL, TRANSFER TO AN AIRTIGHT CONTAINER AND REFRIGERATE FOR UP TO 1 DAY OR FREEZE FOR UP TO 1 MONTH. THAW AND CONTINUE WITH RECIPE.

TIP: ROASTED RED BELL PEPPERS ARE SOLD IN JARS OR IN THE DELI SECTION OF YOUR SUPERMARKET, BUT IT'S EASY TO ROAST YOUR OWN. PREHEAT OVEN TO 425°F (220°C). CUT PEPPERS INTO QUARTERS, REMOVE SEEDS AND BRUSH WITH OLIVE OIL. PLACE SKIN SIDE DOWN ON A BAKING SHEET LINED WITH PARCHMENT PAPER AND ROAST FOR ABOUT 30 MINUTES OR UNTIL SKINS ARE BLACKENED AND PUFFED. TRANSFER PEPPERS TO A BOWL, COVER AND LET STAND FOR 15 MINUTES TO STEAM, THEN PEEL OFF SKINS. STORE IN AN AIRTIGHT CONTAINER IN THE REFRIGERATOR FOR UP TO 5 DAYS. OR CUT INTO STRIPS, SPREAD IN A SINGLE LAYER ON A BAKING SHEET AND FREEZE. PACK FROZEN PEPPER PIECES INTO FREEZER BAGS AND STORE FOR UP TO 3 MONTHS.

VARIATION: OMIT THE CREAM AND FRESH BASIL AND STIR IN 2 TBSP (25 ML) BASIL PESTO JUST BEFORE SERVING.

ROASTED ASPARAGUS SOUP

MAKE THIS SOUP WHEN ASPARAGUS IS IN SEASON
OR IS ON SPECIAL AT THE GROCERY STORE.

2 CUPS	PEELED ASPARAGUS PIECES (2-INCH/5 CM PIECES)	500 ML
1	POTATO, CHOPPED	1
1	ONION, CHOPPED	1
1 TBSP	VEGETABLE OIL	15 ML
4 CUPS	CHICKEN BROTH	1 L
1 TBSP	FRESHLY SQUEEZED LEMON JUICE	15 ML
1/2 TSP	DRIED MARJORAM	2 ML
	SALT AND FRESHLY GROUND BLACK PEPPER	
1/4 CUP	WHIPPING (35%) CREAM, WARMED	50 ML
	HOMEMADE GARLIC CROUTONS (PAGE 77)	

PREHEAT OVEN TO 375°F (190°C). IN A LARGE BOWL, TOSS
ASPARAGUS, POTATO AND ONION WITH OIL. SPREAD IN A
SINGLE LAYER ON A LARGE RIMMED BAKING SHEET AND
ROAST FOR ABOUT 40 MINUTES OR UNTIL TENDER AND
JUST STARTING TO BROWN. IN A LARGE SAUCEPAN,
COMBINE ROASTED VEGETABLES, CHICKEN BROTH, LEMON
JUICE, MARJORAM AND SALT AND PEPPER TO TASTE;
BRING TO A BOIL. REDUCE HEAT AND SIMMER FOR 10
MINUTES. USING AN IMMERSION BLENDER, OR IN A FOOD
PROCESSOR OR BLENDER IN BATCHES, PURÉE SOUP UNTIL
VERY SMOOTH. RETURN TO PAN, IF NECESSARY. STIR IN
CREAM AND REHEAT OVER MEDIUM HEAT, STIRRING OFTEN,
UNTIL STEAMING. DO NOT LET BOIL OR CREAM MAY
CURDLE. TASTE AND ADJUST SEASONING WITH SALT AND
PEPPER, IF DESIRED. SERVE GARNISHED WITH CROUTONS.
SERVES 4 TO 6.

PEA AND SPINACH SOUP

REALLY GREEN AND REALLY, REALLY GOOD.

I TBSP	BUTTER	15 ML
4	GREEN ONIONS, CHOPPED	4
PINCH	GROUND NUTMEG	PINCH
I	PACKAGE (ABOUT 6 OZ/175 G) PREWASHED BABY SPINACH LEAVES	I
3 CUPS	FROZEN BABY GREEN PEAS	750 ML
2 1/2 CUPS	CHICKEN BROTH	625 ML
3/4 TSP	SALT	3 ML
1/2 TSP	GRANULATED SUGAR	2 ML
1/4 TSP	FRESHLY GROUND BLACK PEPPER	I ML
1/4 CUP	HALF-AND-HALF (10%) CREAM, WARMED	50 ML
	SNIPPED FRESH CHIVES	

IN A LARGE SAUCEPAN, MELT BUTTER OVER MEDIUM HEAT. SAUTÉ GREEN ONIONS AND NUTMEG FOR 30 SECONDS OR UNTIL FRAGRANT. ADD SPINACH, PEAS, CHICKEN BROTH, SALT, SUGAR AND PEPPER; BRING TO A BOIL. REDUCE HEAT AND SIMMER FOR 10 MINUTES OR UNTIL SPINACH IS WILTED AND PEAS ARE TENDER. USING AN IMMERSION BLENDER, OR IN A FOOD PROCESSOR OR BLENDER IN BATCHES, PURÉE SOUP UNTIL VERY SMOOTH. RETURN TO PAN, IF NECESSARY. STIR IN CREAM AND REHEAT OVER MEDIUM HEAT, STIRRING OFTEN, UNTIL STEAMING. DO NOT LET BOIL OR CREAM MAY CURDLE. TASTE AND ADJUST SEASONING WITH SALT AND PEPPER, IF DESIRED. SERVE IMMEDIATELY, GARNISHED WITH CHIVES. SERVES 6.

TIP: WARMING THE CREAM BEFORE ADDING IT TO THE SOUP HELPS PREVENT IT FROM CURDLING.

CLASSIC PEA SOUP WITH SAUSAGE AND BACON

A SPEEDIER VERSION OF TRADITIONAL SPLIT PEA SOUP.
LOOK, MA — NO HAM BONE!

2	HOT ITALIAN SAUSAGES, CASINGS REMOVED, CRUMBLED	2
8	SLICES BACON, CHOPPED	8
2	CARROTS, CHOPPED	2
2	STALKS CELERY, CHOPPED	2
1	LARGE ONION, CHOPPED	1
10 CUPS	CHICKEN BROTH OR WATER	2.5 L
2 CUPS	DRIED GREEN SPLIT PEAS, WASHED AND PICKED OVER	500 ML
2	BAY LEAVES	2
1 TSP	DRIED THYME	5 ML
1 TSP	SALT	5 ML
1/2 TSP	HOT PEPPER SAUCE	2 ML
1/4 TSP	FRESHLY GROUND BLACK PEPPER	1 ML
1 TBSP	FRESHLY SQUEEZED LEMON JUICE	15 ML

IN A LARGE SAUCEPAN OR DUTCH OVEN, OVER MEDIUM-HIGH HEAT, SAUTÉ SAUSAGES FOR 6 TO 8 MINUTES OR UNTIL BROWNED. USING A SLOTTED SPOON, TRANSFER TO A PLATE LINED WITH PAPER TOWELS TO DRAIN FAT. ADD BACON TO THE PAN AND SAUTÉ UNTIL CRISP. USING A SLOTTED SPOON, TRANSFER TO A SEPARATE PLATE LINED WITH PAPER TOWELS TO DRAIN FAT. POUR OFF ALL BUT 1 TBSP (15 ML) OF THE FAT FROM THE PAN. ADD CARROTS, CELERY AND ONION; SAUTÉ OVER MEDIUM HEAT FOR 5 TO 7 MINUTES OR UNTIL SOFTENED. STIR IN CHICKEN BROTH, PEAS, BAY LEAVES, THYME, SALT,

HOT PEPPER SAUCE AND BLACK PEPPER. RESERVE 2 TBSP (25 ML) BACON FOR GARNISH AND RETURN THE REMAINDER TO THE PAN. BRING TO A BOIL. REDUCE HEAT TO LOW, COVER, LEAVING LID AJAR, AND SIMMER FOR ABOUT 1 HOUR OR UNTIL PEAS ARE VERY SOFT. DISCARD BAY LEAVES. USING AN IMMERSION BLENDER, OR IN A FOOD PROCESSOR OR BLENDER IN BATCHES, PURÉE SOUP (INCLUDING THE BACON THAT'S ALREADY IN IT) UNTIL SMOOTH. RETURN TO PAN, IF NECESSARY. STIR IN RESERVED SAUSAGE AND LEMON JUICE. TASTE AND ADJUST SEASONING WITH SALT, HOT PEPPER SAUCE AND BLACK PEPPER, IF DESIRED. SERVE GARNISHED WITH THE RESERVED BACON. SERVES MANY!

MAKE AHEAD: LET SOUP COOL, TRANSFER TO AN AIRTIGHT CONTAINER AND REFRIGERATE FOR UP TO 1 DAY OR FREEZE FOR UP TO 1 MONTH. THAW AND REHEAT TO SERVE.

THE REAL ART OF CONVERSATION IS NOT ONLY TO SAY THE RIGHT THING AT THE RIGHT TIME, BUT ALSO TO LEAVE UNSAID THE WRONG THING AT THE TEMPTING TIME.

CARROT, LEEK AND TARRAGON SOUP

THE IDEAL SOUP FOR SWEET YOUNG MARKET GARDEN CARROTS. OLDER SUPERMARKET CARROTS NEED ADDED SUGAR — YOU'RE THE CHEF.

1 TBSP	BUTTER	15 ML
5	CARROTS, THINLY SLICED (ABOUT 3 CUPS/750 ML)	5
1	LARGE LEEK OR ONION, THINLY SLICED	1
4 CUPS	CHICKEN BROTH OR WATER	1 L
1 TBSP	PACKED BROWN SUGAR (OPTIONAL)	15 ML
1/2 TO 1 TSP	DRIED TARRAGON	2 TO 5 ML
1/2 TSP	SALT	2 ML
	FRESHLY GROUND BLACK PEPPER	
1 TBSP	FRESHLY SQUEEZED LEMON OR ORANGE JUICE	15 ML
	SNIPPED FRESH CHIVES	

IN A LARGE SAUCEPAN, MELT BUTTER OVER MEDIUM HEAT. ADD CARROTS AND LEEK; COVER, REDUCE HEAT TO LOW AND LET VEGETABLES "SWEAT" FOR 10 TO 12 MINUTES OR UNTIL SOFTENED BUT NOT BROWNED. ADD CHICKEN BROTH, BROWN SUGAR (IF USING), TARRAGON TO TASTE, SALT AND PEPPER TO TASTE; BRING TO A BOIL. REDUCE HEAT AND SIMMER, UNCOVERED, FOR 10 MINUTES OR UNTIL VEGETABLES ARE VERY SOFT. USING AN IMMERSION BLENDER, OR IN A FOOD PROCESSOR OR BLENDER IN BATCHES, PURÉE SOUP UNTIL SMOOTH. RETURN TO

PAN, IF NECESSARY. STIR IN LEMON JUICE AND ADJUST SEASONING WITH SALT AND PEPPER, IF DESIRED. SERVE GARNISHED WITH CHIVES. SERVES 4.

MAKE AHEAD: LET SOUP COOL, TRANSFER TO AN AIRTIGHT CONTAINER AND REFRIGERATE FOR UP TO 1 DAY OR FREEZE FOR UP TO 1 MONTH. THAW AND REHEAT TO SERVE.

TIP: MANY RECIPES CALL FOR ONLY THE WHITE PART OF THE LEEK, BUT WE THINK THIS IS A WASTE. USE AS MUCH OF THE GREEN PART AS YOU WANT! LEEKS GENERALLY CONTAIN DIRT BETWEEN THEIR LAYERS. THE EASIEST WAY TO CLEAN THEM IS TO SWIRL CHOPPED OR SLICED LEEKS IN A LARGE BOWL OF WATER. LET THE DIRT FALL TO THE BOTTOM AND REMOVE LEEKS WITH A SLOTTED SPOON. REPEAT IF NECESSARY.

VARIATION: IF YOU DON'T LIKE, OR DON'T HAVE, TARRAGON, REPLACE IT WITH AN EQUAL AMOUNT OF DRIED THYME, PARSLEY OR DILL.

THE EASIEST WAY TO FIND SOMETHING AROUND THE HOUSE IS TO BUY A REPLACEMENT.

QUICK BROCCOLI CHEESE SOUP

CRUNCHY, FLAVORFUL AND INCREDIBLY FAST.

I LB	BROCCOLI (ABOUT I BUNCH)	500 G
I	BUNCH GREEN ONIONS, CUT INTO I-INCH (2.5 CM) PIECES (ABOUT $3/4$ CUP/175 ML)	I
I TBSP	VEGETABLE OIL	15 ML
3 CUPS	CHICKEN BROTH	750 ML
I CUP	WHOLE OR 2% MILK (SEE TIP, OPPOSITE)	250 ML
I TSP	DIJON MUSTARD	5 ML
$1/2$ TSP	WORCESTERSHIRE SAUCE	2 ML
$1/4$ TSP	HOT PEPPER SAUCE	I ML
I TSP	CORNSTARCH (OPTIONAL)	5 ML
I TBSP	COLD WATER (OPTIONAL)	15 ML
I CUP	SHREDDED SHARP (OLD) CHEDDAR CHEESE	250 ML
	SALT AND FRESHLY GROUND BLACK PEPPER	
	SHREDDED CHEDDAR CHEESE	

CUT BROCCOLI FLORETS INTO SMALL PIECES. PEEL AND COARSELY CHOP STEMS. IN A FOOD PROCESSOR, PULSE BROCCOLI FLORETS AND STEMS WITH GREEN ONIONS UNTIL FINELY CHOPPED. (ALTERNATIVELY, CHOP WITH A KNIFE; THE FOOD PROCESSOR IS JUST QUICKER).
IN A LARGE SAUCEPAN, HEAT OIL OVER MEDIUM HEAT. SAUTÉ BROCCOLI MIXTURE UNTIL BRIGHT GREEN, ABOUT 3 MINUTES. ADD CHICKEN BROTH, MILK, MUSTARD, WORCESTERSHIRE SAUCE AND HOT PEPPER SAUCE; BRING TO A BOIL, STIRRING, THEN REDUCE HEAT TO SIMMER. IF YOU WANT SLIGHTLY THICKER SOUP, DISSOLVE

CORNSTARCH IN COLD WATER AND ADD TO SOUP, STIRRING FOR 2 MINUTES OR UNTIL THICKENED. ADD CHEESE, $\frac{1}{2}$ CUP (125 ML) AT A TIME, STIRRING AFTER EACH ADDITION UNTIL JUST MELTED. DO NOT LET BOIL OR THE CHEESE WILL CURDLE. SEASON TO TASTE WITH SALT AND PEPPER. SERVE IMMEDIATELY, GARNISHED WITH CHEESE. SERVES 4.

TIP: DON'T SUBSTITUTE SKIM MILK IN THIS RECIPE OR THE SOUP WILL TASTE WATERY.

TIP: SHRED CHEESE IN BATCHES AND FREEZE IT SO THAT YOU ALWAYS HAVE SOME ON HAND. SPREAD SHREDDED CHEESE IN A SINGLE LAYER ON A BAKING SHEET AND FREEZE UNTIL HARD, THEN TRANSFER CHEESE TO RESEALABLE FREEZER BAGS. IT WILL KEEP FOR UP TO 2 MONTHS.

VARIATION: USE I CUP (250 ML) SHREDDED GOUDA OR $\frac{1}{2}$ CUP (125 ML) CRUMBLED STILTON CHEESE IN PLACE OF THE CHEDDAR.

HE WHO HESITATES IS SMART.

125

CHILLED BUTTERNUT SQUASH AND MANGO SOUP

THIS EXOTIC, FRUITY CHILLED SOUP FITS THE BILL ON ONE OF THOSE WARM FALL DAYS WHEN BUTTERNUT SQUASH IS IN SEASON BUT YOU'RE STILL WEARING SHORTS. IT'S ALSO GOOD SERVED HOT.

1 TBSP	BUTTER OR VEGETABLE OIL	15 ML
2 TBSP	GRATED GINGERROOT	25 ML
1 TSP	GROUND CUMIN	5 ML
1 TSP	GROUND CORIANDER	5 ML
1	LARGE ONION, CHOPPED	1
2 CUPS	CHOPPED PEELED BUTTERNUT SQUASH (ABOUT 1 SMALL)	500 ML
2 CUPS	FROZEN MANGO CHUNKS (SEE TIP, OPPOSITE)	500 ML
1	CAN (14 OZ/400 ML) COCONUT MILK	1
2 CUPS	CHICKEN BROTH	500 ML
1 TBSP	LIQUID HONEY OR PACKED BROWN SUGAR	15 ML
1 TO 2 TBSP	FRESHLY SQUEEZED LIME JUICE	15 TO 25 ML
	SALT AND FRESHLY GROUND BLACK PEPPER	
	MANGO CHUNKS, THAWED AND DICED	
	UNSWEETENED SHREDDED COCONUT, TOASTED (SEE TIP, PAGE 87)	

IN A LARGE SAUCEPAN, MELT BUTTER OVER MEDIUM HEAT. SAUTÉ GINGER, CUMIN AND CORIANDER UNTIL FRAGRANT, ABOUT 15 SECONDS. ADD ONION, SQUASH AND MANGO CHUNKS; SAUTÉ FOR ABOUT 5 MINUTES OR UNTIL JUST STARTING TO SOFTEN. ADD COCONUT MILK, CHICKEN BROTH AND HONEY; BRING TO A BOIL. REDUCE HEAT AND

SIMMER FOR 25 MINUTES OR UNTIL VEGETABLES ARE SOFT. USING AN IMMERSION BLENDER, OR IN A FOOD PROCESSOR OR BLENDER IN BATCHES, PURÉE SOUP UNTIL VERY SMOOTH. RETURN TO PAN, IF NECESSARY, AND STIR IN LIME JUICE, SALT AND PEPPER TO TASTE. LET COOL, THEN COVER AND REFRIGERATE FOR AT LEAST I HOUR, UNTIL CHILLED, OR FOR UP TO I DAY. SERVE IN CHILLED BOWLS, GARNISHED WITH DICED MANGO AND COCONUT. SERVES 4 TO 6.

TIP: FROZEN, READY-PEELED MANGO CHUNKS ARE NOW SOLD IN MOST SUPERMARKETS, USUALLY IN 2I-OZ (600 G) PACKAGES. KEEP A BAG IN THE FREEZER AND YOU'LL FIND WAYS TO USE MANGO IN SOUPS, SAUCES, DESSERTS AND SMOOTHIES.

VARIATION: USE CHOPPED FROZEN PEACH SLICES IN PLACE OF THE MANGO.

DID YOU EVER NOTICE THE ROMAN NUMERALS FOR FORTY ARE XL?

MUSHROOM BARLEY SOUP

WHILE THIS RECIPE IS PERFECT FOR THE
SLOW COOKER, IT ALSO WORKS WELL ON THE
STOVETOP (SEE TIP, OPPOSITE). SOAKING THE BARLEY
IN HOT WATER WHILE YOU PREPARE THE VEGETABLES
SPEEDS UP THE COOKING TIME.

1/4 CUP	PEARL OR POT BARLEY	50 ML
I CUP	BOILING WATER	250 ML
1 1/2 TBSP	VEGETABLE OIL	22 ML
I	LARGE ONION, FINELY CHOPPED	I
I	STALK CELERY, FINELY CHOPPED	I
I	CARROT, FINELY CHOPPED	I
6 CUPS	SLICED WHITE MUSHROOMS (ABOUT I LB/500 G)	1.5 L
2	CLOVES GARLIC, MINCED	2
I TBSP	TOMATO PASTE	15 ML
5 CUPS	BEEF OR CHICKEN BROTH	1.25 L
I TBSP	SOY SAUCE	15 ML
1/2 TO 1 TSP	DRIED OREGANO	2 TO 5 ML
1/2 TSP	SALT	2 ML
	FRESHLY GROUND BLACK PEPPER	
1/2 TSP	WORCESTERSHIRE SAUCE	2 ML
I TBSP	DRY SHERRY (OPTIONAL)	15 ML
	CHOPPED FRESH PARSLEY	

PREHEAT A 4- TO 6-QUART SLOW COOKER. PLACE BARLEY
IN A BOWL AND POUR IN BOILING WATER; SET ASIDE. IN A
LARGE SAUCEPAN, HEAT OIL OVER MEDIUM HEAT. SAUTÉ
ONION, CELERY AND CARROT FOR 5 TO 7 MINUTES OR
UNTIL SOFTENED. ADD MUSHROOMS AND SAUTÉ UNTIL

STARTING TO BROWN AND ANY LIQUID HAS EVAPORATED, ABOUT 5 MINUTES. DRAIN BARLEY, DISCARDING SOAKING WATER, AND ADD TO PAN ALONG WITH GARLIC AND TOMATO PASTE; COOK, STIRRING, FOR 15 SECONDS. ADD BEEF BROTH, SOY SAUCE, OREGANO TO TASTE, SALT, PEPPER TO TASTE AND WORCESTERSHIRE SAUCE; BRING TO A BOIL. TRANSFER TO SLOW COOKER. COVER AND COOK ON HIGH FOR ABOUT 3 HOURS OR ON LOW FOR ABOUT 6 HOURS, UNTIL BARLEY IS TENDER. JUST BEFORE SERVING, STIR IN SHERRY (IF USING). SERVE GARNISHED WITH PARSLEY. SERVES 4.

MAKE AHEAD: LET SOUP COOL, TRANSFER TO AN AIRTIGHT CONTAINER AND REFRIGERATE FOR UP TO 1 DAY. REHEAT TO SERVE.

TIP: TO COOK THIS SOUP ON THE STOVETOP, LEAVE IT IN THE SAUCEPAN INSTEAD OF TRANSFERRING TO A SLOW COOKER. REDUCE HEAT, COVER, LEAVING LID AJAR, AND SIMMER FOR 45 TO 60 MINUTES OR UNTIL BARLEY IS TENDER.

THE SOLE PURPOSE FOR A CHILD'S MIDDLE NAME IS SO HE CAN TELL WHEN HE'S REALLY IN TROUBLE.

HUNTER'S WILD RICE SOUP

THIS EXCELLENT SOUP ENDURES THE INDIGNITY OF REHEATING QUITE WELL. SERVE WITH RUSTIC CHEDDAR AND HERB SCONES (PAGE 28).

2 TBSP	BUTTER	25 ML
2	STALKS CELERY, DICED	2
1	CARROT, FINELY CHOPPED	1
1	ONION, FINELY CHOPPED	1
3 TBSP	ALL-PURPOSE FLOUR	45 ML
3 1/2 CUPS	CHICKEN BROTH	875 ML
1 CUP	HALF-AND-HALF (10%) CREAM, WARMED	250 ML
1/3 CUP	DRY SHERRY	75 ML
1 TSP	SALT	5 ML
1/2 TSP	FRESHLY GROUND BLACK PEPPER	2 ML
1 CUP	HOT COOKED WILD RICE	250 ML
1/3 CUP	SLIVERED ALMONDS, TOASTED (SEE TIP, PAGE 149)	75 ML
1/4 CUP	CHOPPED FRESH PARSLEY	50 ML

IN A LARGE SAUCEPAN, MELT BUTTER OVER MEDIUM-HIGH HEAT. SAUTÉ CELERY, CARROT AND ONION FOR 5 TO 7 MINUTES OR UNTIL SOFTENED. WHISK IN FLOUR AND COOK, STIRRING CONSTANTLY, FOR 2 MINUTES OR UNTIL LIGHTLY BROWNED. GRADUALLY ADD CHICKEN BROTH, STIRRING UNTIL SOUP THICKENS. STIR IN CREAM, SHERRY, SALT AND PEPPER. STIR IN COOKED RICE. JUST BEFORE SERVING, STIR IN ALMONDS AND PARSLEY. SERVES 6.

MAKE AHEAD: AFTER STIRRING IN THE RICE, LET SOUP COOL, TRANSFER TO AN AIRTIGHT CONTAINER AND REFRIGERATE FOR UP TO 1 DAY. REHEAT TO SERVE.

FISH AND SEAFOOD

— PARMESAN-CRUSTED HALIBUT —

HALIBUT IS PRICEY, SO YOU NEED A RECIPE
WORTHY OF YOUR PURCHASE — THIS IS IT! SERVE
WITH STEAMED RICE OR BABY POTATOES AND
STIR-FRIED SPINACH (PAGE 243).

1	EGG WHITE, LIGHTLY BEATEN	1
1	CLOVE GARLIC, MINCED	1
1/2 CUP	PANKO (SEE TIP, OPPOSITE) OR DRY BREAD CRUMBS	125 ML
1 1/2 TBSP	FRESHLY GRATED PARMESAN CHEESE	22 ML
2 TSP	CHOPPED FRESH PARSLEY	10 ML
2 TSP	CHOPPED FRESH BASIL (OR 1/2 TSP/2 ML DRIED)	10 ML
1 LB	SKINLESS HALIBUT FILLET, CUT INTO 4 PIECES	500 G
2 TBSP	VEGETABLE OIL	25 ML

SAUCE

1/3 CUP	FRESHLY SQUEEZED LEMON JUICE	75 ML
1/4 CUP	DRY WHITE WINE	50 ML
3 TBSP	BUTTER	45 ML
2 TBSP	CHOPPED FRESH PARSLEY	25 ML
2 TBSP	PECANS, TOASTED (SEE TIP, PAGE 149) AND FINELY CHOPPED	25 ML
2	GREEN ONIONS, CHOPPED	2

PREHEAT OVEN TO 400°F (200°C). PLACE EGG WHITE IN A
SHALLOW DISH. IN ANOTHER SHALLOW DISH, COMBINE
GARLIC, PANKO, PARMESAN, PARSLEY AND BASIL. RINSE
HALIBUT AND PAT DRY WITH PAPER TOWELS. DIP EACH
PIECE IN EGG WHITE, ALLOWING EXCESS TO DRIP OFF,
THEN DIP IN PANKO MIXTURE. IN A LARGE SKILLET,

HEAT OIL OVER MEDIUM HEAT. BROWN FISH FOR I MINUTE PER SIDE. TRANSFER TO AN II- BY 7-INCH (28 BY 18 CM) BAKING DISH. BAKE FOR 5 TO 7 MINUTES OR UNTIL FISH IS OPAQUE AND FLAKES EASILY WITH A FORK. DO NOT OVERCOOK.

SAUCE: IN THE SAME SKILLET, BRING LEMON JUICE, WINE, BUTTER, PARSLEY, PECANS AND GREEN ONIONS TO A SIMMER OVER MEDIUM HEAT. SIMMER, STIRRING, FOR ABOUT 2 MINUTES OR UNTIL SLIGHTLY REDUCED. POUR OVER FISH AND SERVE. SERVES 4.

TIP: PANKO IS ALSO KNOWN AS JAPANESE BREAD CRUMBS. SLIGHTLY COARSER THAN REGULAR DRY BREAD CRUMBS, PANKO IS THE CHEF'S CHOICE FOR A BEAUTIFULLY LIGHT AND CRISP COATING FOR FRIED FOODS. GOOD SUBSTITUTES ARE CRACKER CRUMBS OR CRUSHED MELBA TOASTS.

THE OLDER WE GET, THE FEWER THINGS SEEM WORTH WAITING IN LINE FOR.

SALMON WITH HONEY LIME GLAZE

ZINGS FOR YOUR SUPPER.

HONEY LIME GLAZE

3 TBSP	LIQUID HONEY	45 ML
1/4 TSP	GRATED LIME ZEST	1 ML
1 TBSP	FRESHLY SQUEEZED LIME JUICE	15 ML
1/2 TSP	MINCED GARLIC	2 ML
1/2 TSP	MINCED GINGERROOT	2 ML
1/4 TSP	SALT	1 ML
4	SKIN-ON SALMON FILLETS (EACH ABOUT 4 OZ/125 G)	4
2 TBSP	CHOPPED FRESH PARSLEY	25 ML

PREHEAT OVEN TO 425°F (220°C). LINE A RIMMED BAKING SHEET WITH PARCHMENT PAPER OR GREASED FOIL.

HONEY LIME GLAZE: IN A SMALL BOWL, COMBINE HONEY, LIME ZEST, LIME JUICE, GARLIC, GINGER AND SALT. RESERVE HALF THE GLAZE IN A SEPARATE BOWL.

RINSE SALMON AND PAT DRY WITH PAPER TOWELS. PLACE SKIN SIDE DOWN ON PREPARED BAKING SHEET AND BRUSH WITH GLAZE. BAKE FOR 4 MINUTES, THEN REMOVE FROM OVEN AND BRUSH AGAIN WITH GLAZE. BAKE FOR 4 TO 6 MINUTES OR UNTIL FISH IS OPAQUE AND FLAKES EASILY WITH A FORK. BRUSH SALMON WITH THE RESERVED GLAZE AND SERVE SPRINKLED WITH PARSLEY. SERVES 4.

TERIYAKI SALMON

THIS TERIYAKI MARINADE LENDS A WONDERFUL
TANG TO SALMON. SERVE WITH STEAMED RICE AND
STIR-FRIED SPINACH (PAGE 243).

3 TBSP	PACKED BROWN SUGAR	45 ML
3 TBSP	DRY SHERRY	45 ML
2 TBSP	WATER	25 ML
2 TBSP	VEGETABLE OIL	25 ML
1½ TSP	MINCED GINGERROOT	7 ML
2	CLOVES GARLIC, MINCED	2
4	SKINLESS SALMON FILLETS (EACH ABOUT 4 OZ/125 G)	4
2 TSP	SESAME SEEDS	10 ML

IN A BOWL, WHISK TOGETHER BROWN SUGAR, SHERRY,
WATER, OIL, GINGER AND GARLIC. RINSE SALMON AND PAT
DRY. PLACE IN A SINGLE LAYER IN A SHALLOW DISH AND
POUR MARINADE OVER TOP. COVER AND REFRIGERATE FOR
AT LEAST 20 MINUTES OR FOR UP TO 1 HOUR.

MEANWHILE, PREHEAT OVEN TO 425°F (220°C). LINE A
RIMMED BAKING SHEET WITH PARCHMENT PAPER OR
GREASED FOIL. REMOVE SALMON FROM MARINADE,
RESERVING MARINADE. PLACE SALMON ON PREPARED
BAKING SHEET AND SPRINKLE WITH SESAME SEEDS.
BAKE FOR ABOUT 10 MINUTES OR UNTIL FISH IS OPAQUE
AND FLAKES EASILY WITH A FORK.

MEANWHILE, POUR MARINADE INTO A SMALL SAUCEPAN
AND BRING TO A BOIL. REDUCE HEAT AND SIMMER FOR
5 TO 7 MINUTES OR UNTIL THICKENED AND SYRUPY.
SERVE SALMON DRIZZLED WITH SAUCE. SERVES 4.

SALMON WELLINGTON
WITH WHITE WINE SAUCE

*IMPRESSIVE AND NOT AS DIFFICULT
TO MAKE AS YOU MIGHT THINK. FROZEN
PUFF PASTRY IS THE ANSWER.*

1	LARGE LEEK	1
1 TBSP	BUTTER	15 ML
2 TBSP	DRY WHITE WINE	25 ML
	SALT AND FRESHLY GROUND BLACK PEPPER	
1 CUP	WHIPPING (35%) CREAM	250 ML
1	PACKAGE (14 OZ/398 G) FROZEN PUFF PASTRY, THAWED	1
1	SKINLESS SALMON FILLET (12 TO 14 OZ/375 TO 400 G)	1
1	EGG, LIGHTLY BEATEN	1

WHITE WINE SAUCE

1/2 CUP	DRY WHITE WINE	125 ML
1 TSP	FRESHLY SQUEEZED LEMON JUICE	5 ML
1	SMALL SHALLOT, MINCED	1
1/2 CUP	WHIPPING (35%) CREAM	125 ML
1 TSP	DRIED TARRAGON OR DILLWEED	5 ML
	SALT AND FRESHLY GROUND BLACK PEPPER	

TRIM ROOT FROM LEEK AND REMOVE THE DARK GREEN
LEAVES AT THE TOP. CUT LEEK IN HALF LENGTHWISE.
STARTING AT THE BOTTOM OF EACH HALF, SLICE INTO
VERY THIN SEMICIRCLES. WASH WELL IN COLD WATER AND
DRAIN THOROUGHLY (A SALAD SPINNER DOES A GOOD JOB).
IN A LARGE SKILLET, MELT BUTTER OVER MEDIUM HEAT.
SAUTÉ LEEK FOR 5 MINUTES OR UNTIL TENDER. ADD WINE
AND SALT AND PEPPER TO TASTE; REDUCE HEAT AND

SIMMER FOR 3 TO 4 MINUTES OR UNTIL LIQUID IS ALMOST EVAPORATED. ADD CREAM AND SIMMER, STIRRING OFTEN, UNTIL REDUCED BY HALF. DO NOT LET BOIL. REMOVE FROM HEAT AND LET COOL COMPLETELY.

MEANWHILE, PREHEAT OVEN TO 425°F (220°C). LINE A LARGE RIMMED BAKING SHEET WITH PARCHMENT PAPER. ON A FLOURED SURFACE, CUT BLOCK OF PUFF PASTRY IN HALF (IT IS USUALLY PARTIALLY PRECUT). ROLL OUT EACH HALF INTO A 12- BY 10-INCH (30 BY 25 CM) RECTANGLE. PLACE ONE RECTANGLE ON PREPARED BAKING SHEET. RINSE SALMON AND PAT DRY WITH PAPER TOWELS. PLACE SALMON IN THE CENTER OF THE PASTRY, LEAVING A 2-INCH (5 CM) BORDER ALL AROUND. SPOON LEEK MIXTURE OVER SALMON. BRUSH EDGES OF PASTRY WITH EGG. PLACE SECOND PASTRY RECTANGLE ON TOP AND PRESS THE EDGES TO SEAL, LIKE A PILLOW. TRIM THE EDGES, LEAVING A 1-INCH (2.5 CM) BORDER OF PASTRY AROUND THE FISH. PRESS EDGES WITH A FORK TO RESEAL. CUT 3 OR 4 SLITS IN THE TOP TO ALLOW STEAM TO ESCAPE. BRUSH TOP WITH BEATEN EGG. BAKE FOR 20 TO 25 MINUTES OR UNTIL PASTRY IS PUFFY AND GOLDEN. LET REST FOR 5 MINUTES.

WHITE WINE SAUCE: MEANWHILE, IN A SMALL SAUCEPAN, BRING WINE, LEMON JUICE AND SHALLOT TO A BOIL OVER MEDIUM HEAT. REDUCE HEAT AND SIMMER FOR ABOUT 5 MINUTES OR UNTIL REDUCED BY HALF. ADD CREAM AND SIMMER, STIRRING OFTEN, UNTIL SLIGHTLY THICKENED. DO NOT LET BOIL. STRAIN INTO A SMALL BOWL AND WHISK IN TARRAGON AND SALT AND PEPPER TO TASTE. SLICE SALMON AND SERVE DRIZZLED WITH SAUCE. SERVES 4.

SALMON WITH PISTACHIO CRUST

*YUMMY! IT'S EQUALLY DELICIOUS
MADE WITH SEA BASS OR SABLEFISH.*

4	SKIN-ON SALMON FILLETS (EACH ABOUT 4 OZ/125 G)	4
	SALT AND FRESHLY GROUND BLACK PEPPER	
3 TBSP	GRAINY DIJON MUSTARD	45 ML
3 TBSP	PURE MAPLE SYRUP	45 ML
1/4 CUP	PISTACHIOS, FINELY CHOPPED	50 ML

PREHEAT OVEN TO 425°F (220°C). LINE A RIMMED BAKING SHEET WITH PARCHMENT PAPER OR GREASED FOIL. RINSE SALMON AND PAT DRY WITH PAPER TOWELS. SEASON SALMON WITH SALT AND PEPPER. PLACE SKIN SIDE DOWN ON PREPARED BAKING SHEET. IN A SMALL BOWL, COMBINE MUSTARD AND MAPLE SYRUP; SPREAD OVER SALMON. BAKE FOR 8 TO 10 MINUTES OR UNTIL FISH IS OPAQUE AND FLAKES EASILY WITH A FORK. PAT PISTACHIOS ON TOP OF THE SALMON. SERVE IMMEDIATELY. SERVES 4.

*I'M AS STRONG AS THE COFFEE I DRINK
AND THE HAIRSPRAY I USE.*

SOLE WITH ORANGE NUT BUTTER

A QUICK DINNER, AND HEALTHY TOO.

1 LB	FRESH OR THAWED FROZEN SKINLESS SOLE FILLETS (4 TO 8)	500 G
1/2 CUP	ALL-PURPOSE FLOUR	125 ML
1/2 TSP	SALT	2 ML
1/4 TSP	FRESHLY GROUND BLACK PEPPER	1 ML
1/2 CUP	SLICED ALMONDS	125 ML
2 TBSP	VEGETABLE OIL	25 ML
3 TBSP	BUTTER	45 ML
2 TBSP	CHOPPED FRESH PARSLEY	25 ML
2 TBSP	FRESHLY SQUEEZED ORANGE JUICE OR LEMON JUICE	25 ML

RINSE SOLE AND PAT DRY. (IF THE FISH HAS BEEN FROZEN AND THAWED, IT WILL BE QUITE WET, SO DRY IT WELL.) IN A SHALLOW DISH, COMBINE FLOUR, SALT AND PEPPER. DIP FISH IN SEASONED FLOUR, SHAKING OFF EXCESS. PLACE ON A PLATE AND SET ASIDE. HEAT A LARGE NONSTICK SKILLET OVER MEDIUM HEAT. TOAST ALMONDS, SHAKING OR STIRRING FREQUENTLY, UNTIL AROMATIC AND LIGHT BROWN AT THE EDGES. TRANSFER TO A COLD PLATE AND SET ASIDE. IN THE SAME SKILLET, HEAT OIL OVER MEDIUM-HIGH HEAT. WORKING IN BATCHES AS NECESSARY, FRY FISH FOR ABOUT 2 MINUTES PER SIDE OR UNTIL COATING IS LIGHTLY BROWNED AND FISH FLAKES EASILY WITH A FORK. TRANSFER TO A PLATE LINED WITH PAPER TOWELS AND KEEP HOT. WIPE OUT SKILLET AND MELT BUTTER OVER MEDIUM HEAT. ADD PARSLEY, ORANGE JUICE AND RESERVED ALMONDS, SWIRLING PAN TO COMBINE. SERVE SOLE WITH SAUCE SPOONED OVER TOP. SERVES 4.

CRISPY SOLE FINGERS WITH TARTAR SAUCE

FISH STICKS, BUT BETTER. THE TARTAR SAUCE CAN BE WHISKED TOGETHER IN MINUTES, OR YOU CAN USE STORE-BOUGHT, IF YOU MUST.

TARTAR SAUCE

1/2 CUP	MAYONNAISE	125 ML
2 TBSP	WHIPPING (35%) CREAM OR MILK	25 ML
2 TBSP	FINELY CHOPPED DILL PICKLES	25 ML
2 TBSP	FINELY CHOPPED GREEN ONION	25 ML
1 TBSP	CAPERS	15 ML
2 TSP	JUICE FROM CAPER JAR	10 ML
1/4 TSP	SALT	1 ML
	FRESHLY GROUND BLACK PEPPER	

SOLE FINGERS

1 LB	FRESH OR THAWED FROZEN SKINLESS SOLE FILLETS (4 TO 8)	500 G
1 CUP	ALL-PURPOSE FLOUR	250 ML
1 TSP	PAPRIKA	5 ML
1 TSP	SALT	5 ML
2	EGGS	2
3 TBSP	MILK	45 ML
2 CUPS	PANKO (SEE TIP, PAGE 133) OR DRY BREAD CRUMBS	500 ML
1/4 CUP	VEGETABLE OIL	50 ML

TARTAR SAUCE: IN A SMALL BOWL, WHISK TOGETHER MAYONNAISE, CREAM, PICKLES, GREEN ONION, CAPERS, CAPER JUICE, SALT AND PEPPER TO TASTE. COVER AND REFRIGERATE FOR 2 HOURS TO LET FLAVORS DEVELOP.

SOLE FINGERS: RINSE SOLE AND PAT DRY WITH PAPER TOWELS. (IF THE FISH HAS BEEN FROZEN AND THAWED, IT WILL BE QUITE WET, SO BE SURE TO DRY IT WELL.) CUT EACH FILLET IN HALF LENGTHWAYS, THEN CUT EACH HALF INTO 2 TO 3 STRIPS, DEPENDING ON THE SIZE OF THE FILLET. EACH STRIP SHOULD BE NO MORE THAN I INCH (2.5 CM) WIDE. IN A SHALLOW DISH, COMBINE FLOUR, PAPRIKA AND SALT. IN ANOTHER DISH, WHISK TOGETHER EGGS AND MILK. PLACE PANKO IN A THIRD DISH. WORKING WITH A FEW STRIPS AT A TIME, DIP FISH IN SEASONED FLOUR, SHAKING OFF EXCESS, THEN IN THE EGG MIXTURE AND FINALLY IN PANKO, COATING EVENLY. REPEAT UNTIL ALL FISH STRIPS ARE COATED. IN A LARGE SKILLET, HEAT OIL OVER MEDIUM-HIGH HEAT. WORKING IN BATCHES, FRY FISH STRIPS FOR ABOUT I MINUTE PER SIDE OR UNTIL BATTER IS GOLDEN AND FISH FLAKES EASILY WITH A FORK. TRANSFER TO A PLATE LINED WITH PAPER TOWELS AND KEEP HOT WHILE COOKING THE REMAINING FISH. SERVE WITH TARTAR SAUCE. SERVES 4.

MAKE AHEAD: THE TARTAR SAUCE CAN BE STORED IN THE REFRIGERATOR FOR UP TO 3 DAYS.

PAN-FRIED TILAPIA WITH TOMATO CAPER SALSA

FISH IS BEST ENJOYED WHEN IT IS PREPARED SIMPLY. THIS PAN-FRIED DISH WORKS WELL WITH THIN MILD FISH FILLETS SUCH AS TILAPIA, SOLE OR OCEAN PERCH. THE TOMATO CAPER SALSA IS A FRESH-TASTING ACCOMPANIMENT.

TOMATO CAPER SALSA

2	SMALL TOMATOES, CHOPPED	2
2	GREEN ONIONS, FINELY CHOPPED	2
I	CLOVE GARLIC, MINCED	I
2 TBSP	DRAINED CAPERS	25 ML
2 TBSP	CHOPPED FRESH PARSLEY	25 ML
I TBSP	RED WINE VINEGAR	15 ML
	SALT AND FRESHLY GROUND BLACK PEPPER	
1/2 CUP	ALL-PURPOSE FLOUR	125 ML
I TSP	PAPRIKA	5 ML
	SALT AND FRESHLY GROUND BLACK PEPPER	
I LB	SKINLESS TILAPIA FILLETS, CUT INTO 4 PIECES	500 G
2 TBSP	VEGETABLE OIL	25 ML

TOMATO CAPER SALSA: IN A MEDIUM BOWL, COMBINE TOMATOES, GREEN ONIONS, GARLIC, CAPERS, PARSLEY, VINEGAR AND SALT AND PEPPER TO TASTE. COVER AND REFRIGERATE FOR AT LEAST I HOUR, UNTIL CHILLED, OR FOR UP TO I DAY.

IN A SHALLOW DISH, COMBINE FLOUR, PAPRIKA AND SALT AND PEPPER TO TASTE. RINSE TILAPIA AND PAT DRY WITH PAPER TOWELS. DIP FISH IN SEASONED FLOUR, SHAKING OFF EXCESS. IN A LARGE SKILLET, HEAT OIL OVER MEDIUM-HIGH HEAT. ADD FISH, TOP SIDE DOWN, AND FRY FOR ABOUT 1 MINUTE OR UNTIL COATING IS GOLDEN BROWN. TURN FISH OVER, ADJUSTING HEAT IF NECESSARY, AND FRY FOR 3 TO 4 MINUTES OR UNTIL FISH FLAKES EASILY WITH A FORK. SERVE WITH SALSA SPOONED OVER TOP. SERVES 4.

TIP: FOR A MORE GOLDEN COATING, DIP THE FISH IN COLD MILK BEFORE DIPPING IT IN FLOUR. WHEN YOU FRY THE FISH, THE NATURAL SUGARS IN THE MILK WILL CARAMELIZE, GIVING THE FISH A NICELY COLORED, CRISP COATING.

I CHILDPROOFED THE HOUSE, BUT THEY KEEP GETTING BACK IN.

MEDITERRANEAN FISH BAKE

PUT PIZZAZZ INTO INEXPENSIVE FROZEN FISH
SUCH AS TILAPIA OR BASA. THE FLAVORFUL SAUCE AND
FRAGRANT PARSLEY-LEMON GARNISH IS POSITIVELY
GREEK. SIMPLIFY YOUR SCHEDULE AND MAKE
THE SAUCE A DAY AHEAD.

SAUCE

2 TBSP	OLIVE OIL	25 ML
1	ONION, THINLY SLICED	1
1	RED BELL PEPPER, THINLY SLICED	1
3	CLOVES GARLIC, MINCED	3
2	ZUCCHINI, CHOPPED (ABOUT 2 CUPS/500 ML)	2
1	EGGPLANT, CHOPPED (ABOUT 2 CUPS/500 ML)	1
1 1/4 CUPS	TOMATO SAUCE	300 ML
1/3 CUP	DRY WHITE WINE OR CHICKEN BROTH	75 ML
1/2 TSP	DRIED THYME	2 ML
	SALT AND FRESHLY GROUND BLACK PEPPER	
1 1/2 LBS	FRESH OR THAWED FROZEN SKINLESS TILAPIA FILLETS, CUT INTO 4 PIECES	750 G
1 TBSP	OLIVE OIL	15 ML
	SALT AND FRESHLY GROUND BLACK PEPPER	
2 TBSP	FRESHLY SQUEEZED LEMON JUICE (OR TO TASTE)	25 ML

GARNISH

3 TBSP	CHOPPED FRESH PARSLEY	45 ML
1 TBSP	GRATED LEMON ZEST	15 ML
1	CLOVE GARLIC, MINCED	1

SAUCE: IN A LARGE SKILLET, HEAT OIL OVER MEDIUM-HIGH HEAT. SAUTÉ ONION AND RED PEPPER UNTIL SOFTENED, ABOUT 5 MINUTES. ADD GARLIC, ZUCCHINI AND EGGPLANT; SAUTÉ FOR 5 TO 7 MINUTES OR UNTIL LIGHTLY BROWNED. ADD TOMATO SAUCE, WINE, THYME AND SALT AND PEPPER TO TASTE; BRING TO A BOIL. REDUCE HEAT AND SIMMER FOR 20 TO 25 MINUTES OR UNTIL SAUCE IS THICK AND VEGETABLES ARE VERY SOFT.

MEANWHILE, PREHEAT OVEN TO 400°F (200°C). GREASE A 13- BY 9-INCH (33 BY 23 CM) BAKING DISH. RINSE TILAPIA AND PAT DRY WITH PAPER TOWELS. (IF THE FISH HAS BEEN FROZEN AND THAWED, IT WILL BE QUITE WET, SO BE SURE TO DRY IT WELL.) BRUSH WITH OIL AND SPRINKLE WITH SALT AND PEPPER. TRANSFER SAUCE TO PREPARED BAKING DISH AND LAY TILAPIA ON TOP. BAKE FOR 12 TO 15 MINUTES OR UNTIL FISH IS OPAQUE AND FLAKES EASILY WITH A FORK AND SAUCE IS BUBBLING. DRIZZLE LEMON JUICE OVER FISH.

GARNISH: IN A SMALL BOWL, COMBINE PARSLEY, LEMON ZEST AND GARLIC. SPRINKLE OVER FISH AND SERVE IMMEDIATELY. SERVES 4.

MAKE AHEAD: LET THE SAUCE COOL, TRANSFER TO AN AIRTIGHT CONTAINER AND REFRIGERATE FOR UP TO 1 DAY. BRING BACK TO A BOIL IN A SAUCEPAN AND TRANSFER TO BAKING DISH BEFORE PROCEEDING WITH RECIPE.

RAINBOW TROUT BAKED WITH FENNEL AND POTATOES

WHOLE FISH COOKED ON A BED OF FLAVORFUL, JUICY VEGETABLES — AN IMPRESSIVE, EASY ONE-DISH DINNER.

4	WHOLE SMALL RAINBOW TROUT (EACH ABOUT 8 OZ/250 G), CLEANED	4
	SALT AND FRESHLY GROUND BLACK PEPPER	
4	SMALL SPRIGS FRESH DILL OR PARSLEY	4
1½ LBS	POTATOES, PEELED AND THINLY SLICED	750 G
24	CHERRY TOMATOES	24
3	CLOVES GARLIC, MINCED	3
2	FENNEL BULBS, HALVED, CORED AND THINLY SLICED	2
1 TSP	FENNEL SEEDS (OPTIONAL)	5 ML
4 TBSP	EXTRA VIRGIN OLIVE OIL, DIVIDED	60 ML
	JUICE OF 1 LEMON	
	CHOPPED FRESH PARSLEY	

PREHEAT OVEN TO 375°F (190°C). RINSE TROUT AND PAT DRY WITH PAPER TOWELS. MAKE THREE SMALL DIAGONAL SLASHES THROUGH THE SKIN ON BOTH SIDES. SEASON INSIDE AND OUT WITH SALT AND PEPPER. TUCK A SPRIG OF DILL INSIDE EACH TROUT. COVER AND PLACE IN REFRIGERATOR.

IN A 13- BY 9-INCH (33 BY 23 CM) BAKING DISH, GENTLY COMBINE POTATOES, TOMATOES, GARLIC, SLICED FENNEL, FENNEL SEEDS, SALT AND PEPPER TO TASTE AND 3 TBSP (45 ML) OF THE OIL. BAKE FOR 25 TO 30 MINUTES OR UNTIL POTATOES ARE TENDER AND STARTING TO BROWN AROUND THE EDGES OF THE DISH.

PLACE TROUT ON TOP OF THE VEGETABLES AND DRIZZLE WITH THE REMAINING OIL. BAKE FOR 10 TO 20 MINUTES OR UNTIL FISH IS OPAQUE AND FLAKES EASILY WITH A FORK. DRIZZLE LEMON JUICE OVER FISH AND VEGETABLES. SERVE SPRINKLED WITH PARSLEY. SERVES 4.

TIP: SCORING THE SKIN HELPS PREVENT IT FROM SPLITTING — AND LOOKING UNATTRACTIVE — WHILE THE TROUT IS ROASTING.

NORMAL IS JUST A SETTING ON THE WASHING MACHINE.

PAN-FRIED RAINBOW TROUT WITH LEMON DILL SAUCE

HERE'S A TASTY AND NUTRITIOUS MEAL THAT'S ON THE TABLE IN MINUTES. SERVE WITH BUTTERY BABY POTATOES AND A GREEN SALAD.

1/2 CUP	ALL-PURPOSE FLOUR	125 ML
1 TSP	PAPRIKA	5 ML
1 TSP	SALT	5 ML
1/4 TSP	FRESHLY GROUND BLACK PEPPER	1 ML
1 1/2 LBS	SKIN-ON RAINBOW TROUT FILLETS (4 TO 8)	750 G
1/4 CUP	OLIVE OIL	50 ML
1/2 CUP	DRY WHITE WINE	125 ML
	JUICE OF 1 LEMON	
1/4 CUP	CHOPPED FRESH PARSLEY	50 ML
2 TBSP	CHOPPED FRESH DILL	25 ML
2 TBSP	BUTTER	25 ML
1/4 CUP	SLICED ALMONDS, TOASTED (SEE TIP, OPPOSITE)	50 ML

IN A SHALLOW DISH, COMBINE FLOUR, PAPRIKA, SALT AND PEPPER. RINSE TROUT AND PAT DRY WITH PAPER TOWELS. DIP FISH IN SEASONED FLOUR, SHAKING OFF EXCESS. IN A LARGE SKILLET, HEAT OIL OVER MEDIUM-HIGH HEAT. ADD FISH, SKIN SIDE UP, AND FRY FOR ABOUT 1 MINUTE OR UNTIL COATING IS GOLDEN BROWN. TURN FISH OVER AND FRY FOR 3 TO 4 MINUTES OR UNTIL FISH FLAKES EASILY WITH A FORK. TRANSFER TO A PLATE LINED WITH PAPER TOWELS AND KEEP WARM. ADD WINE TO SKILLET AND SIMMER UNTIL ALMOST EVAPORATED. ADD LEMON JUICE, PARSLEY AND DILL; SAUTÉ FOR 15 TO 20 SECONDS

OR UNTIL FRAGRANT. REMOVE FROM HEAT AND SWIRL IN BUTTER UNTIL MELTED. SERVE TROUT DRIZZLED WITH SAUCE AND SPRINKLED WITH ALMONDS. SERVES 4.

TIP: TOASTING NUTS HELPS BRING OUT THEIR FLAVOR. THE QUICKEST METHOD IS ON THE STOVETOP. SPREAD NUTS OUT IN AN UNGREASED NONSTICK SKILLET AND PLACE OVER MEDIUM HEAT. SHAKE OR STIR FREQUENTLY, TO PREVENT BURNING, FOR 4 TO 5 MINUTES OR UNTIL FRAGRANT AND STARTING TO BROWN. TIP ONTO A COLD PLATE TO STOP THE COOKING PROCESS AND LET COOL COMPLETELY.

VARIATION: INSTEAD OF PREPARING THE LEMON DILL SAUCE, SERVE THE PAN-FRIED TROUT DRIZZLED WITH ORANGE-WALNUT DRESSING (PAGE 69).

WHOEVER SAYS MONEY CAN'T BUY HAPPINESS
DOESN'T KNOW WHERE TO SHOP.

CAJUN FISH WITH CORN AND BLACK BEAN MEDLEY

SENSATIONAL SOUTHWESTERN FLAVORS — USE COD, HALIBUT OR RED SNAPPER. ENJOY WITH SOME FRESH CRUSTY BREAD.

4	SKINLESS FIRM WHITE FISH FILLETS (EACH ABOUT 5 OZ/150 G)	4
4 TSP	CAJUN SEASONING (SEE TIP, OPPOSITE)	20 ML
2 TBSP	VEGETABLE OIL	25 ML
1 TBSP	BUTTER	15 ML
2 CUPS	FROZEN CORN KERNELS	500 ML
4	TOMATOES, SEEDED AND ROUGHLY CHOPPED	4
1½ CUPS	DRAINED RINSED CANNED BLACK BEANS	375 ML
4	GREEN ONIONS, THINLY SLICED	4
	SALT AND FRESHLY GROUND BLACK PEPPER	
2 TBSP	CHOPPED FRESH CILANTRO OR PARSLEY	25 ML

PREHEAT OVEN TO 400°F (200°C). LINE A RIMMED BAKING SHEET WITH PARCHMENT PAPER OR GREASED FOIL. RINSE FISH AND PAT DRY WITH PAPER TOWELS. RUB TOPS WITH CAJUN SEASONING. IN A LARGE SKILLET, HEAT OIL OVER MEDIUM HEAT. ADD FISH, SEASONED SIDE DOWN, AND FRY FOR 1 TO 2 MINUTES OR UNTIL QUITE DARK BROWN (YOU ARE AIMING FOR A CAJUN "BLACKENED" LOOK). TRANSFER FISH, BROWNED SIDE UP, TO PREPARED BAKING SHEET. BAKE FOR 7 TO 10 MINUTES OR UNTIL FISH IS OPAQUE AND FLAKES EASILY WITH A FORK.

MEANWHILE, IN ANOTHER LARGE SKILLET, MELT BUTTER OVER MEDIUM-HIGH HEAT. SAUTÉ CORN UNTIL STARTING TO BROWN, ABOUT 5 MINUTES. ADD TOMATOES AND BLACK BEANS; SAUTÉ FOR 2 TO 3 MINUTES OR UNTIL SLIGHTLY THICKENED. STIR IN GREEN ONIONS AND SALT AND PEPPER TO TASTE. REMOVE FROM HEAT AND STIR IN CILANTRO. TO SERVE, SPOON CORN MEDLEY INTO THE CENTER OF EACH PLATE AND PLACE A FISH FILLET ON TOP. SERVES 4.

TIP: CAJUN SEASONING IS A BLEND OF LOUISIANA HERBS AND SPICES AND IS AN EASY, QUICK WAY TO ENLIVEN MEAT OR FISH. IT'S ONE OF MANY SEASONING BLENDS THAT ARE NOW WIDELY AVAILABLE, INCLUDING BARBECUE, ITALIAN, MONTREAL STEAK AND OLD BAY SEAFOOD. THESE SPICE MIXES TAKE THE GUESSWORK OUT OF SEASONING WHEN YOU'RE TRYING TO CAPTURE A PARTICULAR FLAVOR — AND THEY SAVE YOU FROM HAVING TO BUY A DOZEN DIFFERENT JARS OF HERBS AND SPICES FOR ONE RECIPE!

"I SHOULDN'T HAVE TOLD MY GIRLFRIEND HOW RICH MY GRANDFATHER IS."
"WHY NOT?"
"NEXT SATURDAY SHE'S BECOMING MY STEP-GRANDMOTHER."

FISH TACOS

BLAST YOUR TASTE BUDS WITH THESE FANTASTIC
FISH TACOS FROM THE BAJA REGION OF MEXICO.

CHIPOTLE SAUCE

1/2 CUP	MAYONNAISE	125 ML
1/2 CUP	SOUR CREAM	125 ML
2	CLOVES GARLIC, MINCED	2
2 TBSP	CHOPPED FRESH CILANTRO	25 ML
1 TSP	PURÉED CANNED CHIPOTLE PEPPER (SEE TIP, OPPOSITE)	5 ML
1/2 TSP	SALT	2 ML
1 LB	SKINLESS COD OR OTHER FIRM WHITEFISH FILLETS, CUT INTO 4 PIECES	500 G
2 TBSP	VEGETABLE OIL	25 ML
1 TBSP	FRESHLY SQUEEZED LIME JUICE	15 ML
1/4 TSP	CAYENNE PEPPER	1 ML
1/4 TSP	SALT	1 ML
8	SOFT CORN OR FLOUR TORTILLAS	8
4	TOMATOES, CHOPPED	4
4 CUPS	SHREDDED GREEN AND/OR RED CABBAGE	1 L
	TOMATO SALSA	

CHIPOTLE SAUCE: IN A MEDIUM BOWL, WHISK TOGETHER
MAYONNAISE, SOUR CREAM, GARLIC, CILANTRO, CHIPOTLE
PEPPER AND SALT. COVER AND REFRIGERATE FOR AT LEAST
1 HOUR, UNTIL CHILLED.

RINSE FISH AND PAT DRY WITH PAPER TOWELS. PLACE IN A
SHALLOW DISH. IN A SMALL BOWL, WHISK TOGETHER OIL,
LIME JUICE, CAYENNE AND SALT. POUR OVER FISH. COVER
AND REFRIGERATE FOR 30 MINUTES, UNTIL CHILLED.

PREHEAT OVEN TO 425°F (220°C). LINE A LARGE RIMMED BAKING SHEET WITH GREASED FOIL. WRAP TORTILLAS IN FOIL AND PLACE IN OVEN. REMOVE FISH FROM MARINADE, ALLOWING EXCESS TO DRIP OFF AND DISCARDING MARINADE. PLACE FISH ON PREPARED BAKING SHEET. BAKE FOR 5 TO 7 MINUTES OR UNTIL FISH IS OPAQUE AND FLAKES EASILY WITH A FORK. LET COOL SLIGHTLY, THEN USE A FORK TO FLAKE FISH INTO BITE-SIZE PIECES. TRANSFER TO A SERVING BOWL AND STIR IN ENOUGH CHIPOTLE SAUCE TO MOISTEN. REMOVE TORTILLAS FROM OVEN. LET EVERYONE MAKE THEIR OWN TACOS WITH THE TORTILLAS, FISH MIXTURE, TOMATOES AND CABBAGE. SERVE EXTRA CHIPOTLE SAUCE AND SALSA ON THE SIDE. SERVES 4.

TIP: CANNED CHIPOTLE PEPPERS ARE SMOKED JALAPEÑO PEPPERS PACKED IN MEXICAN ADOBO SAUCE. THE CANS ARE TYPICALLY 7 OZ (198 ML) AND CAN BE FOUND NEAR OTHER MEXICAN FOODS IN MAJOR SUPERMARKETS. THE EASIEST WAY TO USE CHIPOTLES IS TO PURÉE THE PEPPERS WITH THEIR SAUCE. PLACE IN A CLEAN SCREW-TOP JAR AND STORE IN THE REFRIGERATOR, WHERE THE PURÉE WILL KEEP FOR SEVERAL MONTHS, UNTIL YOU ARE READY TO USE IT. CHIPOTLES ARE FIERY LITTLE DEVILS, SO USE THEM IN SMALL QUANTITIES AND WASH YOUR HANDS THOROUGHLY AFTER PREPARING THEM. YOU DON'T WANT TO TOUCH YOUR EYES OR ANY OTHER BODY PART WITH CHIPOTLE ON YOUR FINGERS!

FISHERMAN'S PIE

SHEPHERDS AND FISHERMEN AGREE — YOU'VE GOTTA HAVE MASHED POTATOES ON YOUR PIE.

TOPPING

2 LBS	POTATOES, PEELED AND CHOPPED	1 KG
3 TBSP	BUTTER	45 ML
1/3 TO 1/2 CUP	MILK, WARMED	75 TO 125 ML
	SALT AND FRESHLY GROUND BLACK PEPPER	

FILLING

3 TBSP	BUTTER	45 ML
2	STALKS CELERY, THINLY SLICED	2
1	LARGE LEEK, TRIMMED AND THINLY SLICED	1
3 TBSP	ALL-PURPOSE FLOUR	45 ML
1 1/2 CUPS	MILK	375 ML
1 1/2 LBS	SKINLESS COD OR OTHER FIRM WHITE FISH FILLETS, CUT INTO BITE-SIZE PIECES	750 G
1 CUP	FROZEN CORN KERNELS	250 ML
1/2 CUP	FROZEN PEAS	125 ML
1/2 CUP	WHIPPING (35%) CREAM	125 ML
2 TBSP	CHOPPED FRESH DILL	25 ML
1 TBSP	DIJON MUSTARD	15 ML
1/2 TO 1 TSP	HOT PEPPER SAUCE	2 TO 5 ML
PINCH	GROUND CLOVES	PINCH
	SALT AND FRESHLY GROUND BLACK PEPPER	
2 TO 4 TBSP	FRESHLY SQUEEZED LEMON JUICE	25 TO 60 ML
1/2 CUP	SHREDDED SHARP (OLD) CHEDDAR CHEESE	125 ML

TOPPING: IN A LARGE POT OF BOILING WATER, COOK POTATOES UNTIL FORK-TENDER. DRAIN AND MASH WITH BUTTER AND ENOUGH MILK TO MAKE CREAMY. SEASON TO TASTE WITH SALT AND PEPPER. SET ASIDE.

PREHEAT OVEN TO 375°F (190°C). GREASE A 10-CUP (2.5 L) BAKING DISH.

FILLING: IN A LARGE SAUCEPAN OR DUTCH OVEN, MELT BUTTER OVER MEDIUM-HIGH HEAT. SAUTÉ CELERY AND LEEK UNTIL SOFTENED BUT NOT BROWNED, ABOUT 5 MINUTES. ADD FLOUR AND SAUTÉ FOR 30 SECONDS. GRADUALLY WHISK IN MILK, STIRRING UNTIL SMOOTH. BRING TO A BOIL, STIRRING. REDUCE HEAT AND SIMMER, STIRRING FREQUENTLY, FOR 5 MINUTES OR UNTIL THICKENED. GENTLY STIR IN FISH, CORN, PEAS, CREAM, DILL, MUSTARD, HOT PEPPER SAUCE TO TASTE, CLOVES AND SALT AND PEPPER TO TASTE. ADD LEMON JUICE, 1 TBSP (15 ML) AT A TIME, TASTING BETWEEN EACH ADDITION, UNTIL MIXTURE HAS THE DESIRED FLAVOR. BRING BACK TO A BOIL, STIRRING. REMOVE FROM HEAT. (FISH WILL BE ONLY PARTIALLY COOKED.)

TRANSFER FISH MIXTURE TO PREPARED BAKING DISH AND SPREAD MASHED POTATO OVER TOP. SPRINKLE WITH CHEESE. BAKE FOR ABOUT 30 MINUTES OR UNTIL FILLING IS BUBBLING AND TOP IS BROWNED. SERVES 4 TO 6.

VARIATION: REPLACE SOME OF THE COD WITH AN EQUAL AMOUNT OF PEELED, DEVEINED SHRIMP. YOU COULD ALSO ADD 2 PEELED AND CHOPPED HARD-BOILED EGGS TO THE FILLING.

SEAFOOD PASTA BAKE

A CREAMY ONE-DISH DINNER AND A GREAT MAKE-AHEAD.

5 TBSP	BUTTER, DIVIDED	75 ML
2 CUPS	SLICED WHITE MUSHROOMS	500 ML
2	CLOVES GARLIC, MINCED	2
I	SHALLOT, MINCED	I
I LB	IMITATION CRABMEAT, CUT INTO BITE-SIZE PIECES	500 G
1/2 CUP	DRY WHITE WINE	125 ML
	SALT AND FRESHLY GROUND BLACK PEPPER	
2 TBSP	ALL-PURPOSE FLOUR	25 ML
PINCH	GROUND NUTMEG	PINCH
2 CUPS	MILK	500 ML
8 OZ	MEDIUM SHRIMP, PEELED AND DEVEINED (ABOUT 25)	250 G
3/4 CUP	FRESHLY GRATED PARMESAN CHEESE, DIVIDED	175 ML
3 CUPS	PENNE OR SMALL SHELL-SHAPED PASTA	750 ML
I CUP	SHREDDED MOZZARELLA CHEESE	250 ML

PREHEAT OVEN TO 375°F (190°C). GREASE AN 8-CUP (2 L) BAKING DISH. IN A MEDIUM SKILLET, MELT 2 TBSP (25 ML) OF THE BUTTER OVER MEDIUM HEAT. SAUTÉ MUSHROOMS, GARLIC AND SHALLOT FOR ABOUT 5 MINUTES OR UNTIL SOFTENED AND ANY LIQUID HAS EVAPORATED. STIR IN CRABMEAT AND WINE. REMOVE FROM HEAT AND SEASON TO TASTE WITH SALT AND PEPPER; SET ASIDE. IN A LARGE SAUCEPAN, MELT 2 TBSP (25 ML) BUTTER OVER MEDIUM HEAT. STIR IN FLOUR AND NUTMEG; COOK, STIRRING, FOR I TO 2 MINUTES OR UNTIL GRAINY-LOOKING.

GRADUALLY WHISK IN MILK AND BRING TO A BOIL, STIRRING CONSTANTLY. REDUCE HEAT AND SIMMER FOR 3 TO 4 MINUTES OR UNTIL THICKENED. FOLD IN MUSHROOM MIXTURE, SHRIMP AND 1/4 CUP (50 ML) OF THE PARMESAN. REMOVE FROM HEAT.

MEANWHILE, COOK PASTA ACCORDING TO PACKAGE INSTRUCTIONS. DRAIN AND ADD TO SAUCE, STIRRING WELL TO COMBINE. SPOON HALF THE PASTA MIXTURE INTO PREPARED BAKING DISH AND SPRINKLE WITH HALF THE MOZZARELLA AND 1/4 CUP (50 ML) PARMESAN. MAKE ANOTHER LAYER WITH THE REMAINING SAUCE, MOZZARELLA AND PARMESAN. DOT WITH THE REMAINING BUTTER. BAKE FOR 30 TO 40 MINUTES OR UNTIL BUBBLING AND BROWNED ON TOP. SERVES 4 TO 6.

Cover after awhile

MAKE AHEAD: AFTER ASSEMBLING THE CASSEROLE BUT BEFORE DOTTING WITH BUTTER, LET COOL, COVER AND REFRIGERATE FOR UP TO 1 DAY. OR WRAP THE BAKING DISH IN HEAVY-DUTY FOIL AND FREEZE FOR UP TO 2 WEEKS. THAW IN THE REFRIGERATOR FOR 48 HOURS BEFORE DOTTING WITH BUTTER AND BAKING.

do not overcook - it dries out

"ANYONE WHO LIVES WITHIN THEIR MEANS SUFFERS FROM A LACK OF IMAGINATION."
— OSCAR WILDE

SHRIMP IN WINE AND MUSHROOM SAUCE

WITH SHRIMP IN THE FREEZER, YOU ARE ALWAYS READY FOR COMPANY. SERVE THIS LIGHT AND EASY SEAFOOD DISH WITH STEAMED RICE.

1 TBSP	BUTTER	15 ML
1 TBSP	OLIVE OIL	15 ML
1	SMALL ONION, FINELY CHOPPED	1
3	CLOVES GARLIC, MINCED	3
6 CUPS	SLICED WHITE MUSHROOMS (ABOUT 12 OZ/375 G)	1.5 L
1/2 CUP	DRY WHITE WINE	125 ML
2 TBSP	TOMATO PASTE	25 ML
1 LB	LARGE SHRIMP, PEELED AND DEVEINED (ABOUT 30)	500 G
	SALT AND FRESHLY GROUND BLACK PEPPER	
1/4 CUP	CHOPPED FRESH PARSLEY	50 ML

IN A LARGE SKILLET, HEAT BUTTER AND OIL OVER MEDIUM HEAT. SAUTÉ ONION AND GARLIC UNTIL SOFTENED, ABOUT 5 MINUTES. ADD MUSHROOMS AND SAUTÉ FOR 5 TO 7 MINUTES OR UNTIL STARTING TO BROWN AND ANY LIQUID HAS EVAPORATED. STIR IN WINE AND TOMATO PASTE; BRING TO A BOIL. REDUCE HEAT AND SIMMER FOR 2 MINUTES OR UNTIL SAUCE IS SLIGHTLY REDUCED. ADD SHRIMP AND SIMMER FOR 3 TO 4 MINUTES OR UNTIL PINK AND OPAQUE. SEASON TO TASTE WITH SALT AND PEPPER. SPRINKLE WITH PARSLEY. SERVES 4.

CHICKEN AND TURKEY

CHICKEN ON A BEER CAN

IT DOESN'T LOOK VERY ELEGANT, BUT THIS POPULAR METHOD OF COOKING A WHOLE CHICKEN SITTING UPRIGHT ON A CAN OF BEER (OR GINGER ALE) MAKES THE MEAT SO INCREDIBLY MOIST YOU WON'T BELIEVE IT.

1	WHOLE ROASTING CHICKEN (ABOUT 4 LBS/2 KG), GIBLETS REMOVED	1
1/4 CUP	CAJUN SEASONING (SEE TIP, OPPOSITE), 50 ML DIVIDED	
1	CAN (12 OZ/341 ML) BEER OR GINGER ALE	1
2 TBSP	VEGETABLE OIL	25 ML
1	SMALL POTATO OR ONION	1

PREHEAT OVEN TO 350°F (180°C). RINSE CHICKEN INSIDE AND OUT AND BLOT DRY WITH PAPER TOWELS. OPEN CAN OF BEER, MAKING TWO ADDITIONAL HOLES WITH A BOTTLE OPENER. DISCARD (OR DRINK) ABOUT 1/4 CUP (50 ML). SPOON 1 TBSP (15 ML) CAJUN SEASONING INTO BEER CAN (IT WILL PROBABLY FROTH SLIGHTLY). SPRINKLE 1 TBSP (15 ML) CAJUN SEASONING INTO THE CAVITY OF THE CHICKEN. BRUSH THE OUTSIDE OF THE CHICKEN WITH OIL AND RUB WITH THE REMAINING CAJUN SEASONING. PLACE BEER CAN IN A ROASTING PAN AND PUSH THE CHICKEN ONTO IT SO THAT THE CAN ALMOST DISAPPEARS INTO THE CAVITY. ADJUST THE CHICKEN LEGS TO STABILIZE THE BIRD. STUFF THE POTATO IN THE NECK CAVITY TO SEAL IN VAPORS. CAREFULLY PLACE IN OVEN AND BAKE FOR ABOUT 2 HOURS OR UNTIL THE SKIN IS BEAUTIFULLY BROWN AND CRISP, THE JUICES RUN CLEAR WHEN CHICKEN IS PIERCED AND A MEAT THERMOMETER

CONTINUED ON PAGE 161...

Salmon with Pistachio Crust (page 138)

Pan-Fried Tilapia with Tomato Caper Salsa (page 142)

Madras Chicken Skewers (page 176) and Coconut Mango Rice (page 274)

Thai Chicken and Mango Stir-Fry (page 182)

INSERTED IN THE THICKEST PART OF A THIGH REGISTERS 175°F (80°C). REMOVE PAN FROM OVEN AND LET REST FOR 10 MINUTES. PROTECT YOUR HANDS WITH SILICONE OVEN GLOVES OR THICK WADS OF PAPER TOWEL WHEN REMOVING THE CHICKEN FROM THE CAN. DISCARD BEER IN CAN AND THE POTATO. CARVE CHICKEN WHILE PATTING YOURSELF ON THE BACK. SERVES 4 TO 5.

TIP: CAJUN SEASONING IS A BLEND OF LOUISIANA HERBS AND SPICES AND IS AN EASY, QUICK WAY TO ENLIVEN MEAT OR FISH. IT'S ONE OF MANY SEASONING BLENDS THAT ARE NOW WIDELY AVAILABLE, INCLUDING BARBECUE, ITALIAN, MONTREAL STEAK AND OLD BAY SEAFOOD. THESE SPICE MIXES TAKE THE GUESSWORK OUT OF SEASONING WHEN YOU'RE TRYING TO CAPTURE A PARTICULAR FLAVOR — AND THEY SAVE YOU FROM HAVING TO BUY A DOZEN DIFFERENT JARS OF HERBS AND SPICES FOR ONE RECIPE!

VARIATION: THIS CHICKEN CAN ALSO BE GRILLED ON THE BARBECUE. LIGHT ONE SIDE OF THE BARBECUE. PLACE CHICKEN IN A FOIL PAN, ADD $\frac{1}{4}$ CUP (50 ML) WATER AND PLACE PAN ON THE UNLIT SIDE. CLOSE THE LID AND COOK OVER LOW TO MEDIUM HEAT FOR $1\frac{1}{4}$ TO 2 HOURS.

FIVE-YEAR-OLD IN THE MIDST OF A SWORDFIGHT: "ONE FOR ALL AND GOOD FOR NOTHING!"

CHEESE AND WALNUT-STUFFED CHICKEN BREASTS

EVERYONE YOU KNOW WILL WANT THIS RECIPE!

1	PACKAGE (5 OZ/142 G) BOURSIN GARLIC-AND-HERB-FLAVORED FRESH SOFT CHEESE (SEE TIP, PAGE 39)	1
1/3 CUP	GRATED CARROTS	75 ML
1/3 CUP	CHOPPED WALNUTS	75 ML
1 TBSP	ALL-PURPOSE FLOUR	15 ML
1 CUP	SEASONED DRY BREAD CRUMBS	250 ML
1/4 CUP	FRESHLY GRATED PARMESAN CHEESE	50 ML
1/4 CUP	CHOPPED FRESH PARSLEY	50 ML
6	BONELESS SKINLESS CHICKEN BREASTS	6
1/4 CUP	MELTED BUTTER	50 ML

PREHEAT OVEN TO 325°F (160°C). LINE A BAKING SHEET WITH PARCHMENT PAPER. IN A MEDIUM BOWL, COMBINE SOFT CHEESE, CARROTS, WALNUTS AND FLOUR. IN A SHALLOW DISH, COMBINE BREAD CRUMBS, PARMESAN AND PARSLEY. MAKE A DEEP SLIT OR POCKET IN THE THICK END OF THE CHICKEN BREASTS AND STUFF WITH CHEESE MIXTURE. BRUSH CHICKEN ALL OVER WITH MELTED BUTTER, THEN ROLL IN CRUMB MIXTURE. PLACE ON PREPARED BAKING SHEET AND BAKE FOR 35 TO 45 MINUTES OR UNTIL NO LONGER PINK INSIDE. SERVES 6.

MAKE AHEAD: AFTER STUFFING THE CHICKEN BREASTS, PLACE ON A PLATE, COVER AND REFRIGERATE FOR UP TO 4 HOURS.

CHICKEN IN TARRAGON CREAM SAUCE

IF TARRAGON IS YOUR THING...

2 TBSP	ALL-PURPOSE FLOUR	25 ML
1/2 TSP	SALT	2 ML
	FRESHLY GROUND BLACK PEPPER	
4	BONELESS SKINLESS CHICKEN BREASTS, CUT INTO BITE-SIZE PIECES	4
2 TBSP	BUTTER, DIVIDED	25 ML
1	SMALL ONION, FINELY CHOPPED	1
3/4 CUP	UNSWEETENED APPLE JUICE	175 ML
1 1/4 CUPS	CHICKEN BROTH	300 ML
1 TSP	DRIED TARRAGON	5 ML
1 TSP	DIJON MUSTARD	5 ML
1/2 CUP	WHIPPING (35%) CREAM, WARMED	125 ML
1/4 CUP	CHOPPED FRESH PARSLEY (OPTIONAL)	50 ML

IN A LARGE BOWL, WHISK TOGETHER FLOUR, SALT AND PEPPER TO TASTE. ADD CHICKEN AND TOSS TO COAT. IN A LARGE SKILLET, MELT 1 TBSP (15 ML) OF THE BUTTER OVER MEDIUM-HIGH HEAT. BROWN CHICKEN AND TRANSFER TO A PLATE. IN THE SAME SKILLET, HEAT THE REMAINING BUTTER OVER MEDIUM-HIGH HEAT. SAUTÉ ONION FOR 3 TO 4 MINUTES OR UNTIL SOFTENED. ADD APPLE JUICE AND BRING TO A BOIL. REDUCE HEAT AND SIMMER UNTIL REDUCED BY HALF. ADD BROTH, TARRAGON AND MUSTARD. RETURN CHICKEN TO SKILLET AND BRING TO A BOIL. REDUCE HEAT, COVER, LEAVING LID AJAR, AND SIMMER FOR ABOUT 5 MINUTES OR UNTIL CHICKEN IS NO LONGER PINK INSIDE AND SAUCE IS THICKENED. STIR IN CREAM. SERVE SPRINKLED WITH PARSLEY, IF DESIRED. SERVES 4.

LEMON CHICKEN

YOU'LL LIKE THIS — A LOT!

3 TBSP	BUTTER, DIVIDED	45 ML
4 CUPS	SLICED WHITE MUSHROOMS (ABOUT 8 OZ/250 G)	1 L
6	GREEN ONIONS, SLICED	6
2	CLOVES GARLIC, MINCED	2
1/4 CUP	ALL-PURPOSE FLOUR	50 ML
1/4 TSP	PAPRIKA	1 ML
1/4 TSP	SALT	1 ML
1/4 TSP	FRESHLY GROUND BLACK PEPPER	1 ML
3 TO 4	BONELESS SKINLESS CHICKEN BREASTS, CUT INTO BITE-SIZE PIECES	3 TO 4
1/2 CUP	CHICKEN BROTH	125 ML
1/4 CUP	DRY WHITE WINE	50 ML
1 TBSP	GRANULATED SUGAR	15 ML
1 TSP	GRATED LEMON ZEST	5 ML
1/4 CUP	FRESHLY SQUEEZED LEMON JUICE	50 ML
1/4 CUP	SLICED ALMONDS, TOASTED (SEE TIP, OPPOSITE)	50 ML

PREHEAT OVEN TO 350°F (180°C). IN A LARGE SKILLET, MELT 2 TBSP (25 ML) OF THE BUTTER OVER MEDIUM HEAT. SAUTÉ MUSHROOMS, GREEN ONIONS AND GARLIC FOR ABOUT 5 MINUTES OR UNTIL JUST SOFTENED. TRANSFER TO A 12-CUP (3 L) CASSEROLE DISH. IN A LARGE BOWL, COMBINE FLOUR, PAPRIKA, SALT AND PEPPER. ADD CHICKEN AND TOSS TO COAT. REMOVE CHICKEN TO A PLATE, RESERVING THE REMAINING FLOUR MIXTURE. WIPE OUT SKILLET AND MELT THE REMAINING BUTTER OVER MEDIUM-HIGH HEAT. BROWN CHICKEN AND TRANSFER

TO CASSEROLE. IN THE SKILLET, WHISK TOGETHER RESERVED FLOUR MIXTURE, CHICKEN BROTH, WINE, SUGAR, LEMON ZEST AND LEMON JUICE. BRING TO A BOIL, STIRRING CONSTANTLY. REDUCE HEAT AND SIMMER, STIRRING OCCASIONALLY, FOR 2 TO 3 MINUTES OR UNTIL THICKENED. POUR OVER CHICKEN. COVER AND BAKE FOR 20 MINUTES. SPRINKLE WITH ALMONDS AND BAKE, UNCOVERED, FOR 10 MINUTES OR UNTIL CHICKEN IS NO LONGER PINK INSIDE. SERVES 4.

TIP: TOASTING NUTS HELPS BRING OUT THEIR FLAVOR. THE QUICKEST METHOD IS ON THE STOVETOP. SPREAD NUTS OUT IN AN UNGREASED NONSTICK SKILLET AND PLACE OVER MEDIUM HEAT. SHAKE OR STIR FREQUENTLY, TO PREVENT BURNING, FOR 4 TO 5 MINUTES OR UNTIL FRAGRANT AND STARTING TO BROWN. TIP ONTO A COLD PLATE TO STOP THE COOKING PROCESS AND LET COOL COMPLETELY.

"DON'T CRY BECAUSE IT'S OVER — SMILE
BECAUSE IT HAPPENED."
— DR. SEUSS

SPEEDY SKILLET CHICKEN

READY IN LESS THAN 30 MINUTES, THIS RECIPE
IS PERFECT FOR THOSE HECTIC WEEKNIGHTS.
SERVE WITH MASHED POTATOES OR COUSCOUS
AND A GREEN VEGETABLE.

3 TBSP	ALL-PURPOSE FLOUR	45 ML
1/2 TSP	PAPRIKA	2 ML
1/2 TSP	SALT	2 ML
	FRESHLY GROUND BLACK PEPPER	
4	BONELESS SKINLESS CHICKEN BREASTS, CUT INTO BITE-SIZE PIECES	4
4	SLICES BACON, CHOPPED	4
2 TBSP	BUTTER, DIVIDED	25 ML
1	SMALL ONION, FINELY CHOPPED	1
2	CLOVES GARLIC, MINCED	2
1/4 CUP	DRY WHITE WINE	50 ML
1 1/2 CUPS	CHICKEN BROTH	375 ML
1 TBSP	TOMATO PASTE	15 ML
1/2 TSP	DRIED THYME	2 ML
1/4 CUP	CHOPPED FRESH PARSLEY	50 ML

IN A LARGE BOWL, WHISK TOGETHER FLOUR, PAPRIKA,
SALT AND PEPPER TO TASTE. ADD CHICKEN AND TOSS
TO COAT; SET ASIDE. IN A LARGE SKILLET, OVER
MEDIUM-HIGH HEAT, SAUTÉ BACON UNTIL CRISP. USING
A SLOTTED SPOON, TRANSFER TO A PLATE LINED WITH
PAPER TOWELS. DRAIN FAT AND WIPE OUT SKILLET. MELT
1 TBSP (15 ML) OF THE BUTTER OVER MEDIUM-HIGH HEAT.
BROWN CHICKEN AND TRANSFER TO A PLATE. IN THE
SKILLET, MELT THE REMAINING BUTTER OVER MEDIUM
HEAT. SAUTÉ ONION AND GARLIC FOR ABOUT 5 MINUTES

OR UNTIL SOFTENED. ADD WINE AND BRING TO A BOIL. REDUCE HEAT AND SIMMER FOR 3 TO 4 MINUTES OR UNTIL ALMOST EVAPORATED. STIR IN CHICKEN BROTH, TOMATO PASTE AND THYME. RETURN CHICKEN AND BACON TO PAN AND BRING TO A BOIL, STIRRING. REDUCE HEAT, COVER, LEAVING LID AJAR, AND SIMMER FOR ABOUT 5 MINUTES OR UNTIL CHICKEN IS NO LONGER PINK INSIDE AND SAUCE IS THICKENED. SERVE SPRINKLED WITH PARSLEY. SERVES 4.

TIP: FREEZE LEFTOVER TOMATO PASTE IN AN ICE CUBE TRAY, THEN TRANSFER THE CUBES TO AN AIRTIGHT CONTAINER OR RESEALABLE FREEZER BAGS. EACH CUBE IS EQUIVALENT TO ABOUT 1 TBSP (15 ML) TOMATO PASTE AND CAN BE ADDED FROZEN TO SOUPS AND SAUCES.

VARIATION: INSTEAD OF DRY WHITE WINE, USE AN EQUAL AMOUNT OF UNSWEETENED APPLE JUICE.

I'M A QUEEN — AT LEAST, THAT'S WHAT MY PANTYHOSE SAY.

SPANISH CHICKEN AND RICE

READY IN ABOUT 30 MINUTES. THE RICH FLAVOR COMES FROM FRESH CHORIZO, A PAPRIKA-SPICED SAUSAGE THAT IS WIDELY AVAILABLE IN GROCERY STORES. SERVE IN LARGE BOWLS, WITH A GREEN SALAD ON THE SIDE.

I TBSP	VEGETABLE OIL	15 ML
I LB	BONELESS SKINLESS CHICKEN BREASTS (ABOUT 3), CUT INTO I-INCH (2.5 CM) CHUNKS	500 G
2	FRESH CHORIZO SAUSAGES (SEE TIP, OPPOSITE), SLICED	2
I	ONION, CHOPPED	I
I	RED OR GREEN BELL PEPPER, CHOPPED	I
2	CLOVES GARLIC, MINCED	2
I TBSP	TOMATO PASTE	15 ML
2 TSP	PAPRIKA	10 ML
1/4 TSP	HOT PEPPER FLAKES (OPTIONAL)	I ML
1 1/2 CUPS	LONG-GRAIN WHITE RICE	375 ML
3 TO 4 CUPS	CHICKEN BROTH	750 ML TO I L
2	TOMATOES, CHOPPED	2
I	BAG (10 OZ/300 G) PREWASHED BABY SPINACH	I

IN A LARGE NONSTICK SKILLET OR WOK, HEAT OIL OVER MEDIUM-HIGH HEAT. BROWN CHICKEN AND TRANSFER TO A PLATE. ADD SAUSAGES, ONION AND RED PEPPER TO SKILLET AND SAUTÉ FOR ABOUT 5 MINUTES OR UNTIL SAUSAGE IS BROWNED. ADD GARLIC, TOMATO PASTE, PAPRIKA AND HOT PEPPER FLAKES (IF USING); SAUTÉ FOR 15 SECONDS. ADD RICE, 3 CUPS (750 ML) CHICKEN BROTH AND TOMATOES, SCRAPING UP ANY BROWN BITS AT

THE BOTTOM OF THE PAN. BRING TO A BOIL, STIRRING OCCASIONALLY. REDUCE HEAT, COVER AND SIMMER, STIRRING OCCASIONALLY, FOR 10 MINUTES OR UNTIL THE LIQUID IS PARTIALLY ABSORBED. RETURN CHICKEN TO PAN, COVER AND SIMMER, ADDING MORE BROTH IF NECESSARY, FOR 10 MINUTES OR UNTIL RICE IS TENDER, LIQUID IS ABSORBED AND CHICKEN IS NO LONGER PINK INSIDE. REMOVE FROM HEAT AND, USING A FORK, GENTLY STIR IN SPINACH. COVER AND LET STAND FOR ABOUT 5 MINUTES OR UNTIL SPINACH IS WILTED. SERVES 4.

TIP: IF YOU CAN'T FIND FRESH CHORIZO, YOU CAN SUBSTITUTE COOKED CHORIZO, WHICH IS MORE LIKE PEPPERONI. ALTERNATIVELY, YOU CAN USE HOT ITALIAN SAUSAGES, THOUGH THE DISH WILL TASTE SOMEWHAT DIFFERENT.

VARIATION: REPLACE THE SPINACH WITH 1 CUP (250 ML) FROZEN BABY PEAS.

WHAT IF THE HOKEY-POKEY REALLY
IS WHAT IT'S ALL ABOUT?

CHICKEN PARMIGIANA

SERVE WITH A GREEN SALAD AND FRESH CRUSTY BREAD.

I	JAR (24 OZ/700 ML) SPAGHETTI SAUCE	I
1/2 CUP	WHIPPING (35%) CREAM (OPTIONAL)	125 ML
4	BONELESS SKINLESS CHICKEN BREASTS	4
	SALT AND FRESHLY GROUND BLACK PEPPER	
I	EGG	I
2 TBSP	WATER	25 ML
I CUP	PANKO (SEE TIP, PAGE 133) OR DRY BREAD CRUMBS	250 ML
3/4 CUP	FRESHLY GRATED PARMESAN CHEESE	175 ML
1/4 CUP	OLIVE OIL	50 ML
I CUP	SHREDDED MOZZARELLA CHEESE	250 ML

PREHEAT OVEN TO 375°F (190°C). COMBINE SPAGHETTI SAUCE AND CREAM (IF USING) AND SPREAD IN A 13- BY 9-INCH (33 BY 23 CM) BAKING DISH. CUT EACH CHICKEN BREAST IN HALF, PLACE BETWEEN TWO SHEETS OF PLASTIC WRAP AND POUND LIGHTLY WITH A ROLLING PIN OR THE BOTTOM OF A SKILLET TO FLATTEN. SEASON EACH PIECE WITH SALT AND PEPPER. IN A SHALLOW DISH, WHISK TOGETHER EGG AND WATER. IN ANOTHER SHALLOW DISH, COMBINE PANKO AND PARMESAN. DIP CHICKEN PIECES IN EGG WASH, SHAKING OFF EXCESS, THEN ROLL IN PANKO MIXTURE. IN A LARGE SKILLET, HEAT OIL OVER MEDIUM-HIGH HEAT. FRY CHICKEN, IN BATCHES IF NECESSARY, UNTIL GOLDEN ON BOTH SIDES. TRANSFER CHICKEN TO THE BAKING DISH, NESTLING BUT NOT IMMERSING IT IN THE SAUCE. SPRINKLE WITH MOZZARELLA. BAKE FOR ABOUT 20 MINUTES OR UNTIL SAUCE IS BUBBLING AND CHICKEN IS NO LONGER PINK INSIDE. SERVE IMMEDIATELY. SERVES 4.

BAKED BALSAMIC CHICKEN

THE BALSAMIC VINEGAR ADDS A SWEET, INTRIGUING FLAVOR TO THE PAN JUICES — TERRIFIC WITH MASHED POTATOES OR STEAMED RICE.

MARINADE

1/4 CUP	BALSAMIC VINEGAR	50 ML
2 TBSP	DIJON MUSTARD	25 ML
2 TBSP	FRESHLY SQUEEZED LEMON JUICE	25 ML
2 TBSP	OLIVE OIL	25 ML
2 TBSP	GRANULATED SUGAR	25 ML
5	BONELESS SKINLESS CHICKEN THIGHS	5
1/2 CUP	CHICKEN BROTH	125 ML

MARINADE: IN A MEDIUM BOWL, WHISK TOGETHER VINEGAR, MUSTARD, LEMON JUICE, OIL AND SUGAR.

PLACE CHICKEN IN A SEALABLE PLASTIC BAG AND POUR IN MARINADE. SEAL AND REFRIGERATE OVERNIGHT.

PREHEAT OVEN TO 375°F (190°C). GREASE A ROASTING PAN. REMOVE CHICKEN FROM MARINADE, DISCARDING MARINADE, AND PLACE IN ROASTING PAN. BAKE FOR 30 MINUTES OR UNTIL JUICES RUN CLEAR WHEN CHICKEN IS PIERCED. REMOVE CHICKEN TO A SERVING PLATE AND KEEP WARM. ADD CHICKEN BROTH TO PAN, SCRAPING UP ANY BROWN BITS, AND BRING TO A BOIL. REDUCE HEAT AND SIMMER GENTLY UNTIL REDUCED TO A RICH GRAVY. SPOON OVER CHICKEN. SERVES 2 TO 3.

HUNGARIAN CHICKEN CASSEROLE

THIS CHICKEN HAS PIZZAZZ. SERVE WITH MASHED POTATO TO FORK INTO THE LOVELY THICK SAUCE, RICH WITH THE FLAVORS OF TOMATO, ROASTED RED PEPPER AND PAPRIKA.

8	BONELESS SKINLESS CHICKEN THIGHS	8
1/4 CUP	ALL-PURPOSE FLOUR	50 ML
1/2 TSP	SALT	2 ML
1/4 TSP	FRESHLY GROUND BLACK PEPPER	1 ML
2 TBSP	VEGETABLE OIL	25 ML
1 TBSP	BUTTER	15 ML
1	LARGE ONION, THINLY SLICED	1
1	CARROT, THINLY SLICED	1
2 TBSP	PAPRIKA	25 ML
1	CAN (14 OZ/398 ML) WHOLE TOMATOES WITH JUICE (SEE TIP, OPPOSITE), CHOPPED	1
1/2 CUP	CHOPPED ROASTED RED BELL PEPPERS (SEE TIP, PAGE 117)	125 ML
1/2 CUP	CHICKEN BROTH OR WATER	125 ML
1/4 CUP	DRY WHITE WINE	50 ML
1 TSP	GRANULATED SUGAR	5 ML
1/2 CUP	SOUR CREAM	125 ML
	CHOPPED FRESH PARSLEY	

PREHEAT OVEN TO 350°F (180°C). IN A LARGE BOWL, WHISK TOGETHER FLOUR, SALT AND PEPPER. ADD CHICKEN AND TURN TO COAT. IN A LARGE SKILLET, HEAT OIL AND BUTTER OVER MEDIUM-HIGH HEAT. BROWN CHICKEN AND, USING A SLOTTED SPOON, TRANSFER TO A 12-CUP (3 L) CASSEROLE DISH. ADD ONION AND CARROT TO OIL REMAINING IN SKILLET AND SAUTÉ FOR 5 TO 7 MINUTES

OR UNTIL SOFTENED. ADD PAPRIKA AND SAUTÉ FOR 15 SECONDS. ADD TOMATOES, ROASTED PEPPERS, CHICKEN BROTH, WINE AND SUGAR; BRING TO A BOIL. POUR OVER CHICKEN. COVER AND BAKE FOR 45 MINUTES OR UNTIL SAUCE IS THICK AND JUICES RUN CLEAR WHEN CHICKEN IS PIERCED. SERVE DOLLOPED WITH SOUR CREAM AND SPRINKLED WITH PARSLEY. SERVES 4.

TIP: WHEN COOKING WITH CANNED TOMATOES, WE PREFER TO USE WHOLE TOMATOES PACKED IN JUICE, WITH NO ADDED SALT OR SEASONINGS. THEY ARE CLOSEST TO FRESH TOMATOES IN TASTE AND TEXTURE, AND WE LIKE TO ADD OUR OWN SALT AND OTHER SEASONINGS. DICED, CRUSHED OR STEWED TOMATOES MAY HAVE ADDED WATER, ACID AND FLAVORINGS, WHICH CAN AFFECT THE OUTCOME OF A RECIPE. IF YOU DON'T HAVE WHOLE CANNED TOMATOES, YOU CAN SUBSTITUTE DICED OR CRUSHED TOMATOES, BUT TASTE THE DISH AS YOU COOK IT TO ADJUST THE SEASONINGS ACCORDINGLY. IF YOU HAVE WHOLE TOMATOES PACKED IN WATER, DRAIN OFF THE WATER AND USE EXTRA TOMATOES TO GET THE AMOUNT CALLED FOR IN THE RECIPE.

A BALANCED DIET IS A COOKIE IN BOTH HANDS.

CHICKEN DATE TAGINE

A TAGINE IS A TYPE OF MOROCCAN CASSEROLE NAMED AFTER THE COOKING POT WITH A FUNNEL-SHAPED TOP IT'S TRADITIONALLY COOKED IN. YOU DON'T NEED TO GO SHOPPING IN A BAZAAR, THOUGH — A REGULAR BAKING DISH WILL DO. SERVE WITH STEAMED COUSCOUS.

I TBSP	BUTTER OR OLIVE OIL	15 ML
8	BONELESS SKINLESS CHICKEN THIGHS	8
I	SMALL ONION, FINELY CHOPPED	I
2	CLOVES GARLIC, MINCED	2
I TBSP	MINCED GINGERROOT	15 ML
I TSP	GROUND CORIANDER	5 ML
I TSP	GROUND CUMIN	5 ML
I TSP	CHILI POWDER	5 ML
I	SMALL BUTTERNUT SQUASH, PEELED AND DICED (ABOUT 3 CUPS/750 ML)	I
I	CAN (14 OZ/398 ML) WHOLE TOMATOES WITH JUICE, CHOPPED (SEE TIP, PAGE 173)	I
I CUP	CHICKEN BROTH	250 ML
2 TBSP	CHOPPED FRESH CILANTRO	25 ML
I TBSP	LIQUID HONEY	15 ML
I TSP	SALT	5 ML
	GRATED ZEST AND JUICE OF I LEMON	
12	SOFT DRIED DATES (SUCH AS MEDJOOL), PITTED AND HALVED	12
1/4 CUP	SLICED ALMONDS, TOASTED (SEE TIP, PAGE 165)	50 ML

PREHEAT OVEN TO 350°F (180°C). IN A LARGE SKILLET, MELT BUTTER OVER MEDIUM-HIGH HEAT. BROWN CHICKEN AND, USING A SLOTTED SPOON, TRANSFER TO AN 11- BY 7-INCH (28 BY 18 CM) BAKING DISH. ADD ONION, GARLIC,

GINGER, CORIANDER, CUMIN AND CHILI POWDER TO OIL REMAINING IN SKILLET AND SAUTÉ FOR 1 MINUTE OR UNTIL FRAGRANT. ADD SQUASH, TOMATOES, CHICKEN BROTH, CILANTRO, HONEY, SALT, LEMON ZEST AND LEMON JUICE; BRING TO A BOIL. POUR OVER CHICKEN. COVER AND BAKE FOR 30 MINUTES. PUSH DATES INTO SAUCE AND BAKE, UNCOVERED, FOR 20 MINUTES OR UNTIL JUICES RUN CLEAR WHEN CHICKEN IS PIERCED. SERVE SPRINKLED WITH ALMONDS. SERVES 4.

TIP: GROUND SPICES SUCH AS CUMIN, CORIANDER AND TURMERIC HAVE A SHORT SHELF LIFE AND STAY FRESH FOR ONLY A FEW WEEKS. LIGHT AND HEAT MAKE THEM GO STALE. SO SCRAP THAT TRENDY SPICE RACK ON THE KITCHEN COUNTER! INSTEAD, STORE YOUR SPICES IN AIRTIGHT CONTAINERS IN A CUPBOARD AWAY FROM THE WARMTH OF THE STOVE. IF POSSIBLE, BUY SPICES IN SMALL QUANTITIES.

IF OLDER IS BETTER, I'M APPROACHING MAGNIFICENT.

MADRAS CHICKEN SKEWERS

MARINATE THE CHICKEN OVERNIGHT, AND YOU'RE GOOD TO GO THE NEXT DAY. SERVE WITH COCONUT MANGO RICE (PAGE 274), GREEN SALAD WITH TOASTED PECANS AND CITRUS DRESSING (PAGE 70) AND WARM PITAS OR NAAN.

4	BONELESS SKINLESS CHICKEN BREASTS	4

MARINADE

1/3 CUP	MAYONNAISE	75 ML
1/3 CUP	MANGO CHUTNEY	75 ML
2	CLOVES GARLIC, MINCED	2
2 TBSP	FRESHLY SQUEEZED LEMON JUICE	25 ML
2 TBSP	FRESHLY SQUEEZED LIME JUICE	25 ML
1 TSP	CHILI POWDER	5 ML
1/2 TSP	GROUND CUMIN	2 ML
1/2 TSP	GROUND CORIANDER	2 ML
1/4 TSP	SALT	1 ML

PLACE CHICKEN BREASTS BETWEEN TWO PIECES OF PLASTIC WRAP AND POUND LIGHTLY WITH A ROLLING PIN OR THE BOTTOM OF A SKILLET TO FLATTEN. CUT CHICKEN INTO 1-INCH (2.5 CM) LONG STRIPS.

MARINADE: IN A LARGE BOWL, WHISK TOGETHER MAYONNAISE, CHUTNEY, GARLIC, LEMON JUICE, LIME JUICE, CHILI POWDER, CUMIN, CORIANDER AND SALT.

ADD CHICKEN TO MARINADE AND TURN TO COAT. COVER AND REFRIGERATE FOR AT LEAST 4 HOURS OR OVERNIGHT.

SOAK EIGHT 10-INCH (25 CM) WOODEN SKEWERS IN WATER FOR 30 MINUTES (OR USE METAL SKEWERS). MEANWHILE,

PREHEAT BARBECUE GRILL TO MEDIUM. REMOVE CHICKEN FROM MARINADE, DISCARDING MARINADE, AND THREAD ONTO SKEWERS. GRILL FOR ABOUT 10 MINUTES, TURNING OCCASIONALLY, UNTIL CHICKEN IS BROWNED AND NO LONGER PINK INSIDE. SERVES 4.

TIP: WATCH THE CHICKEN CAREFULLY WHILE YOU'RE GRILLING IT — IT WILL COOK QUICKLY.

VARIATION: APRICOT OR PEACH JAM MAY BE USED IN PLACE OF THE MANGO CHUTNEY.

I AM WOMAN. I AM STRONG. I AM SO TIRED.

BUTTER CHICKEN

THIS POPULAR INDIAN DISH IN TOMATO CREAM SAUCE IS JUST AS DELICIOUS AS THE RESTAURANT VERSION, AND THE FRAGRANT SPICES WILL FILL YOUR KITCHEN WITH THE MOST HEAVENLY AROMA. LOOK AT YOU — AN EXOTIC COOK (OR, AT LEAST, A COOKER OF EXOTIC FOOD). SERVE OVER STEAMED BASMATI RICE (FLAVORED WITH A FEW THREADS OF SAFFRON, IF YOU HAVE IT), WITH WARMED PITAS OR NAAN ON THE SIDE.

1 TBSP	MADRAS CURRY POWDER	15 ML
1 TBSP	MINCED GINGERROOT	15 ML
1/4 TSP	CAYENNE PEPPER	1 ML
1/4 CUP	BUTTER	50 ML
1	LARGE ONION, CHOPPED	1
4	CLOVES GARLIC, MINCED	4
1 TBSP	TOMATO PASTE	15 ML
8	BONELESS SKINLESS CHICKEN THIGHS, CUT INTO BITE-SIZE PIECES	8
1	CAN (14 OZ/398 ML) TOMATO SAUCE	1
1	CAN (14 OZ/398 ML) DICED TOMATOES WITH JUICE	1
	SALT	
2 CUPS	FROZEN BABY PEAS	500 ML
1	CAN (12 OZ OR 370 ML) EVAPORATED MILK (APPROX.)	1

IN A SMALL BOWL, COMBINE CURRY POWDER, GINGER AND CAYENNE; SET ASIDE. IN A LARGE SKILLET, MELT BUTTER OVER MEDIUM HEAT. SAUTÉ ONION FOR 5 TO 7 MINUTES OR UNTIL SOFTENED. ADD GARLIC, TOMATO PASTE AND SPICE MIXTURE; SAUTÉ FOR 30 SECONDS OR UNTIL FRAGRANT. ADD CHICKEN AND STIR TO COAT. ADD

TOMATO SAUCE, DICED TOMATOES AND SALT TO TASTE;
BRING TO A SIMMER. REDUCE HEAT, COVER AND SIMMER
FOR 30 MINUTES OR UNTIL CHICKEN IS NO LONGER
PINK INSIDE AND SAUCE IS THICKENED. STIR IN PEAS
AND EVAPORATED MILK; HEAT GENTLY UNTIL STEAMING.
DO NOT LET BOIL. IF THE SAUCE IS TOO THICK, STIR IN
MORE EVAPORATED MILK. SERVES 4 TO 6.

MAKE AHEAD: BEFORE STIRRING IN THE PEAS AND MILK,
LET BUTTER CHICKEN COOL, TRANSFER TO AN AIRTIGHT
CONTAINER AND REFRIGERATE FOR UP TO 2 DAYS. REHEAT
IN SKILLET OVER MEDIUM-LOW HEAT UNTIL BUBBLING.
ADD PEAS AND MILK AND CONTINUE WITH RECIPE.

VARIATION: TO GIVE THIS RECIPE SOME EXTRA HEAT, ADD
$\frac{1}{4}$ TO $\frac{1}{2}$ TSP (1 TO 2 ML) HOT PEPPER FLAKES (OR MORE,
IF YOU LIKE IT REALLY FIERY) TO THE CURRY POWDER
MIXTURE.

*I KNOW GOD WOULDN'T GIVE ME MORE THAN I CAN HANDLE.
I JUST WISH HE DIDN'T TRUST ME SO MUCH.*

CHICKEN PAPRIKASH

A HUNGARIAN CLASSIC. SERVE OVER BUTTERED BROAD NOODLES WITH A GREEN VEGETABLE.

2 TBSP	VEGETABLE OIL	25 ML
12	BONELESS SKINLESS CHICKEN THIGHS	12
1	ONION, CHOPPED	1
2	CLOVES GARLIC, MINCED	2
1 CUP	CHICKEN BROTH	250 ML
2 TBSP	PAPRIKA	25 ML
	SALT AND FRESHLY GROUND BLACK PEPPER	
1/3 CUP	SOUR CREAM	75 ML

PREHEAT OVEN TO 325°F (160°C). IN A HEAVY SKILLET, HEAT OIL OVER MEDIUM-HIGH HEAT. BROWN CHICKEN AND, USING A SLOTTED SPOON, TRANSFER TO A 12-CUP (3 L) CASSEROLE DISH. ADD ONION AND GARLIC TO OIL REMAINING IN SKILLET AND SAUTÉ FOR 5 TO 7 MINUTES OR UNTIL SOFTENED. STIR IN CHICKEN BROTH, PAPRIKA AND SALT AND PEPPER TO TASTE; BRING TO A BOIL. POUR OVER CHICKEN, COVER AND BAKE FOR 1 HOUR OR UNTIL JUICES RUN CLEAR WHEN CHICKEN IS PIERCED. TRANSFER CHICKEN TO A SERVING PLATE AND KEEP WARM. POUR SAUCE INTO A SMALL SAUCEPAN, ADD SOUR CREAM AND HEAT GENTLY OVER MEDIUM-LOW HEAT, STIRRING. DO NOT LET BOIL OR THE SOUR CREAM WILL SEPARATE. SERVES 4 TO 6.

ASIAN STICKY CHICKEN

EXCELLENT — THE PERFECT MIDWEEK MEAL.
SERVE WITH STEAMED RICE.

8	BONELESS SKINLESS CHICKEN THIGHS	8
	ALL-PURPOSE FLOUR	
1 TBSP	OLIVE OIL OR VEGETABLE OIL	15 ML
1/4 CUP	ORANGE JUICE	50 ML
3 TBSP	LIQUID HONEY	45 ML
3 TBSP	HOISIN SAUCE	45 ML
2 TSP	RICE OR CIDER VINEGAR	10 ML
1	CLOVE GARLIC, MINCED	1
2 TSP	MINCED GINGERROOT	10 ML
1 TSP	CORNSTARCH	5 ML
1/4 CUP	TOASTED SESAME SEEDS (SEE TIP, PAGE 93)	50 ML
4	GREEN ONIONS, CHOPPED	4

PREHEAT OVEN TO 375°F (190°C). GREASE AN 8-INCH
(20 CM) SQUARE BAKING DISH. DUST CHICKEN WITH FLOUR.
IN A SKILLET, HEAT OIL OVER MEDIUM-HIGH HEAT. BROWN
CHICKEN AND TRANSFER TO BAKING DISH. IN A SMALL
BOWL, WHISK TOGETHER ORANGE JUICE, HONEY, HOISIN
SAUCE, VINEGAR, GARLIC, GINGER AND CORNSTARCH.
POUR OVER CHICKEN. BAKE FOR 15 MINUTES. FLIP CHICKEN
OVER, SPRINKLE WITH SESAME SEEDS AND BAKE FOR
15 MINUTES OR UNTIL JUICES RUN CLEAR WHEN CHICKEN
IS PIERCED. SERVE SPRINKLED WITH GREEN ONIONS.

SERVES 4.

THAI CHICKEN AND MANGO STIR-FRY

HERE'S A YUMMY YET EASY DINNER FOR GUESTS THAT WE'VE THAI'D AND TESTED!

I CUP	FROZEN MANGO CUBES (SEE TIP, OPPOSITE)	250 ML
I CUP	COCONUT MILK	250 ML
1/2 CUP	CHICKEN BROTH	125 ML
I TBSP	FRESHLY SQUEEZED LIME JUICE	15 ML
2 TSP	SOY SAUCE	10 ML
I TSP	PACKED BROWN SUGAR	5 ML
I TBSP	VEGETABLE OIL	15 ML
4	BONELESS SKINLESS CHICKEN BREASTS, CUT INTO BITE-SIZE PIECES	4
2	GREEN ONIONS, CHOPPED	2
1	RED BELL PEPPER, THINLY SLICED	1
2 TSP	THAI RED CURRY PASTE	10 ML
I CUP	SNOW PEAS	250 ML
2 TSP	CORNSTARCH	10 ML
2 TSP	WATER	10 ML
2 TBSP	CHOPPED FRESH CILANTRO	25 ML

IN A LARGE BOWL, COMBINE MANGO, COCONUT MILK, CHICKEN BROTH, LIME JUICE, SOY SAUCE AND BROWN SUGAR; SET ASIDE. IN A LARGE SKILLET OR WOK, HEAT OIL OVER MEDIUM HEAT. LIGHTLY BROWN CHICKEN AND, USING A SLOTTED SPOON, TRANSFER TO A PLATE. ADD GREEN ONIONS, RED PEPPER AND CURRY PASTE TO OIL REMAINING IN SKILLET AND SAUTÉ FOR I MINUTE. RETURN CHICKEN TO PAN. ADD MANGO MIXTURE, REDUCE HEAT AND SIMMER FOR 3 TO 5 MINUTES OR UNTIL CHICKEN IS NO LONGER

PINK INSIDE. ADD SNOW PEAS AND SIMMER FOR 1 MINUTE. DISSOLVE CORNSTARCH IN WATER AND ADD TO PAN. SIMMER, STIRRING, FOR 1 MINUTE OR UNTIL THICKENED. SERVE SPRINKLED WITH CILANTRO. SERVES 4.

TIP: FROZEN, READY-PEELED MANGO CHUNKS ARE NOW SOLD IN MOST SUPERMARKETS, USUALLY IN 21-OZ (600 G) PACKAGES. KEEP A BAG IN THE FREEZER AND YOU'LL FIND WAYS TO USE MANGO IN SOUPS, SAUCES, DESSERTS AND SMOOTHIES. THERE'S NO NEED TO THAW THEM FOR THIS RECIPE.

VARIATION: REDUCE THE CHICKEN BREASTS FROM 4 TO 2. ADD 2 CUPS (500 ML) RINSED DRAINED CANNED CHICKPEAS WITH THE MANGO.

SPEAK THE TRUTH BUT LEAVE IMMEDIATELY AFTER.

ZIPPY CHICKEN STIR-FRY

*COLORFUL, QUICK AND TASTY, THIS DISH IS SURE
TO BE A HIT. SERVE WITH STEAMED RICE.*

SAUCE

2 TBSP	CHICKEN BROTH OR WATER	25 ML
2 TBSP	HOISIN SAUCE	25 ML
1 TBSP	LIQUID HONEY OR GRANULATED SUGAR	15 ML
1 TSP	CORNSTARCH	5 ML
1/2 TSP	SESAME OIL	2 ML
1/2 TSP	ASIAN CHILI PASTE (SEE TIP, PAGE 231)	2 ML
2 TBSP	VEGETABLE OIL, DIVIDED	25 ML
1 LB	BONELESS SKINLESS CHICKEN BREASTS (ABOUT 2 LARGE), CUT INTO BITE-SIZE PIECES	500 G
2	CARROTS, CUT INTO THIN MATCHSTICKS (SEE TIP, BELOW)	2
1	LARGE ONION, THINLY SLICED	1
1	RED BELL PEPPER, THINLY SLICED	1
1/2 CUP	FROZEN CORN KERNELS	125 ML
1 TBSP	CHICKEN BROTH OR WATER	15 ML
3	GREEN ONIONS, CHOPPED	3
2	CLOVES GARLIC, MINCED	2
1 TBSP	FINELY CHOPPED GINGERROOT	15 ML

SAUCE: IN A SMALL BOWL, COMBINE CHICKEN BROTH, HOISIN SAUCE, HONEY, CORNSTARCH, SESAME OIL AND CHILI PASTE; SET ASIDE.

IN A LARGE SKILLET OR WOK, HEAT 1 TBSP (15 ML) OF THE OIL OVER MEDIUM HEAT. SAUTÉ CHICKEN FOR ABOUT 5 MINUTES OR UNTIL BROWNED AND NO LONGER

PINK INSIDE. TRANSFER TO A PLATE AND SET ASIDE. IN THE SKILLET, HEAT THE REMAINING OIL OVER MEDIUM-HIGH HEAT. ADD CARROTS, ONION, RED PEPPER, CORN AND CHICKEN BROTH; COVER AND SIMMER FOR ABOUT 3 MINUTES TO STEAM THE VEGETABLES. ADD GREEN ONIONS, GARLIC AND GINGER; SAUTÉ FOR 15 SECONDS OR UNTIL FRAGRANT. POUR IN SAUCE, RETURN CHICKEN AND ANY JUICES TO PAN AND COOK FOR 2 TO 3 MINUTES OR UNTIL HOT, BUBBLING AND SLIGHTLY THICKENED. SERVES 4.

TIP: TO SAVE TIME, LOOK FOR BAGS OF PRECUT CARROT MATCHSTICKS (SOMETIMES LABELED FRENCH-CUT COOKING CARROTS) IN THE PRODUCE AISLE.

I TRY TO WATCH WHAT I EAT, BUT I'M NOT FAST ENOUGH.

GRILLED CHICKEN AND ZUCCHINI SANDWICH WITH LEMON TARRAGON MAYONNAISE

FAST, FRESH AND HEALTHY.

LEMON TARRAGON MAYONNAISE

1/4 CUP	MAYONNAISE	50 ML
1 TBSP	FRESHLY SQUEEZED LEMON JUICE	15 ML
1 TSP	DRIED TARRAGON	5 ML
1	CLOVE GARLIC, MINCED	1
	SALT AND FRESHLY GROUND BLACK PEPPER	
2	BONELESS SKINLESS CHICKEN BREASTS	2
1	ZUCCHINI, CUT ON A DIAGONAL INTO 1/4-INCH (0.5 CM) SLICES	1
2 TBSP	OLIVE OIL	25 ML
	SALT AND FRESHLY GROUND BLACK PEPPER	
2 TBSP	FRESHLY SQUEEZED LEMON JUICE	25 ML
2	LARGE MULTIGRAIN KAISER BUNS, SLICED IN HALF AND TOASTED	2
	TORN GREEN LEAF LETTUCE	

LEMON TARRAGON MAYONNAISE: IN A SMALL BOWL, WHISK TOGETHER MAYONNAISE, LEMON JUICE, TARRAGON AND GARLIC. SEASON TO TASTE WITH SALT AND PEPPER. COVER AND REFRIGERATE FOR AT LEAST 1 HOUR, UNTIL CHILLED, OR FOR UP TO 2 DAYS.

PREHEAT BARBECUE GRILL TO MEDIUM. PLACE CHICKEN BREASTS BETWEEN TWO SHEETS OF PLASTIC WRAP AND POUND LIGHTLY WITH A ROLLING PIN OR THE BOTTOM OF A SKILLET TO UNIFORM THICKNESS. BRUSH CHICKEN AND

ZUCCHINI WITH OIL AND SPRINKLE WITH SALT AND PEPPER. PLACE CHICKEN AND ZUCCHINI ON GREASED GRILL AND COOK FOR 6 TO 8 MINUTES PER SIDE OR UNTIL CHICKEN IS NO LONGER PINK INSIDE AND ZUCCHINI IS LIGHTLY BROWNED AND TENDER-CRISP. TRANSFER CHICKEN AND ZUCCHINI TO A PLATE AND SPRINKLE WITH LEMON JUICE. SLICE CHICKEN INTO $\frac{1}{2}$-INCH (1 CM) WIDE STRIPS. SPREAD LEMON TARRAGON MAYONNAISE ON BUNS AND MAKE SANDWICHES WITH LETTUCE, SLICED CHICKEN AND ZUCCHINI. SERVES 2.

TIP: FREEZE LEFTOVER LEMON JUICE IN AN ICE CUBE TRAY, THEN TRANSFER THE CUBES TO AN AIRTIGHT CONTAINER OR RESEALABLE FREEZER BAGS. EACH CUBE IS EQUIVALENT TO ABOUT 1 TBSP (15 ML) LEMON JUICE AND CAN BE ADDED FROZEN TO SOUPS AND SAUCES OR THAWED IN THE MICROWAVE AND ADDED TO SALAD DRESSINGS.

REMEMBER, AS FAR AS ANYONE KNOWS, WE'RE
A NICE NORMAL FAMILY.

NEW TURKEY POT PIE

HERE IT IS — A GREAT WAY TO USE UP LEFTOVER TURKEY. A CRUNCHY HOMEMADE BREAD TOPPING PUTS A NEW TWIST ON AN OLD FAVORITE. IT'S IMPRESSIVE ENOUGH FOR COMPANY. SERVE WITH STEAMED GREEN BEANS OR BROCCOLI.

TOPPING

1 TBSP	VEGETABLE OIL	15 ML
2	STALKS CELERY, CHOPPED	2
1	LARGE ONION, CHOPPED	1
8 CUPS	CUBED STALE WHITE BREAD	2 L
1 1/4 CUPS	CHICKEN BROTH (APPROX.)	300 ML
2 TSP	DRIED SAGE	10 ML
1/4 TO 1/2 TSP	DRIED THYME	1 TO 2 ML

FILLING

1 TBSP	BUTTER	15 ML
2	STALKS CELERY, THINLY SLICED	2
1	LARGE ONION, CHOPPED	1
2 CUPS	THINLY SLICED WHITE MUSHROOMS	500 ML
1/4 CUP	ALL-PURPOSE FLOUR	50 ML
2 CUPS	CHICKEN BROTH	500 ML
1/2 CUP	DRY WHITE WINE	125 ML
1/4 TO 1/2 TSP	DRIED THYME	1 TO 2 ML
	SALT AND FRESHLY GROUND BLACK PEPPER	
4 CUPS	CHOPPED COOKED TURKEY (ABOUT 1 1/2 LBS/750 G)	1 L
2 CUPS	FROZEN PEA AND CARROT MEDLEY	500 ML
1/2 CUP	WHIPPING (35%) CREAM, WARMED	125 ML

TOPPING: IN A LARGE SAUCEPAN, HEAT OIL OVER MEDIUM HEAT. SAUTÉ CELERY AND ONION FOR 5 TO 7 MINUTES OR UNTIL SOFTENED. REMOVE FROM HEAT AND ADD BREAD, CHICKEN BROTH, SAGE AND THYME, STIRRING UNTIL BREAD CUBES ARE JUST MOISTENED. IF NECESSARY, ADD A LITTLE MORE CHICKEN BROTH. SET ASIDE.

FILLING: IN A LARGE SKILLET, MELT BUTTER OVER MEDIUM-HIGH HEAT. SAUTÉ CELERY, ONION AND MUSHROOMS FOR 5 TO 7 MINUTES OR UNTIL LIQUID RELEASED FROM MUSHROOMS EVAPORATES. SPRINKLE WITH FLOUR AND SAUTÉ FOR 1 MINUTE. GRADUALLY WHISK IN CHICKEN BROTH, WINE, THYME AND SALT AND PEPPER TO TASTE; BRING TO A BOIL, THEN REDUCE HEAT TO LOW. ADD TURKEY, PEA AND CARROT MEDLEY AND CREAM; SIMMER GENTLY UNTIL SAUCE IS SLIGHTLY THICKENED. REMOVE FROM HEAT AND LET COOL.

PREHEAT OVEN TO 350°F (180°C). GREASE A 13- BY 9-INCH (33 BY 23 CM) BAKING DISH. POUR IN FILLING AND SPOON TOPPING OVER TOP. BAKE FOR ABOUT 45 MINUTES OR UNTIL FILLING IS BUBBLING AND TOP IS BROWNED AND CRISP. SERVES 6 TO 8.

MAKE AHEAD: PREPARE AND ASSEMBLE POT PIE. COVER AND REFRIGERATE FOR UP TO 1 DAY BEFORE BAKING. INCREASE BAKING TIME TO 50 TO 55 MINUTES.

TURKEY, BRIE AND CRANBERRY PANINI

THE DAY AFTER THANKSGIVING OR CHRISTMAS, THESE SANDWICHES WILL BE A BIG HIT WITH THE WHOLE FAMILY. PANINI ARE ITALY'S VERSION OF GRILLED CHEESE SANDWICHES. COOK THESE DINNER-SIZED SANDWICHES IN AN ELECTRIC SANDWICH MAKER, IF YOU HAVE ONE; IF YOU DON'T, A SKILLET WILL WORK JUST FINE (SEE TIP, BELOW).

2 TBSP	BUTTER, AT ROOM TEMPERATURE	25 ML
4	THICK SLICES WHOLE WHEAT OR MULTIGRAIN BREAD	4
4	THIN SLICES LEFTOVER OR DELI TURKEY	4
4 TO 6 OZ	BRIE CHEESE, THINLY SLICED	125 TO 175 G
4 TBSP	CRANBERRY JELLY OR SAUCE	60 ML
	SALT AND FRESHLY GROUND BLACK PEPPER	

PREHEAT SANDWICH MAKER TO MEDIUM-HIGH. LIGHTLY SPREAD BUTTER ON ONE SIDE OF EACH BREAD SLICE. PLACE BREAD ON A WORK SURFACE, BUTTERED SIDE DOWN. ON BOTTOM HALVES, LAYER WITH 1 TURKEY SLICE, BRIE, CRANBERRY JELLY AND ANOTHER TURKEY SLICE. SEASON TO TASTE WITH SALT AND PEPPER. COVER WITH TOP HALVES. PLACE SANDWICHES IN GRILL AND COOK FOR 3 TO 4 MINUTES OR UNTIL BREAD IS BROWNED AND CHEESE IS MELTING. SERVES 2.

TIP: IF YOU DON'T HAVE A PANINI GRILL OR OTHER ELECTRIC SANDWICH MAKER, COOK THE SANDWICHES IN A LARGE NONSTICK SKILLET, PRESSING DOWN GENTLY WITH A SPATULA AND TURNING ONCE.

BEEF, PORK AND LAMB

BEEF-IN-BEER POT ROAST

EVERYTHING TASTES BETTER WITH BEER.
THE RICH GRAVY IS SO GOOD WITH CRUSTY BREAD.

1 TSP	PAPRIKA	5 ML
1 TSP	DRIED THYME	5 ML
1 TSP	SALT	5 ML
1/4 TSP	FRESHLY GROUND BLACK PEPPER	1 ML
3 TO 4 LB	BONELESS BEEF CROSS RIB OR BLADE ROAST	1.5 TO 2 KG
1 TBSP	VEGETABLE OIL	15 ML
1	LARGE ONION, CHOPPED	1
2	CLOVES GARLIC, MINCED	2
2 TBSP	ALL-PURPOSE FLOUR	25 ML
1	BOTTLE (12 OZ/341 ML) LIGHT-COLORED BEER (NOT DARK ALE)	1
1 CUP	BEEF BROTH	250 ML
2 TBSP	TOMATO PASTE	25 ML
1 TBSP	WORCESTERSHIRE SAUCE	15 ML
1 LB	SWEET POTATOES, PEELED AND CHOPPED	500 G
1 LB	NEW POTATOES	500 G
3	CARROTS, CHOPPED	3
1 CUP	FROZEN PEAS	250 ML
1 TBSP	BALSAMIC VINEGAR	15 ML
1 TBSP	PACKED BROWN SUGAR	15 ML
	CHOPPED FRESH PARSLEY	

IN A SMALL BOWL, COMBINE PAPRIKA, THYME, SALT AND PEPPER. RUB OVER ALL SIDES OF BEEF AND SET ASIDE. IN A LARGE DUTCH OVEN, HEAT OIL OVER MEDIUM-HIGH HEAT.

CONTINUED ON PAGE 193...

Turkey, Brie and Cranberry Panini (page 190)

Southwestern
Beef Chili (page 214)

Pork Chops with Apples and Butternut Squash (page 228)

Orange-Chili Pork Stir-Fry (page 230)

SAUTÉ ONION AND GARLIC FOR 5 TO 7 MINUTES OR UNTIL SOFTENED. ADD FLOUR AND SAUTÉ FOR 1 MINUTE. GRADUALLY ADD BEER, BEEF BROTH, TOMATO PASTE AND WORCESTERSHIRE SAUCE, STIRRING TO SCRAPE UP FLOUR AND BROWN BITS. ADD SWEET POTATOES, POTATOES AND CARROTS. PLACE BEEF ON TOP. COVER AND SIMMER (OR BAKE IN A 325°F/160°C OVEN) FOR $2\frac{1}{2}$ TO 3 HOURS OR UNTIL BEEF IS FORK-TENDER, BASTING BEEF WITH SAUCE AT LEAST TWICE. ABOUT 20 MINUTES BEFORE THE END OF COOKING TIME, ADD PEAS, VINEGAR AND BROWN SUGAR. SEASON TO TASTE WITH SALT AND PEPPER. TRANSFER BEEF TO A CUTTING BOARD, SLICE AND SERVE WITH THE VEGETABLES AND SAUCE. GARNISH WITH PARSLEY. SERVES 6.

TIP: FREEZE LEFTOVER TOMATO PASTE IN AN ICE CUBE TRAY, THEN TRANSFER THE CUBES TO AN AIRTIGHT CONTAINER OR RESEALABLE FREEZER BAGS. EACH CUBE IS EQUIVALENT TO ABOUT 1 TBSP (15 ML) TOMATO PASTE AND CAN BE ADDED FROZEN TO SOUPS AND SAUCES.

WINE IMPROVES WITH AGE. I IMPROVE WITH WINE.

PAN-FRIED STEAK WITH BRANDIED MUSHROOM SAUCE

FAST ENOUGH FOR ANY WEEKNIGHT,
SPECIAL ENOUGH FOR COMPANY.

1 LB	BONELESS BEEF TOP SIRLOIN GRILLING STEAK	500 G
	SALT AND FRESHLY GROUND BLACK PEPPER	
1 TBSP	VEGETABLE OIL	15 ML
2	CLOVES GARLIC, MINCED	2
1	SMALL ONION, CHOPPED	1
1 CUP	SLICED WHITE MUSHROOMS	250 ML
1 TBSP	BRANDY	15 ML
1 TBSP	SOUR CREAM	15 ML
1 TSP	DIJON MUSTARD	5 ML
	CHOPPED FRESH PARSLEY	

SEASON STEAK ON BOTH SIDES WITH SALT AND PEPPER. IN A LARGE SKILLET, HEAT OIL OVER MEDIUM-HIGH HEAT. FRY STEAK FOR 3 TO 4 MINUTES PER SIDE FOR MEDIUM-RARE, OR UNTIL DESIRED DONENESS. TRANSFER STEAK TO A CUTTING BOARD AND COVER LOOSELY WITH FOIL. ADD GARLIC, ONION AND MUSHROOMS TO JUICES IN PAN AND COOK FOR 7 TO 8 MINUTES OR UNTIL BROWNED. ADD BRANDY AND COOK FOR 1 MINUTE. COMBINE SOUR CREAM AND MUSTARD; ADD TO PAN, REDUCE HEAT TO LOW AND COOK, STIRRING, FOR 1 TO 2 MINUTES OR UNTIL SAUCE IS THICKENED AND HEATED THROUGH. THINLY SLICE STEAK ACROSS THE GRAIN AND SERVE WITH SAUCE. SPRINKLE WITH PARSLEY. *SERVES 2 TO 3.*

BISTECCA TOSCANA

THE CLASSIC ITALIAN STEAK — SIMPLE IS BEST.

1½ LB	BONE-IN BEEF RIB STEAK, CUT 2 INCHES (5 CM) THICK	750 G
1 TO 2 TBSP	OLIVE OIL	15 TO 25 ML
	COARSE SALT	
	FRESHLY GROUND BLACK PEPPER	
	JUICE OF ½ LEMON	
3 CUPS	ARUGULA	750 ML
1 TBSP	BALSAMIC VINEGAR	15 ML

PREHEAT BARBECUE GRILL TO HIGH. BRUSH STEAK WITH OLIVE OIL AND SEASON GENEROUSLY WITH SALT AND PEPPER. PLACE ON GREASED GRILL AND SEAR STEAK ON BOTH SIDES. CONTINUE GRILLING FOR 8 TO 10 MINUTES, TURNING ONCE, FOR MEDIUM-RARE, OR UNTIL DESIRED DONENESS. TRANSFER TO A CUTTING BOARD AND LET STAND FOR 5 MINUTES. BRUSH STEAK WITH OLIVE OIL, SPRINKLE WITH LEMON JUICE AND SEASON TO TASTE WITH SALT AND PEPPER. THINLY SLICE STEAK ACROSS THE GRAIN. SPREAD ARUGULA ON PLATES OR A SERVING PLATTER, SPRINKLE WITH VINEGAR AND ARRANGE STEAK SLICES ON TOP. SERVES 2.

TIP: DON'T TRY TO SPEED UP COOKING BY PUSHING DOWN ON THE STEAK WITH A SPATULA — THIS WILL FORCE OUT ALL THE DELICIOUS JUICES, AND YOUR STEAK WILL BE DRY.

STIR-FRIED BEEF AND GREEN BEANS

YOU CAN NEVER HAVE TOO MANY STIR-FRIES IN YOUR REPERTOIRE. HERE'S ONE FOR BEEF LOVERS. SERVE WITH STEAMED RICE OR NOODLES.

1 LB	BONELESS BEEF TOP SIRLOIN GRILLING STEAK, CUT ACROSS THE GRAIN INTO 1/8-INCH (3 MM) WIDE STRIPS (SEE TIP, OPPOSITE)	500 G
4 TBSP	SOY SAUCE, DIVIDED	60 ML
4 TBSP	OYSTER SAUCE	60 ML
3 TBSP	WATER, DIVIDED	45 ML
1 TBSP	DRY SHERRY	15 ML
1 TBSP	LIQUID HONEY	15 ML
1 TSP	CORNSTARCH	5 ML
1/2 TSP	ASIAN CHILI PASTE (SEE TIP, PAGE 231)	2 ML
2	CARROTS, THINLY SLICED	2
3 CUPS	GREEN BEANS, CUT INTO 1/2-INCH (1 CM) LENGTHS	750 ML
1 TBSP	OLIVE OR VEGETABLE OIL	15 ML
1	LARGE ONION, THINLY SLICED	1
1	RED BELL PEPPER, THINLY SLICED	1
3	CLOVES GARLIC, MINCED	3
3	GREEN ONIONS, CHOPPED	3
1 TBSP	CHOPPED GINGERROOT	15 ML

IN A LARGE BOWL, TOSS STEAK WITH 1 TBSP (15 ML) OF THE SOY SAUCE; SET ASIDE. IN A MEDIUM BOWL, WHISK TOGETHER THE REMAINING SOY SAUCE, OYSTER SAUCE, 2 TBSP (25 ML) OF THE WATER, SHERRY, HONEY, CORNSTARCH AND CHILI PASTE; SET ASIDE. IN A LARGE POT OF BOILING WATER, BLANCH CARROTS AND GREEN

BEANS FOR 2 MINUTES OR UNTIL TENDER-CRISP. DRAIN AND PLUNGE INTO ICE-COLD WATER TO STOP THE COOKING; DRAIN AGAIN. IN A WOK OR LARGE SKILLET, HEAT OIL OVER MEDIUM-HIGH HEAT. STIR-FRY STEAK UNTIL WELL BROWNED BUT STILL SLIGHTLY PINK INSIDE. USING A SLOTTED SPOON, TRANSFER TO A PLATE. ADD ONION AND RED PEPPER TO JUICES IN PAN AND STIR-FRY FOR 2 MINUTES OR UNTIL JUST STARTING TO SOFTEN. MAKE A WELL IN THE CENTER AND ADD GARLIC, GREEN ONIONS, GINGER AND THE REMAINING WATER; STIR-FRY FOR 15 SECONDS OR UNTIL FRAGRANT. ADD BLANCHED VEGETABLES. RETURN STEAK AND ANY ACCUMULATED JUICES TO THE PAN. STIR IN THE SOY SAUCE MIXTURE, INCREASE HEAT TO HIGH AND STIR-FRY FOR ABOUT 1 MINUTE OR UNTIL SAUCE IS THICKENED AND HEATED THROUGH. SERVES 4.

TIP: TO MAKE THE STEAK EASIER TO SLICE, FREEZE IT FOR 30 MINUTES.

AT OUR AGE, BRIDGE IS THE ONLY WAY TO GET TO FOUR CLUBS IN ONE NIGHT.

SLOW COOKER HUNGARIAN GOULASH

HI HO, HI HO, IT'S OFF TO WORK I GO.
THE STEW'S IN THE COOKER
AND THE HOUSE'LL SMELL GOOD
I KNOW, I KNOW, I KNOW, I KNOW . . .
AND YOU DON'T EVEN HAVE TO BROWN THE MEAT.

1 TBSP	OLIVE OIL OR VEGETABLE OIL	15 ML
2	ONIONS, THINLY SLICED	2
1	RED BELL PEPPER, CHOPPED	1
4	CLOVES GARLIC, MINCED	4
3 TBSP	PAPRIKA	45 ML
1 TSP	DRIED MARJORAM	5 ML
1 TSP	SALT	5 ML
1 TSP	CARAWAY SEEDS (OPTIONAL)	5 ML
1/4 CUP	ALL-PURPOSE FLOUR	50 ML
1 1/2 CUPS	BEEF BROTH	375 ML
1/4 CUP	TOMATO-BASED CHILI SAUCE	50 ML
4 LB	BONELESS BEEF CROSS RIB OR BLADE ROAST, CUT INTO 1-INCH (2.5 CM) CUBES	2 KG
1/2 CUP	SOUR CREAM	125 ML
1/4 CUP	CHOPPED FRESH PARSLEY	50 ML

PREHEAT A LARGE (MINIMUM 5-QUART) SLOW COOKER.
IN A LARGE SAUCEPAN OR DUTCH OVEN, HEAT OIL OVER
MEDIUM HEAT. SAUTÉ ONIONS AND RED PEPPER FOR 5
TO 7 MINUTES OR UNTIL SOFTENED AND STARTING TO
BROWN. ADD GARLIC, PAPRIKA, MARJORAM, SALT AND
CARAWAY SEEDS (IF USING); SAUTÉ FOR 15 SECONDS OR
UNTIL FRAGRANT. ADD FLOUR AND SAUTÉ FOR 1 MINUTE
OR UNTIL BROWNED. GRADUALLY WHISK IN BEEF BROTH.

ADD CHILI SAUCE AND BEEF; BRING TO A BOIL, STIRRING OCCASIONALLY. TRANSFER TO SLOW COOKER. COVER AND COOK ON HIGH FOR 4 TO 5 HOURS OR ON LOW FOR 8 TO 10 HOURS, UNTIL BEEF IS FORK-TENDER. LADLE $\frac{1}{2}$ CUP (125 ML) OF THE SAUCE INTO A MEDIUM BOWL AND WHISK IN SOUR CREAM. STIR BACK INTO GOULASH. (THIS PREVENTS THE SOUR CREAM FROM CURDLING.) STIR IN PARSLEY. SERVES 6 TO 8.

MAKE AHEAD: AFTER SLOW COOKING BUT BEFORE ADDING THE SOUR CREAM, LET COOL, TRANSFER TO AN AIRTIGHT CONTAINER AND REFRIGERATE FOR UP TO 1 DAY OR FREEZE FOR UP TO 1 MONTH. THAW, REHEAT AND PROCEED WITH RECIPE.

TIP: ALTHOUGH MEAT IS TRADITIONALLY BROWNED AT THE START OF A STEW, WE SAVE TIME BY SKIPPING THIS STEP — AND WE DON'T EVEN TASTE THE DIFFERENCE.

MEN ARE FROM MARS; WOMEN ARE FROM VISA.

SPICY BEEF SKEWERS

FLAVORFUL BUT NOT FIERY. THE YOGURT AND CUCUMBER HELP COOL YOUR MOUTH AS YOUR TASTE BUDS TINGLE. SERVE ON A BED OF STEAMED RICE WITH WARMED PITA BREAD. FATTOUSH (PAGE 72) IS A GREAT SALAD TO SERVE WITH THESE KEBABS.

MARINADE

1/2 CUP	PLAIN YOGURT (NOT LOW-FAT)	125 ML
2 TBSP	MADRAS CURRY PASTE	25 ML
2 TBSP	FRESHLY SQUEEZED LIME JUICE	25 ML
2	CLOVES GARLIC, MINCED	2
1 TSP	SALT	5 ML
1/4 TSP	FRESHLY GROUND BLACK PEPPER	1 ML
1 LB	BONELESS BEEF TOP SIRLOIN GRILLING STEAK, CUT INTO 1-INCH (2.5 CM) CUBES	500 G

YOGURT CUCUMBER SAUCE

1/2 CUP	PLAIN YOGURT (NOT LOW-FAT)	125 ML
1/2 CUP	CHOPPED ENGLISH CUCUMBER	125 ML
2 TBSP	CHOPPED FRESH CILANTRO	25 ML
1	CLOVE GARLIC, MINCED	1
1/4 TSP	SALT	1 ML
1/4 TSP	GROUND CUMIN	1 ML
2	TOMATOES, CHOPPED	2
1/2	RED ONION, VERY THINLY SLICED	1/2

MARINADE: IN A LARGE BOWL, COMBINE YOGURT, CURRY PASTE, LIME JUICE, GARLIC, SALT AND PEPPER.

ADD BEEF TO MARINADE AND TOSS TO COAT. COVER AND REFRIGERATE FOR AT LEAST 2 HOURS OR OVERNIGHT.

YOGURT CUCUMBER SAUCE: IN A SMALL BOWL, COMBINE YOGURT, CUCUMBER, CILANTRO, GARLIC, SALT AND CUMIN. COVER AND REFRIGERATE FOR AT LEAST 1 HOUR, UNTIL CHILLED, OR FOR UP TO 4 HOURS.

SOAK FOUR 10-INCH (25 CM) WOODEN SKEWERS IN WATER FOR 30 MINUTES (OR USE METAL SKEWERS). MEANWHILE, PREHEAT BARBECUE GRILL TO MEDIUM-HIGH. REMOVE BEEF FROM MARINADE, DISCARDING MARINADE, AND THREAD ONTO SKEWERS. PLACE SKEWERS ON GREASED GRILL AND GRILL FOR 6 TO 8 MINUTES, TURNING OCCASIONALLY, FOR MEDIUM-RARE, OR UNTIL DESIRED DONENESS. SERVE GARNISHED WITH TOMATOES AND ONION AND A BIG DOLLOP OF YOGURT CUCUMBER SAUCE. SERVES 4.

IF IT'S ON SALE, I NEED IT.

PARSLEY-WALNUT PESTO — BEEF KEBABS

SIRLOIN TIP IS A GOOD CHOICE FOR KEBABS — IT LENDS ITSELF TO BEING CUT INTO NICE EVEN CUBES. SERVE WITH LEMON COUSCOUS SALAD (PAGE 98) AND WARMED PITA BREAD.

PARSLEY-WALNUT PESTO

I CUP	CHOPPED FRESH PARSLEY	250 ML
1/4 CUP	WALNUTS	50 ML
1/4 CUP	FRESHLY GRATED PARMESAN CHEESE	50 ML
2	CLOVES GARLIC, MINCED	2
	GRATED ZEST AND JUICE OF 1 LEMON	
	SALT AND FRESHLY GROUND BLACK PEPPER	
1/2 CUP	WALNUT OR OLIVE OIL	125 ML
1 1/4 LB	BONELESS BEEF SIRLOIN TIP, CUT INTO 1-INCH (2.5 CM) CUBES	625 G

PARSLEY-WALNUT PESTO: IN A FOOD PROCESSOR, COMBINE PARSLEY, WALNUTS, PARMESAN, GARLIC, LEMON ZEST, LEMON JUICE AND SALT AND PEPPER TO TASTE; PROCESS UNTIL SMOOTH. SCRAPE DOWN THE SIDES. WITH THE MOTOR RUNNING, THROUGH THE FEED TUBE, GRADUALLY ADD OIL UNTIL A RUNNY PASTE FORMS. YOU'LL HAVE ABOUT 3/4 CUP (175 ML) PESTO.

PLACE BEEF IN A LARGE BOWL. ADD PESTO AND STIR TO THOROUGHLY COAT MEAT. COVER AND REFRIGERATE FOR AT LEAST 4 HOURS OR OVERNIGHT.

SOAK FOUR 10-INCH (25 CM) WOODEN SKEWERS IN WATER FOR 30 MINUTES (OR USE METAL SKEWERS). MEANWHILE,

PREHEAT BARBECUE GRILL TO MEDIUM-HIGH. REMOVE BEEF FROM PESTO, SHAKING OFF AND DISCARDING EXCESS, AND THREAD ONTO SKEWERS. PLACE SKEWERS ON GREASED GRILL AND GRILL FOR 6 TO 8 MINUTES, TURNING OCCASIONALLY, FOR MEDIUM-RARE, OR UNTIL DESIRED DONENESS. SERVES 4.

TIP: PARSLEY-WALNUT PESTO IS A GREAT ALTERNATIVE TO BASIL PESTO AND CAN BE USED IN MANY WAYS. STIR IT INTO STEAMED RICE, BRUSH IT ON FISH BEFORE BAKING OR SPREAD IT ON PIZZA CRUST BEFORE ADDING OTHER TOPPINGS. IT KEEPS IN THE REFRIGERATOR FOR UP TO 2 DAYS OR CAN BE FROZEN FOR UP TO 1 MONTH.

LITTLE GIRL ARRIVING HOME FROM HER FIRST DAY OF KINDERGARTEN: "I DIDN'T LEARN TO READ AND I DIDN'T LEARN TO WRITE AND I HAD TO TAKE A NAP."

CHIMICHURRI FLANK STEAK

IN ARGENTINA, A SAUCE CALLED CHIMICHURRI IS OFTEN SERVED ALONGSIDE MEAT. HERE, IT'S USED AS A MARINADE TO TENDERIZE INEXPENSIVE FLANK STEAK. TO ENJOY THIS CUT OF MEAT AT ITS BEST, BE SURE TO COOK IT TO NO MORE THAN MEDIUM-RARE; OTHERWISE, IT WILL BE DRY AND CHEWY.

1 CUP	PACKED FRESH PARSLEY, CHOPPED	250 ML
1/2 CUP	OLIVE OIL	125 ML
1/4 CUP	RED WINE VINEGAR	50 ML
6	CLOVES GARLIC, MINCED	6
2 TBSP	CHOPPED FRESH CILANTRO	25 ML
1 TSP	DRIED OREGANO	5 ML
1/2 TSP	HOT PEPPER FLAKES	2 ML
1/2 TSP	SALT	2 ML
1/4 TSP	FRESHLY GROUND BLACK PEPPER	1 ML
1 LB	BEEF FLANK STEAK	500 G

IN A MEDIUM BOWL, WHISK TOGETHER PARSLEY, OIL, VINEGAR, GARLIC, CILANTRO, OREGANO, HOT PEPPER FLAKES, SALT AND PEPPER. PIERCE STEAK ALL OVER WITH A FORK. PLACE IN A SEALABLE PLASTIC BAG AND POUR IN MARINADE. SEAL AND REFRIGERATE OVERNIGHT OR FOR UP TO 24 HOURS.

PREHEAT BARBECUE GRILL TO MEDIUM-HIGH. REMOVE STEAK FROM MARINADE, DISCARDING MARINADE, AND PAT DRY. PLACE STEAK ON GREASED GRILL AND GRILL FOR ABOUT 5 MINUTES PER SIDE, TURNING ONCE, UNTIL MEDIUM-RARE. TRANSFER TO A CUTTING BOARD AND LET STAND FOR 10 MINUTES. THINLY SLICE STEAK ACROSS THE GRAIN. SERVES 4.

PORTOBELLO-STUFFED HAMBURGERS

CRUSTY ON THE OUTSIDE, MOIST ON THE INSIDE — THE ULTIMATE BURGER. SERVE WITH YOUR FAVORITE FIXINS.

1	PORTOBELLO MUSHROOM (ABOUT 4 OZ/125 G)	1
1	EGG, LIGHTLY BEATEN	1
6 TBSP	FRESH BREAD CRUMBS	90 ML
2 TBSP	MILK	25 ML
2 TSP	CREAMED HORSERADISH	10 ML
1 TSP	WORCESTERSHIRE SAUCE	5 ML
1 TSP	SALT	5 ML
1/2 TSP	FRESHLY GROUND BLACK PEPPER	2 ML
1 LB	LEAN GROUND BEEF	500 G
1	ONION, FINELY CHOPPED	1

IN A FOOD PROCESSOR, PULSE MUSHROOM UNTIL VERY FINELY CHOPPED; SET ASIDE. IN A MEDIUM BOWL, WHISK TOGETHER EGG, BREAD CRUMBS, MILK, HORSERADISH, WORCESTERSHIRE SAUCE, SALT AND PEPPER. PLACE BEEF IN A LARGE BOWL. ADD EGG MIXTURE AND MUSHROOM. STIR OR USE CLEAN HANDS TO MIX THOROUGHLY. SHAPE INTO 4 PATTIES (OR MORE IF YOU LIKE SMALLER BURGERS). PLACE ON A PLATE, COVER AND REFRIGERATE FOR AT LEAST 1 HOUR OR UP TO 4 HOURS.

BARBECUE OR PAN-FRY BURGERS OVER MEDIUM-HIGH HEAT FOR ABOUT 10 MINUTES, TURNING ONLY ONCE, UNTIL NO LONGER PINK INSIDE. MAKES 4 BURGERS.

TIP: DO NOT FLATTEN BURGERS WITH A SPATULA AS YOU COOK THEM — THIS FORCES OUT ALL THE YUMMY JUICES, RESULTING IN A DRY BURGER.

MAKE-AHEAD MEATBALLS, THREE WAYS

MEALS THAT CAN BE MADE AHEAD OF TIME ARE THE SECRET TO SURVIVING WEEKNIGHT DINNERS. VERSATILE MEATBALLS ARE PERFECT: THEY FREEZE WELL AND ARE DELICIOUS WITH A VARIETY OF SAUCES. WE'VE GIVEN YOU THREE SAUCE IDEAS TO GET STARTED. DOUBLE OR TRIPLE THESE RECIPES, FREEZING THE MEATBALLS AND SAUCES SEPARATELY, AND YOU'LL ALWAYS HAVE A QUICK MEAL ON HAND.

MEATBALLS

FOR A QUICK MEAL, TAKE OUT AS MANY MEATBALLS AS YOU NEED AND REHEAT FROM FROZEN IN YOUR SAUCE OF CHOICE.

I	EGG	I
1/4 CUP	MILK	50 ML
1/2 TSP	WORCESTERSHIRE SAUCE	2 ML
3/4 CUP	FRESH BREAD CRUMBS	175 ML
I LB	LEAN GROUND BEEF (OR A MIXTURE OF BEEF AND PORK)	500 G
2 TBSP	CHOPPED FRESH PARSLEY (OPTIONAL)	25 ML
1/2 TSP	DRIED OREGANO	2 ML
	SALT AND FRESHLY GROUND BLACK PEPPER	

PREHEAT OVEN TO 375°F (190°C). LINE A RIMMED BAKING SHEET WITH FOIL. IN A MEDIUM BOWL, WHISK TOGETHER EGG, MILK AND WORCESTERSHIRE SAUCE. ADD BREAD CRUMBS AND LET SOAK FOR 5 MINUTES. IN A LARGE BOWL, COMBINE BEEF, EGG MIXTURE, PARSLEY,

OREGANO AND SALT AND PEPPER TO TASTE. SCOOP TABLESPOONFULS (15 ML) OF MEAT MIXTURE AND, USING CLEAN HANDS, ROLL INTO MEATBALLS. PLACE ON PREPARED BAKING SHEET AND BAKE FOR 15 MINUTES OR UNTIL NO LONGER PINK INSIDE. MAKES ABOUT 24 MEATBALLS.

MAKE AHEAD: PLACE COOKED AND COOLED MEATBALLS ON A FOIL-LINED BAKING SHEET AND FREEZE, UNCOVERED, UNTIL HARD. TRANSFER TO PLASTIC FREEZER BAGS AND SEAL TIGHTLY.

SWEET-AND-SOUR SAUCE

3/4 CUP	PINEAPPLE JUICE	175 ML
1/2 CUP	CIDER OR RICE VINEGAR	125 ML
1/4 CUP	KETCHUP	50 ML
2 TBSP	SOY SAUCE	25 ML
1 1/2 TSP	CORNSTARCH	7 ML
1/4 TSP	HOT PEPPER FLAKES	1 ML

IN A SMALL SAUCEPAN, WHISK TOGETHER PINEAPPLE JUICE, VINEGAR, KETCHUP, SOY SAUCE, CORNSTARCH AND HOT PEPPER FLAKES; BRING TO A BOIL. REDUCE HEAT AND SIMMER FOR ABOUT 5 MINUTES OR UNTIL THICK AND GLOSSY. MAKES ABOUT 1 1/2 CUPS (375 ML), ENOUGH FOR 12 TO 18 MEATBALLS.

MAKE AHEAD: LET COOL, TRANSFER TO AN AIRTIGHT CONTAINER AND REFRIGERATE FOR UP TO 2 DAYS OR FREEZE FOR UP TO 2 MONTHS. REHEAT TO SERVE.

CONTINUED ON NEXT PAGE...

SWEDISH MEATBALL SAUCE

1 TBSP	VEGETABLE OIL	15 ML
1	SMALL ONION, FINELY CHOPPED	1
1	STALK CELERY, FINELY CHOPPED	1
1	SMALL CARROT, FINELY CHOPPED	1
2 TBSP	ALL-PURPOSE FLOUR	25 ML
2 1/2 CUPS	BEEF BROTH	625 ML
2 TBSP	TOMATO PASTE	25 ML
1 TSP	WORCESTERSHIRE SAUCE	5 ML
1 TSP	DRIED THYME	5 ML
1	BAY LEAF	1
	SALT AND FRESHLY GROUND BLACK PEPPER	
1/2 CUP	WHIPPING (35%) CREAM, WARMED	125 ML
1 1/2 TBSP	DRY SHERRY (OPTIONAL)	22 ML

IN A SAUCEPAN, HEAT OIL OVER MEDIUM HEAT. SAUTÉ ONION, CELERY AND CARROT FOR 5 TO 7 MINUTES OR UNTIL SOFTENED. ADD FLOUR AND SAUTÉ FOR 1 MINUTE. GRADUALLY WHISK IN BROTH, TOMATO PASTE, WORCESTERSHIRE SAUCE, THYME, BAY LEAF AND SALT AND PEPPER TO TASTE; BRING TO A BOIL, STIRRING CONSTANTLY. REDUCE HEAT AND SIMMER FOR 25 TO 30 MINUTES OR UNTIL SAUCE IS THICKENED. SEASON TO TASTE WITH SALT AND PEPPER AND DISCARD BAY LEAF. STIR IN CREAM AND SHERRY (IF USING). MAKES ABOUT 2 1/2 CUPS (625 ML), ENOUGH FOR 24 MEATBALLS.

MAKE AHEAD: BEFORE ADDING THE CREAM, LET COOL, TRANSFER TO AN AIRTIGHT CONTAINER AND REFRIGERATE FOR UP TO 2 DAYS OR FREEZE FOR UP TO 1 MONTH. TO SERVE, THAW, REHEAT AND PROCEED WITH RECIPE.

SIMPLY SUPER TOMATO SAUCE

2 TBSP	OLIVE OIL	25 ML
2	CLOVES GARLIC, SLIGHTLY CRUSHED	2
PINCH	HOT PEPPER FLAKES	PINCH
1	SMALL ONION, FINELY CHOPPED	1
1	CAN (28 OZ/796 ML) WHOLE TOMATOES WITH JUICE	1
1 TBSP	GRANULATED SUGAR	15 ML
	SALT AND FRESHLY GROUND BLACK PEPPER	
1/4 CUP	SHREDDED FRESH BASIL	50 ML

IN A LARGE SAUCEPAN, HEAT OIL OVER MEDIUM HEAT. SAUTÉ GARLIC AND HOT PEPPER FLAKES FOR 30 TO 45 SECONDS OR UNTIL GARLIC IS GOLDEN. REMOVE GARLIC FROM PAN AND DISCARD. ADD ONION AND SAUTÉ FOR ABOUT 1 MINUTE OR UNTIL SOFTENED. ADD TOMATOES AND SUGAR, BREAKING UP TOMATOES WITH A SPOON. BRING TO A BOIL. REDUCE HEAT AND SIMMER, STIRRING OCCASIONALLY, FOR 20 TO 30 MINUTES OR UNTIL THICKENED. SEASON TO TASTE WITH SALT AND PEPPER. STIR IN BASIL. MAKES ABOUT 3 CUPS (750 ML), ENOUGH FOR 24 MEATBALLS.

MAKE AHEAD: BEFORE ADDING THE BASIL, LET COOL, TRANSFER TO AN AIRTIGHT CONTAINER AND REFRIGERATE FOR UP TO 2 DAYS OR FREEZE FOR UP TO 2 MONTHS. TO SERVE, THAW, REHEAT AND STIR IN BASIL.

VARIATIONS: ONCE THE SAUCE HAS THICKENED BUT BEFORE ADDING THE BASIL, PURÉE SAUCE UNTIL SMOOTH. TO MAKE A ROSE SAUCE, ADD 1/2 CUP (125 ML) WARMED WHIPPING (35%) CREAM JUST BEFORE SERVING.

EMPANADA PIE

HERE'S AN EASY, FAMILY-SIZED, KID-FRIENDLY VERSION OF THE POPULAR LATIN AMERICAN CRESCENT-SHAPED SAVORY PIES. WE CUT DOWN THE PREPARATION TIME BY USING THE WELL-KNOWN REFRIGERATED PIE CRUSTS SOLD IN CANISTERS. SERVE WITH STEAMED GREEN BEANS OR CARROTS.

FILLING

12 OZ	LEAN GROUND BEEF	375 G
1 CUP	SLICED WHITE MUSHROOMS	250 ML
2	CLOVES GARLIC, MINCED	2
1	ONION, FINELY CHOPPED	1
1	GREEN BELL PEPPER, CHOPPED	1
1 TSP	CHILI POWDER (OR TO TASTE)	5 ML
1 TSP	GROUND CUMIN	5 ML
1 TSP	DRIED OREGANO	5 ML
1/2 TSP	SALT	2 ML
1 CUP	CANNED WHOLE TOMATOES WITH JUICE, CHOPPED (SEE TIP, PAGE 173)	250 ML
1/2 CUP	FROZEN CORN KERNELS	125 ML
1	PACKAGE (15 OZ/425 G) REFRIGERATED PIE CRUSTS (CONTAINS 2)	1
1	EGG, LIGHTLY BEATEN	1

FILLING: HEAT A LARGE NONSTICK SKILLET OVER MEDIUM-HIGH HEAT. SAUTÉ BEEF, MUSHROOMS, GARLIC, ONION AND GREEN PEPPER, BREAKING UP BEEF WITH A SPOON, FOR 7 TO 8 MINUTES OR UNTIL BEEF IS NO LONGER PINK. DRAIN OFF EXCESS FAT. ADD CHILI POWDER, CUMIN, OREGANO AND SALT; SAUTÉ FOR 30 SECONDS OR UNTIL

FRAGRANT. ADD TOMATOES AND CORN; BRING TO A BOIL. REDUCE HEAT AND SIMMER FOR 25 MINUTES OR UNTIL SAUCE IS THICKENED. LET COOL COMPLETELY (OTHERWISE, IT WILL MAKE THE PASTRY SOGGY).

MEANWHILE, PREHEAT OVEN TO 425°F (220°C). GREASE A LARGE BAKING SHEET. ON A FLOURED WORK SURFACE, UNFOLD 1 PIE CRUST. SPOON HALF THE MEAT MIXTURE ON ONE SIDE OF THE PASTRY CIRCLE, LEAVING A 1-INCH (2.5 CM) BORDER. FOLD THE OTHER SIDE OF THE PASTRY OVER, MAKING A CRESCENT-SHAPED PIE. MOISTEN THE EDGES WITH WATER AND PRESS TOGETHER TO SEAL. REPEAT WITH THE OTHER PIE CRUST AND THE REMAINING MEAT. USE A SPATULA TO CAREFULLY TRANSFER EMPANADAS TO PREPARED BAKING SHEET. BRUSH WITH BEATEN EGG. BAKE FOR 20 TO 25 MINUTES OR UNTIL CRISPY AND GOLDEN BROWN. SERVES 6 TO 8.

MAKE AHEAD: TRANSFER COOLED FILLING TO AN AIRTIGHT CONTAINER AND REFRIGERATE FOR UP TO 1 DAY OR FREEZE FOR UP TO 1 MONTH. THAW BEFORE FILLING THE PASTRY.

I DON'T REPEAT GOSSIP — SO LISTEN CAREFULLY.

BOLOGNESE PASTA SAUCE

MAMMA MIA! MILK IS THE ITALIAN SECRET FOR THIS
SLOW-SIMMERED, RICH-TASTING MEAT SAUCE. SERVE
OVER SPAGHETTI OR YOUR FAVORITE PASTA.

1 TBSP	OLIVE OIL	15 ML
1/2 CUP	FINELY CHOPPED ONION	125 ML
1/4 CUP	FINELY CHOPPED CARROT	50 ML
1/4 CUP	FINELY CHOPPED CELERY	50 ML
8 OZ	EXTRA-LEAN GROUND BEEF	250 G
8 OZ	GROUND PORK	250 G
1 CUP	WHOLE OR 2% MILK (SEE TIP, OPPOSITE)	250 ML
1/2 CUP	DRY RED OR WHITE WINE	125 ML
1	CAN (28 OZ/796 ML) WHOLE TOMATOES WITH JUICE (SEE TIP, PAGE 173)	1
1 TBSP	TOMATO PASTE	15 ML
PINCH	GROUND NUTMEG	PINCH
1/4 CUP	CHOPPED FRESH PARSLEY	50 ML
	SALT AND FRESHLY GROUND BLACK PEPPER	

IN LARGE SAUCEPAN OR DUTCH OVEN, HEAT OIL OVER
MEDIUM-HIGH HEAT. SAUTÉ ONION, CARROT AND CELERY
FOR ABOUT 5 MINUTES OR UNTIL SOFTENED. ADD BEEF
AND PORK; SAUTÉ, BREAKING UP MEAT WITH A SPOON,
FOR 7 TO 8 MINUTES OR UNTIL MEAT IS NO LONGER
PINK. DRAIN OFF EXCESS FAT. ADD MILK, REDUCE HEAT
AND SIMMER FOR ABOUT 3 MINUTES OR UNTIL ALMOST
EVAPORATED. ADD WINE AND SIMMER FOR ABOUT
5 MINUTES OR UNTIL EVAPORATED. STIR IN TOMATOES,
TOMATO PASTE AND NUTMEG, BREAKING UP TOMATOES

WITH A SPOON. BRING TO A BOIL. REDUCE HEAT AND
SIMMER, STIRRING OCCASIONALLY, FOR 1½ HOURS OR
UNTIL THICKENED. STIR IN PARSLEY AND SEASON TO
TASTE WITH SALT AND PEPPER. SERVES 4.

MAKE AHEAD: LET COOL, TRANSFER TO AN AIRTIGHT
CONTAINER AND REFRIGERATE FOR UP TO 2 DAYS OR
FREEZE FOR UP TO 1 MONTH.

TIP: THE FAT IN WHOLE OR 2% MILK LENDS A LOVELY
MELLOW FLAVOR TO THE SAUCE BY BALANCING OUT THE
ACIDITY OF THE TOMATOES. SKIM MILK WON'T HAVE
THE SAME EFFECT, AS THE FAT HAS BEEN REMOVED.

VARIATION: OMIT THE GROUND PORK AND USE 1 LB (500 G)
GROUND BEEF.

WINE IS PROOF THAT GOD WANTS US TO BE HAPPY.

SOUTHWESTERN BEEF CHILI

BACON AND PURÉED CHIPOTLE PEPPER ADD A SWEET, SMOKY FLAVOR TO THIS RIB-STICKIN' BEEF CHILI. SERVE WITH FRESH CRUSTY MULTIGRAIN BREAD AND PASS SOUR CREAM AND SHREDDED CHEDDAR CHEESE AT THE TABLE.

2	SLICES BACON, CHOPPED	2
1 LB	LEAN GROUND BEEF	500 G
1	LARGE ONION, FINELY CHOPPED	1
1	LARGE CARROT, FINELY CHOPPED	1
1	STALK CELERY, FINELY CHOPPED	1
1	RED BELL PEPPER, CHOPPED	1
2	CLOVES GARLIC, MINCED	2
2 TSP	CHILI POWDER	10 ML
1 TSP	PURÉED CANNED CHIPOTLE PEPPER (SEE TIP, PAGE 153)	5 ML
1 TSP	GROUND CUMIN	5 ML
1 TSP	DRIED OREGANO	5 ML
1	CAN (28 OZ/796 ML) WHOLE TOMATOES WITH JUICE (SEE TIP, PAGE 173), CHOPPED	1
1	CAN (14 TO 19 OZ/398 TO 540 ML) BLACK BEANS, DRAINED AND RINSED	1
1 CUP	FROZEN CORN KERNELS	250 ML
2 TBSP	TOMATO PASTE	25 ML
2 TBSP	PACKED BROWN SUGAR	25 ML
1/4 CUP	CHOPPED FRESH CILANTRO	50 ML
	SALT AND FRESHLY GROUND BLACK PEPPER	

IN A LARGE SAUCEPAN OR DUTCH OVEN, OVER MEDIUM-HIGH HEAT, SAUTÉ BACON UNTIL CRISP. USING A SLOTTED SPOON, TRANSFER TO A PLATE LINED WITH PAPER

TOWELS. DRAIN OFF ALL BUT 1 TBSP (15 ML) OF THE FAT. ADD BEEF, ONION, CARROT, CELERY AND RED PEPPER TO SKILLET AND SAUTÉ, BREAKING UP BEEF WITH A SPOON, FOR 7 TO 8 MINUTES OR UNTIL BEEF IS NO LONGER PINK. DRAIN FAT. RETURN BACON TO PAN AND ADD GARLIC, CHILI POWDER, CHIPOTLE PEPPER, CUMIN AND OREGANO; SAUTÉ FOR 15 SECONDS OR UNTIL FRAGRANT. ADD TOMATOES, BEANS, CORN, TOMATO PASTE AND BROWN SUGAR; BRING TO A BOIL. REDUCE HEAT AND SIMMER, STIRRING OCCASIONALLY, FOR 30 MINUTES OR UNTIL THICKENED. STIR IN CILANTRO AND SEASON TO TASTE WITH SALT AND PEPPER. SERVES 6.

MAKE AHEAD: LET COOL, TRANSFER TO AN AIRTIGHT CONTAINER AND REFRIGERATE FOR UP TO 1 DAY OR FREEZE FOR UP TO 1 MONTH.

TIP: DON'T BE SHY WITH THE SALT. IT MAKES ALL THE DIFFERENCE TO THE FLAVOR OF THIS EXCELLENT CHILI!

"TO GET BACK MY YOUTH I WOULD DO ANYTHING IN THE WORLD EXCEPT EXERCISE, GET UP EARLY OR BE RESPECTABLE."
— OSCAR WILDE

PULLED PORK AND COLESLAW ON A BUN

NOW YOU'RE COOKING SOUTHERN! SHREDDED, OR "PULLED," PORK IS COOKED VERY S-L-O-W-L-Y FOR SEVERAL HOURS ON THE BARBECUE UNTIL IT PRACTICALLY FALLS APART. WE PREFER NOT TO BABYSIT THE MEAT, SO WE USE A SLOW COOKER OR A LOW OVEN. SERVE ON A BUN WITH OUR DELICIOUS, CHIN-DRIBBLIN' BARBECUE SAUCE, TOPPED WITH COLESLAW.

3 TBSP	PAPRIKA	45 ML
I TBSP	CHILI POWDER	15 ML
I TBSP	PACKED BROWN SUGAR	15 ML
I TBSP	DRY MUSTARD	15 ML
I TSP	SALT	5 ML
3 LB	BONELESS PORK SHOULDER BLADE (BUTT) ROAST, CUT INTO 4 LARGE CHUNKS	1.5 KG
I 1/2 CUPS	CHICKEN BROTH	375 ML
I	PACKET (1 1/3 OZ/39 G) DRIED ONION SOUP MIX	I
I 1/2 CUPS	TOMATO-BASED CHILI SAUCE	375 ML
3 TBSP	PACKED BROWN SUGAR	45 ML
3 TBSP	CIDER VINEGAR	45 ML
I TBSP	SOY SAUCE	15 ML
1/4 TO 1/2 TSP	CAYENNE PEPPER	I TO 2 ML
	CELERY ROOT AND APPLE COLESLAW (PAGE 68)	

IN A SMALL BOWL, COMBINE PAPRIKA, CHILI POWDER, BROWN SUGAR, MUSTARD AND SALT. RUB OVER ALL SIDES OF PORK. SET ON A LARGE PLATE, COVER AND REFRIGERATE FOR 2 HOURS.

PREHEAT A LARGE (MINIMUM 5-QUART) SLOW COOKER. PLACE PORK IN SLOW COOKER. WHISK TOGETHER CHICKEN BROTH AND ONION SOUP MIX AND POUR OVER PORK. COVER AND COOK ON LOW FOR 8 TO 10 HOURS OR UNTIL PORK SHREDS VERY EASILY WITH A FORK. USING A SLOTTED SPOON, TRANSFER PORK TO A PLATE AND LET COOL SLIGHTLY. SKIM EXCESS FAT FROM SAUCE, POUR INTO A LARGE SAUCEPAN AND BRING TO A BOIL. REDUCE HEAT AND SIMMER FOR 15 TO 20 MINUTES OR UNTIL REDUCED AND SLIGHTLY THICKENED. ADD CHILI SAUCE, BROWN SUGAR, VINEGAR, SOY SAUCE AND CAYENNE TO TASTE; SIMMER FOR 5 TO 10 MINUTES TO LET THE FLAVORS BLEND. TASTE AND ADJUST SEASONING.

MEANWHILE, TRANSFER PORK TO A CUTTING BOARD AND ADD ACCUMULATED JUICES TO SAUCE. USE TWO FORKS TO REMOVE EXCESS FAT AND SHRED PORK, PLACING PULLED PORK IN A SHALLOW DISH. (THIS IS A SUPER-MESSY JOB BUT WORTH THE EFFORT!) POUR 1 CUP (250 ML) SAUCE OVER SHREDDED MEAT, GENTLY TURNING PORK TO ABSORB THE SAUCE. SERVE PORK TOPPED WITH COLESLAW ON WARMED BUNS, WITH EXTRA SAUCE FOR DIPPING. SERVES 8.

TIP: TO COOK THE PORK IN THE OVEN, PLACE RUBBED PORK IN A ROASTING PAN, POUR IN THE CHICKEN BROTH MIXTURE, COVER AND ROAST AT 300°F (150°C) FOR 3 TO 4 HOURS OR UNTIL PORK SHREDS VERY EASILY WITH A FORK. CHECK ONCE OR TWICE AND ADD MORE BROTH IF THE PAN IS GETTING DRY.

GLAZED ROAST PORK LOIN

THE PERFECT SUNDAY NIGHT SUPPER. SERVE
WITH ROASTED SWEET POTATO AND PARSNIP
PURÉE (PAGE 254) AND GREEN BEANS WITH
TOASTED ALMONDS (PAGE 236).

GLAZE

1/4 CUP	PORT	50 ML
6 TBSP	BLACK CURRANT JELLY	90 ML
2	CLOVES GARLIC, MINCED	2
3 LB	BONELESS PORK CENTER-CUT LOIN ROAST	1.5 KG
	SALT AND FRESHLY GROUND BLACK PEPPER	
1 TBSP	VEGETABLE OIL	15 ML
1 CUP	CHICKEN BROTH	250 ML
1 TSP	CORNSTARCH	5 ML

GLAZE: IN A SMALL SAUCEPAN, COMBINE PORT, BLACK
CURRANT JELLY AND GARLIC; BRING TO A BOIL. REDUCE
HEAT AND SIMMER FOR 10 MINUTES OR UNTIL SLIGHTLY
THICKENED. REMOVE FROM HEAT AND KEEP WARM.

PREHEAT OVEN TO 325°F (160°C). SPRINKLE PORK WITH
SALT AND PEPPER. IN A LARGE SKILLET, HEAT OIL OVER
MEDIUM-HIGH HEAT. BROWN PORK ON ALL SIDES AND
TRANSFER TO A RACK IN A ROASTING PAN. ROAST FOR
30 MINUTES. BRUSH ROAST WITH 2 TBSP (25 ML) OF
THE GLAZE, RESERVING THE REST. BAKE FOR 45 TO
55 MINUTES, BRUSHING AGAIN WITH GLAZE, UNTIL A
MEAT THERMOMETER INSERTED IN THE THICKEST
PART REGISTERS 155°F (68°C) AND JUST A HINT OF PINK

REMAINS INSIDE. TRANSFER TO A CUTTING BOARD AND COVER LOOSELY WITH FOIL. (THE PORK WILL CONTINUE TO "COOK" IN ITS OWN HEAT, AND THE TEMPERATURE WILL RISE BY ABOUT ANOTHER 5°F/3°C.) WHISK CHICKEN BROTH AND CORNSTARCH INTO THE RESERVED GLAZE. ADD TO ROASTING PAN, STIRRING TO SCRAPE UP BROWN BITS, AND SIMMER GENTLY ON THE STOVETOP, OVER LOW HEAT, FOR ABOUT 5 MINUTES OR UNTIL SLIGHTLY THICKENED. SEASON TO TASTE WITH SALT AND PEPPER. STRAIN INTO A SERVING BOWL. SLICE PORK AND ARRANGE ON A SERVING PLATTER. SERVE SAUCE SEPARATELY. SERVES 6.

VARIATION: USE RED CURRANT JELLY IN PLACE OF THE BLACK CURRANT JELLY.

HER LIFE, LIKE HER HAIR, HAS BECOME UNMANAGEABLE.

CHINESE BARBECUE PORK

THIS SUCCULENT PORK TENDERLOIN COOKS
BEAUTIFULLY ON THE BARBECUE OR IN THE OVEN
(SEE TIP, OPPOSITE). SERVE WITH ASIAN NOODLES WITH
VEGETABLES (PAGE 258) OR STEAMED RICE.

I	PORK TENDERLOIN (ABOUT 12 OZ/375 G)	I
2	CLOVES GARLIC, MINCED	2
I TSP	CHOPPED GINGERROOT	5 ML
2 TBSP	GRANULATED SUGAR	25 ML
3 TBSP	SOY SAUCE	45 ML
2 TBSP	HOISIN SAUCE	25 ML
I TBSP	DRY SHERRY	15 ML
I TBSP	KETCHUP	15 ML

REMOVE ANY SILVERY-LOOKING SKIN FROM THE PORK.
IN A MEDIUM BOWL, COMBINE GARLIC, GINGER, SUGAR,
SOY SAUCE, HOISIN SAUCE, SHERRY AND KETCHUP;
DIVIDE SAUCE IN HALF. PLACE PORK IN A SHALLOW
DISH AND BRUSH LIBERALLY ON ALL SIDES WITH HALF
THE SAUCE. COVER AND REFRIGERATE FOR AT LEAST
4 HOURS OR OVERNIGHT. COVER AND REFRIGERATE THE
REMAINING SAUCE.

PREHEAT BARBECUE GRILL TO MEDIUM. REMOVE PORK
FROM MARINADE, DISCARDING MARINADE. PLACE PORK
ON GREASED GRILL AND GRILL FOR 30 TO 35 MINUTES,
TURNING OCCASIONALLY, UNTIL A MEAT THERMOMETER
INSERTED IN THE THICKEST PART REGISTERS 155°F (68°C)
AND JUST A HINT OF PINK REMAINS INSIDE. TRANSFER
TO A CUTTING BOARD, COVER LOOSELY WITH FOIL AND
LET REST FOR 10 MINUTES. (THE PORK WILL CONTINUE TO

"COOK" IN ITS OWN HEAT, AND THE TEMPERATURE WILL RISE BY ABOUT ANOTHER 5°F/3°C.) WARM THE RESERVED SAUCE IN THE MICROWAVE FOR ABOUT 20 SECONDS. THINLY SLICE PORK AND SERVE WITH SAUCE. SERVES 4.

TIP: TO COOK THIS PORK IN THE OVEN, PLACE PORK ON A RIMMED BAKING SHEET LINED WITH GREASED FOIL AND BAKE IN A 375°F (180°C) OVEN FOR 30 TO 40 MINUTES OR UNTIL A MEAT THERMOMETER INSERTED IN THE THICKEST PART REGISTERS 155°F (68°C) AND JUST A HINT OF PINK REMAINS INSIDE.

TIP: WHEN BUYING FRESH GINGERROOT, LOOK FOR FIRM PIECES. IF THE SKIN IS WRINKLY, IT'S PAST ITS BEST. TO PEEL GINGER, HOLD IT IN THE PALM OF YOUR HAND AND USE THE EDGE OF A TEASPOON TO SCRAPE AWAY THE SKIN, GETTING INTO ALL THE CREVICES AND AROUND THE KNOBBY BITS. BREAK THE PEELED GINGER INTO SMALLER PIECES AND WRAP TIGHTLY IN A DOUBLE LAYER OF PLASTIC WRAP. IT WILL KEEP IN THE FRIDGE FOR A COUPLE OF WEEKS AND IN THE FREEZER FOR SEVERAL MONTHS.

THE MOST DIFFICULT YEARS OF MARRIAGE ARE THOSE FOLLOWING THE WEDDING.

APPLE AND PECAN-STUFFED PORK TENDERLOIN

THE PERFECT DISH WHEN YOU FEEL LIKE MAKING A BIT OF AN EFFORT. SERVE WITH SCALLOPED POTATOES WITH FENNEL (PAGE 244).

2	PORK TENDERLOINS (EACH ABOUT 12 OZ/375 G)	2
1 TBSP	BUTTER	15 ML
1/4 CUP	FINELY CHOPPED ONION	50 ML
1/4 CUP	FINELY CHOPPED CELERY	50 ML
1	SMALL GOLDEN DELICIOUS APPLE (UNPEELED), DICED	1
1	SMALL CARROT, GRATED	1
1 1/2 CUPS	FRESH BREAD CRUMBS	375 ML
1/4 CUP	FINELY CHOPPED PECANS	50 ML
2 TBSP	CHOPPED FRESH SAGE (OR 1 TSP/5 ML DRIED)	25 ML
	SALT AND FRESHLY GROUND BLACK PEPPER	
1/4 CUP	HONEY MUSTARD	50 ML
4	SLICES BACON	4

PREHEAT OVEN TO 375°F (190°C). GREASE A ROASTING PAN. REMOVE ANY SILVERY-LOOKING SKIN FROM THE PORK. CUT A DEEP POCKET LENGTHWISE THROUGH EACH PORK TENDERLOIN; SET ASIDE. IN A MEDIUM SKILLET, MELT BUTTER OVER MEDIUM HEAT. SAUTÉ ONION, CELERY, APPLE AND CARROT FOR 5 TO 7 MINUTES OR UNTIL SOFTENED. STIR IN BREAD CRUMBS, PECANS, SAGE AND SALT AND PEPPER TO TASTE, PRESSING WITH A SPATULA SO THAT THE MIXTURE STICKS TOGETHER SLIGHTLY. STUFF PORK WITH ONION MIXTURE, PACKING TIGHTLY.

TUCK THIN ENDS OF TENDERLOINS UNDER AND TIE EACH
TENDERLOIN WITH THREE TO FOUR PIECES OF KITCHEN
STRING TO HOLD PORK AND STUFFING TOGETHER. BRUSH
TOPS WITH HONEY MUSTARD. PLACE TWO STRIPS OF
BACON LENGTHWISE ALONG EACH TENDERLOIN. PLACE
IN PREPARED PAN AND BAKE FOR 45 TO 60 MINUTES
OR UNTIL A MEAT THERMOMETER INSERTED IN THE
THICKEST PART OF A TENDERLOIN REGISTERS 155°F (68°C)
AND JUST A HINT OF PINK REMAINS INSIDE. TRANSFER TO
A CUTTING BOARD AND LET REST FOR 5 MINUTES. (THE
PORK WILL CONTINUE TO "COOK" IN ITS OWN HEAT, AND
THE TEMPERATURE WILL RISE BY ABOUT ANOTHER 5°F/3°C.)
REMOVE STRING AND SLICE. SERVES 6 TO 8.

VARIATION: OMIT THE APPLE, CARROT, PECANS, HONEY
MUSTARD AND BACON. ADD 6 DRIED APRICOTS, FINELY
CHOPPED, 1 ORANGE, PEELED AND FINELY CHOPPED, AND
1 TSP (5 ML) CRUSHED FENNEL SEEDS WITH THE BREAD
CRUMBS. BRUSH THE STUFFED TENDERLOIN WITH $1/4$ CUP
(50 ML) SWEET ASIAN CHILI SAUCE BEFORE ROASTING.

THERAPY HAS TAUGHT ME THAT IT'S ALL HIS FAULT.

HERB AND PARMESAN-CRUSTED PORK TENDERLOIN

HERE'S A TASTY WAY TO DRESS UP QUICK-COOKING PORK TENDERLOIN.

2	PORK TENDERLOINS (EACH ABOUT 12 OZ/375 G)	2
1/2 CUP	DRY BREAD CRUMBS	125 ML
1/2 CUP	CHOPPED FRESH PARSLEY	125 ML
1/3 CUP	FRESHLY GRATED PARMESAN CHEESE	75 ML
1/2 TSP	DRIED THYME	2 ML
1/2 TSP	SALT	2 ML
1/4 TSP	FRESHLY GROUND BLACK PEPPER	1 ML
1/4 CUP	DIJON MUSTARD	50 ML
3/4 TSP	FENNEL SEEDS, CRUSHED	3 ML
1	CLOVE GARLIC, MINCED	1

PREHEAT OVEN TO 375°F (190°C). LINE A BAKING SHEET WITH PARCHMENT PAPER. REMOVE ANY SILVERY-LOOKING SKIN FROM THE PORK. IN A SHALLOW DISH, COMBINE BREAD CRUMBS, PARSLEY, PARMESAN, THYME, SALT AND PEPPER. IN A SMALL BOWL, COMBINE MUSTARD, FENNEL SEEDS AND GARLIC. SPREAD MUSTARD MIXTURE EVENLY OVER PORK. ROLL PORK IN CRUMB MIXTURE. PLACE ON PREPARED BAKING SHEET AND BAKE FOR 35 TO 40 MINUTES OR UNTIL A MEAT THERMOMETER INSERTED IN THE THICKEST PART OF A TENDERLOIN REGISTERS 155°F (68°C) AND JUST A HINT OF PINK REMAINS INSIDE. TRANSFER TO A CUTTING BOARD AND LET REST FOR 5 MINUTES BEFORE SLICING. SERVES 6.

MAKE AHEAD: BEFORE BAKING, COVER AND REFRIGERATE FOR UP TO 4 HOURS.

MAPLE GINGER PORK CHOPS

DELICIOUS AND EASY — MARINATE OVERNIGHT AND GRILL WHEN YOU COME HOME FROM WORK. SERVE WITH ROASTED NEW POTATOES AND STEAMED GREEN BEANS.

1/2 CUP	PURE MAPLE SYRUP	125 ML
1/2 CUP	DARK ALE OR REGULAR BEER	125 ML
1 TBSP	GRATED GINGERROOT	15 ML
4	BONE-IN PORK RIB CHOPS (ABOUT 1 1/4 LBS/625 G TOTAL)	4
	SALT AND FRESHLY GROUND BLACK PEPPER	

IN A BOWL, COMBINE MAPLE SYRUP, BEER AND GINGER. PLACE CHOPS IN A SHALLOW DISH OR A SEALABLE PLASTIC BAG AND POUR IN MARINADE. COVER OR SEAL AND REFRIGERATE FOR AT LEAST 4 HOURS OR OVERNIGHT.

PREHEAT BARBECUE GRILL TO MEDIUM-HIGH. REMOVE PORK FROM MARINADE, DISCARDING MARINADE. PLACE PORK ON GREASED GRILL AND GRILL FOR 8 TO 10 MINUTES, TURNING EVERY 2 MINUTES, UNTIL JUST A HINT OF PINK REMAINS INSIDE AND JUICES RUN CLEAR WHEN PORK IS PIERCED. SERVES 4.

TIP: BONE-IN PORK RIB CHOPS ARE A GOOD CHOICE FOR A SKILLET DINNER AS THEY STAY FAIRLY JUICY. YOU CAN ALSO MAKE THIS DISH WITH BONELESS PORK CENTER-CUT LOIN CHOPS, BUT THE MEAT WILL BE SOMEWHAT DRIER.

SKILLET PORK CHOPS WITH MUSHROOM SAUCE

REMEMBER PORK CHOPS AND MUSHROOM SOUP? WELL, THIS IS THE CONTEMPORARY VERSION. YOU COULD SERVE THESE TO ROYALTY! SERVE WITH STEAMED RICE AND A GREEN VEGETABLE.

2 TBSP	OLIVE OIL	25 ML
1 TBSP	FRESHLY SQUEEZED LEMON JUICE	15 ML
2	CLOVES GARLIC, MINCED	2
1/4 TSP	SALT	1 ML
PINCH	FRESHLY GROUND BLACK PEPPER	PINCH
4	BONE-IN PORK RIB CHOPS (ABOUT 1 1/4 LBS/625 G TOTAL)	4
2 TBSP	BUTTER	25 ML
2 CUPS	SLICED WHITE MUSHROOMS	500 ML
1	ONION, FINELY CHOPPED	1
1 TSP	DRIED SAGE	5 ML
2 TBSP	DRY SHERRY OR UNSWEETENED APPLE JUICE	25 ML
1/2 CUP	WHIPPING (35%) CREAM	125 ML
1/4 CUP	CHOPPED FRESH PARSLEY	50 ML

IN A BOWL, WHISK TOGETHER OIL, LEMON JUICE, GARLIC, SALT AND PEPPER. PLACE PORK IN A LARGE SHALLOW DISH AND POUR IN MARINADE, TURNING TO COAT. COVER AND REFRIGERATE FOR 30 MINUTES.

IN A LARGE SKILLET, MELT BUTTER OVER MEDIUM-HIGH HEAT. SAUTÉ MUSHROOMS, ONION AND SAGE FOR 5 TO 7 MINUTES OR UNTIL VEGETABLES ARE SOFTENED AND ANY LIQUID RELEASED FROM THE MUSHROOMS HAS EVAPORATED. TRANSFER TO A BOWL AND KEEP WARM.

REMOVE PORK FROM MARINADE, DISCARDING MARINADE. IN THE SAME SKILLET, OVER MEDIUM-HIGH HEAT, COOK PORK FOR 4 TO 5 MINUTES PER SIDE OR UNTIL BROWNED ON BOTH SIDES, JUST A HINT OF PINK REMAINS INSIDE AND JUICES RUN CLEAR WHEN PORK IS PIERCED. IF CHOPS START TO BROWN TOO QUICKLY, REDUCE HEAT TO MEDIUM. RETURN MUSHROOM MIXTURE TO PAN, ADD SHERRY AND BRING TO A BOIL. REDUCE HEAT AND SIMMER UNTIL SHERRY IS ALMOST EVAPORATED. STIR IN CREAM AND HEAT GENTLY. SPRINKLE WITH PARSLEY. SERVES 4.

TIP: BONE-IN PORK RIB CHOPS ARE A GOOD CHOICE FOR A SKILLET DINNER AS THEY STAY FAIRLY JUICY. YOU CAN ALSO MAKE THIS DISH WITH BONELESS PORK CENTER-CUT LOIN CHOPS, BUT THE MEAT WILL BE SOMEWHAT DRIER.

I'VE REACHED THE AGE WHERE I NO LONGER CARE WHAT ANYONE THINKS. IS THAT OKAY WITH YOU?

PORK CHOPS WITH APPLES AND BUTTERNUT SQUASH

THE PORK CHOPS, FRUIT AND VEGETABLES COOK TOGETHER IN THE SAME SKILLET TO MAKE A MILD SWEET-AND-SOUR SAUCE. SERVE WITH CREAMY MASHED POTATOES FOR A FAST AND NUTRITIOUS DINNER.

1 1/2 CUPS	UNSWEETENED APPLE JUICE	375 ML
1 TBSP	HONEY MUSTARD	15 ML
1 TBSP	PURE MAPLE SYRUP OR LIQUID HONEY	15 ML
1 TBSP	CIDER VINEGAR	15 ML
	SALT AND FRESHLY GROUND BLACK PEPPER	
4	BONE-IN PORK RIB CHOPS (ABOUT 1 1/4 LBS/625 G TOTAL)	4
1 TBSP	VEGETABLE OIL	15 ML
1 TBSP	BUTTER	15 ML
1	LARGE LEEK OR ONION, THINLY SLICED	1
1/2	SMALL BUTTERNUT SQUASH, PEELED AND GRATED (ABOUT 2 CUPS/500 ML)	1/2
2	RED APPLES (UNPEELED), THINLY SLICED	2
	CHOPPED FRESH PARSLEY	

IN A MEDIUM BOWL, WHISK TOGETHER APPLE JUICE, HONEY MUSTARD, MAPLE SYRUP, VINEGAR AND SALT AND PEPPER TO TASTE; SET ASIDE. SPRINKLE PORK ON BOTH SIDES WITH SALT AND PEPPER. IN A LARGE SKILLET, HEAT OIL OVER MEDIUM HEAT. COOK PORK FOR 4 TO 5 MINUTES PER SIDE OR UNTIL BROWNED ON BOTH SIDES, JUST A HINT OF PINK REMAINS INSIDE AND JUICES RUN CLEAR WHEN PORK IS PIERCED. TRANSFER TO A PLATE AND KEEP WARM. IN THE SAME SKILLET, MELT BUTTER OVER MEDIUM HEAT. SAUTÉ LEEK AND SQUASH FOR

2 MINUTES OR UNTIL SOFTENED. ADD APPLES AND APPLE JUICE MIXTURE; BRING TO A BOIL. REDUCE HEAT, COVER AND SIMMER FOR ABOUT 5 MINUTES OR UNTIL APPLES ARE SOFTENED BUT NOT MUSHY. RETURN PORK AND ANY ACCUMULATED JUICES TO PAN AND BRING SAUCE BACK TO A BOIL. REMOVE FROM HEAT IMMEDIATELY AND SPRINKLE WITH PARSLEY. SERVE PORK HEAPED WITH A COUPLE OF GENEROUS SPOONFULS OF SAUCE. SERVES 4.

TIP: BONE-IN PORK RIB CHOPS ARE A GOOD CHOICE FOR A SKILLET DINNER AS THEY STAY FAIRLY JUICY. YOU CAN ALSO MAKE THIS DISH WITH BONELESS PORK CENTER-CUT LOIN CHOPS, BUT THE MEAT WILL BE SOMEWHAT DRIER.

MINISTER PRONOUNCING CONTEMPORARY WEDDING VOWS: "LOVE, HONOR AND CHERISH BEING TOO LOFTY A GOAL, DO YOU PROMISE TO LOOK UP, NOD AND PRETEND TO BE LISTENING?"

ORANGE-CHILI PORK STIR-FRY

PORK TENDERLOINS VARY QUITE A BIT IN SIZE — LOOK
FOR A LARGE ONE FOR THIS STIR-FRY. SERVE WITH
STEAMED RICE OR BOILED NOODLES.

3/4 CUP	ORANGE JUICE	175 ML
2 TBSP	HOISIN SAUCE	25 ML
2 TBSP	DRY SHERRY	25 ML
1 TSP	CORNSTARCH	5 ML
1/2 TSP	ASIAN CHILI PASTE (SEE TIP, OPPOSITE)	2 ML
1 TBSP	VEGETABLE OIL	15 ML
1	PORK TENDERLOIN (ABOUT 1 LB/500 G), TRIMMED AND CUT INTO THIN SLICES	1
1	ONION, CHOPPED	1
3 CUPS	BROCCOLI FLORETS AND CHOPPED PEELED STEMS (ABOUT 1 BUNCH)	750 ML
3	CARROTS, THINLY SLICED	3
2 TBSP	CHICKEN BROTH	25 ML
2	CLOVES GARLIC, MINCED	2
1 TBSP	CHOPPED GINGERROOT	15 ML
2	GREEN ONIONS, CHOPPED	2

IN A SMALL BOWL, WHISK TOGETHER ORANGE JUICE,
HOISIN SAUCE, SHERRY, CORNSTARCH AND CHILI PASTE;
SET ASIDE. IN A LARGE SKILLET OR WOK, HEAT OIL OVER
MEDIUM-HIGH HEAT. STIR-FRY PORK UNTIL BROWNED AND
JUST A HINT OF PINK REMAINS INSIDE. USING A SLOTTED
SPOON, TRANSFER TO A PLATE AND KEEP WARM. ADD
ONION TO OIL REMAINING IN SKILLET AND STIR-FRY FOR
ABOUT 5 MINUTES OR UNTIL SLIGHTLY SOFTENED. ADD
BROCCOLI, CARROTS AND CHICKEN BROTH, COVER AND
STEAM FOR ABOUT 4 MINUTES OR UNTIL VEGETABLES

ARE TENDER BUT NOT SOGGY. MAKE A WELL IN THE CENTER AND ADD GARLIC AND GINGER; STIR-FRY FOR 15 SECONDS OR UNTIL FRAGRANT. RETURN PORK AND ANY ACCUMULATED JUICES TO PAN. ADD ORANGE JUICE MIXTURE AND BRING TO A BOIL. REDUCE HEAT AND SIMMER, STIRRING, FOR 30 TO 45 SECONDS OR UNTIL SAUCE IS THICKENED AND HEATED THROUGH. SPRINKLE WITH GREEN ONIONS. SERVES 4.

TIP: ASIAN CHILI PASTE (NOT TO BE CONFUSED WITH SWEET ASIAN CHILI SAUCE) IS USUALLY A MIX OF GROUND FRESH CHILE PEPPERS, VINEGAR, SUGAR AND SALT. IT ADDS ZIP TO SOUPS, STIR-FRIES, SAUCES AND PIZZAS, BUT IT PACKS A LOT OF HEAT, SO ADD IT $\frac{1}{4}$ TSP (1 ML) AT A TIME, TASTING AS YOU GO. A POPULAR VERSION, FAVORED BY PROFESSIONAL CHEFS, IS SAMBAL OELEK. LOOK FOR IT IN THE ASIAN AISLE OF THE SUPERMARKET. IF YOU CAN'T FIND ASIAN CHILI PASTE, SUBSTITUTE HOT PEPPER FLAKES TO TASTE.

WE ARE SO OFTEN CAUGHT UP IN THE THICK OF THIN THINGS.

HERBED LAMB CHOPS WITH MINT SAUCE

IT'S FRIDAY NIGHT, SO OPEN UP A GOOD BOTTLE OF RED WINE AND FIRE UP THE OVEN. THESE LAMB CHOPS ARE SO GOOD. SERVE WITH CREAMY GARLIC MASHED POTATOES AND A STEAMED GREEN VEGETABLE.

MINT SAUCE

3 TBSP	FINELY SHREDDED FRESH MINT	45 ML
2 TBSP	BOILING WATER	25 ML
2 TO 3 TSP	PACKED BROWN SUGAR	10 TO 15 ML
2 TBSP	RICE VINEGAR	25 ML
12	LAMB LOIN CHOPS (EACH ABOUT 3 OZ/90 G)	12
	SALT AND FRESHLY GROUND BLACK PEPPER	
2 TBSP	OLIVE OIL	25 ML
2 TBSP	DIJON MUSTARD	25 ML
1	CLOVE GARLIC, MINCED	1
2 TBSP	CHOPPED FRESH MINT	25 ML
2 TBSP	CHOPPED FRESH PARSLEY	25 ML
1 TSP	DRIED ROSEMARY	5 ML
1 TSP	DRIED THYME	5 ML

MINT SAUCE: IN A SMALL BOWL, COMBINE MINT, BOILING WATER AND BROWN SUGAR TO TASTE, STIRRING GENTLY UNTIL SUGAR IS DISSOLVED. STIR IN VINEGAR. LET STAND FOR 1 HOUR TO LET FLAVORS DEVELOP.

PREHEAT OVEN TO 375°F (190°C). GREASE A LARGE RIMMED BAKING SHEET (OR LINE WITH GREASED FOIL FOR EASIER

CLEANUP). SEASON LAMB WITH SALT AND PEPPER. BRUSH ALL OVER WITH OLIVE OIL AND SPREAD WITH MUSTARD. IN A SMALL BOWL, COMBINE GARLIC, MINT, PARSLEY, ROSEMARY AND THYME. SPRINKLE OVER LAMB, PRESSING GENTLY TO MAKE IT STICK. PLACE ON PREPARED BAKING SHEET AND BAKE FOR 12 MINUTES FOR MEDIUM-RARE, OR UNTIL DESIRED DONENESS. SERVE MINT SAUCE ON THE SIDE. SERVES 4.

I HATE HOUSEKEEPING. YOU WASH THE DISHES AND CLEAN THE FLOORS, AND SIX MONTHS LATER YOU HAVE TO DO IT ALL OVER AGAIN.

BRAISED LAMB SHANKS

SLOW FOOD TO SAVOR. SERVE WITH MASHED
POTATOES AND STEAMED BROCCOLI.

1 1/2 TBSP	VEGETABLE OIL	22 ML
3	CARROTS, THINLY SLICED	3
2	ONIONS, THINLY SLICED	2
2	STALKS CELERY, THINLY SLICED	2
4	CLOVES GARLIC, MINCED	4
1 TSP	EACH DRIED ROSEMARY AND THYME	5 ML
2	BAY LEAVES	2
1 TSP	SALT	5 ML
6	LAMB SHANKS (ABOUT 4 LBS/2 KG TOTAL)	6
2 CUPS	DRY RED WINE	500 ML
2 CUPS	CHICKEN BROTH	500 ML
1/4 CUP	BALSAMIC VINEGAR	50 ML
2 TBSP	ALL-PURPOSE FLOUR	25 ML
2 TBSP	TOMATO PASTE	25 ML
	FRESHLY GROUND BLACK PEPPER	
2 TBSP	CHOPPED FRESH PARSLEY	25 ML
2 TBSP	GRATED ORANGE ZEST	25 ML

PREHEAT OVEN TO 325°F (160°C). IN A LARGE DUTCH OVEN,
HEAT OIL OVER MEDIUM-HIGH HEAT. SAUTÉ CARROTS,
ONIONS AND CELERY UNTIL SOFTENED. ADD GARLIC,
ROSEMARY, THYME, BAY LEAVES AND SALT; SAUTÉ FOR
30 SECONDS. PLACE LAMB ON TOP OF VEGETABLES. IN A
BOWL, COMBINE WINE, BROTH, VINEGAR, FLOUR, TOMATO
PASTE AND PEPPER TO TASTE. POUR OVER LAMB AND
BRING TO A BOIL. COVER AND BAKE FOR 2 1/2 HOURS OR
UNTIL LAMB IS FORK-TENDER. SKIM FAT FROM SAUCE AND
SPRINKLE WITH PARSLEY AND ORANGE ZEST. SERVES 6.

VEGETABLES

GREEN BEANS WITH TOASTED ALMONDS

HERE'S A SPEEDY SIDE DISH THAT WORKS ESPECIALLY WELL WITH GRILLED MEAT OR FISH.

1/4 CUP	CHICKEN OR VEGETABLE BROTH, DIVIDED	50 ML
2	GREEN ONIONS, THINLY SLICED	2
1	CLOVE GARLIC, MINCED	1
12 OZ	GREEN BEANS, TRIMMED AND CUT INTO 1-INCH (2.5 CM) LENGTHS (ABOUT 2 1/2 CUPS/625 ML)	375 G
	SALT AND FRESHLY GROUND BLACK PEPPER	
2 TBSP	SLICED ALMONDS, TOASTED (SEE TIP, PAGE 165)	25 ML

IN A LARGE SKILLET, HEAT 1 TBSP (15 ML) OF THE CHICKEN BROTH OVER MEDIUM-HIGH HEAT. COOK GREEN ONIONS AND GARLIC FOR ABOUT 20 SECONDS OR UNTIL FRAGRANT. ADD GREEN BEANS AND THE REMAINING STOCK; BRING TO A SIMMER. COVER AND STEAM FOR 8 TO 10 MINUTES, SHAKING THE PAN OCCASIONALLY, UNTIL BEANS ARE TENDER. ADD MORE BROTH IF BEANS GET TOO DRY BEFORE THEY'RE READY. REMOVE FROM HEAT AND SEASON TO TASTE WITH SALT AND PEPPER. SPRINKLE WITH ALMONDS. SERVES 4.

TIP: A SUPER-FAST WAY TO BRIGHTEN THE FLAVOR OF STEAMED GREEN BEANS IS SIMPLY TO SQUEEZE THE JUICE OF HALF A LEMON OVER TOP JUST BEFORE SERVING.

GLAZED CARROTS

BYE-BYE BORING CARROTS.

1 LB	CARROTS (5 TO 6 MEDIUM), CUT INTO 1/4-INCH (0.5 CM) THICK ROUNDS	500 G
1 TBSP	BUTTER	15 ML
1 TBSP	LIQUID HONEY	15 ML
1 TBSP	ORANGE JUICE	15 ML
1/2 TSP	DRIED THYME	2 ML
	SALT AND FRESHLY GROUND BLACK PEPPER	
1/4 CUP	PISTACHIOS OR ALMONDS, CHOPPED	50 ML

IN A LARGE POT OF BOILING SALTED WATER, COOK CARROTS FOR ABOUT 5 MINUTES OR UNTIL TENDER-CRISP. DRAIN. IN A LARGE SKILLET, MELT BUTTER OVER MEDIUM HEAT. STIR IN HONEY, ORANGE JUICE AND THYME. ADD CARROTS AND SIMMER, STIRRING OCCASIONALLY, FOR 5 MINUTES OR UNTIL CARROTS ARE NICELY COATED AND GLAZE IS SYRUPY. SEASON TO TASTE WITH SALT AND PEPPER. SPRINKLE WITH PISTACHIOS. SERVES 4.

MY LIFE IS A CIRCUS WITHOUT THE TENT.

BAKED CHEESY CAULIFLOWER

MAKE AHEAD FOR A FAMILY DINNER AND YOU WON'T
HAVE TO FUSS WITH LAST-MINUTE VEGETABLES. THIS
DISH ALSO WORKS WELL AS PART OF A HOT BUFFET.

1	LARGE HEAD CAULIFLOWER	1
1/4 CUP	BUTTER	50 ML
1/2 CUP	ALL-PURPOSE FLOUR	125 ML
4 CUPS	WHOLE OR 2% MILK	1 L
1 TBSP	DIJON MUSTARD	15 ML
3 CUPS	SHREDDED CHEDDAR CHEESE	750 ML
1/2 CUP	FRESHLY GRATED PARMESAN CHEESE, DIVIDED	125 ML
1/2 TSP	HOT PEPPER SAUCE	2 ML
	SALT AND FRESHLY GROUND BLACK PEPPER	
3/4 CUP	DRY BREAD CRUMBS	175 ML

PREHEAT OVEN TO 350°F (180°C). GREASE AN 11- BY
7-INCH (28 BY 18 CM) BAKING DISH. BREAK CAULIFLOWER
INTO FLORETS, DISCARDING LEAVES AND HARD CORE.
IN A LARGE POT OF BOILING SALTED WATER, COOK
CAULIFLOWER FOR ABOUT 4 MINUTES OR UNTIL JUST
TENDER. (DO NOT OVERCOOK, AS IT WILL CONTINUE TO
COOK IN THE SAUCE.) DRAIN THOROUGHLY AND TRANSFER
TO PREPARED BAKING DISH. IN A LARGE SAUCEPAN, MELT
BUTTER OVER MEDIUM HEAT. ADD FLOUR AND COOK,
STIRRING, UNTIL IT LOOKS SANDY. GRADUALLY WHISK
IN MILK AND MUSTARD; BRING TO A BOIL. REDUCE HEAT
AND SIMMER, STIRRING CONSTANTLY, FOR 8 MINUTES
OR UNTIL THICKENED. ADD CHEDDAR, 1/4 CUP (50 ML)
OF THE PARMESAN, HOT PEPPER SAUCE AND SALT AND

PEPPER TO TASTE, STIRRING UNTIL CHEESE IS MELTED. POUR OVER CAULIFLOWER. COMBINE BREAD CRUMBS AND THE REMAINING PARMESAN AND SPRINKLE EVENLY OVER TOP. BAKE FOR ABOUT 20 MINUTES OR UNTIL SAUCE IS BUBBLING AND TOP IS NICELY BROWNED. SERVES 4 TO 6.

MAKE AHEAD: PREPARE CAULIFLOWER IN CHEESE SAUCE, BUT DO NOT SPRINKLE WITH BREAD CRUMB MIXTURE. LET COOL, COVER AND REFRIGERATE FOR UP TO 1 DAY. WHEN READY TO REHEAT, SPRINKLE WITH BREAD CRUMB MIXTURE AND BAKE FOR 30 TO 40 MINUTES.

COLORFUL CORN

ALL THE COLOR AND VEGETABLE GOODNESS YOU NEED IN ONE EASY DISH — WHAT A GOOD MOM YOU ARE. SAUTÉING THE CORN MAKES ALL THE DIFFERENCE.

1 TBSP	BUTTER	15 ML
2 CUPS	FROZEN CORN KERNELS	500 ML
16	SPEARS ASPARAGUS, TRIMMED AND CUT INTO 1/2-INCH (1 CM) LENGTHS	16
1	RED BELL PEPPER, CHOPPED	1
	SALT AND FRESHLY GROUND BLACK PEPPER	

IN A LARGE SKILLET, MELT BUTTER OVER MEDIUM-HIGH HEAT. SAUTÉ CORN, ASPARAGUS AND RED PEPPER FOR 5 TO 7 MINUTES OR UNTIL VEGETABLES ARE JUST STARTING TO BROWN AND ARE TENDER BUT NOT MUSHY. SEASON TO TASTE WITH SALT AND PEPPER. SERVES 4.

CORN FRITTERS

THESE CORN FRITTERS ARE SWEET AND CRISP.
SERVE THEM, DRIZZLED WITH REAL MAPLE SYRUP,
ALONGSIDE BACON AND EGGS FOR A HEARTY BRUNCH.
OR MAKE MINI VERSIONS (SEE TIP, OPPOSITE)
AND PAIR THEM WITH SWEET CHILI DIPPING SAUCE
TO SERVE AS AN APPETIZER.

1	CAN (12 OZ/340 ML) CORN KERNELS, WELL DRAINED	1
3	GREEN ONIONS, CHOPPED	3
1	EGG	1
1/4 CUP	ALL-PURPOSE FLOUR	50 ML
2 TBSP	CORNMEAL	25 ML
2 TBSP	CHOPPED FRESH CILANTRO	25 ML
1 TSP	GRANULATED SUGAR	5 ML
1/2 TSP	HOT PEPPER SAUCE	2 ML
1 TSP	SALT	5 ML
1/4 TSP	FRESHLY GROUND BLACK PEPPER	1 ML
	VEGETABLE OIL	

IN A FOOD PROCESSOR, COMBINE 1/2 CUP (125 ML) OF THE
CORN, GREEN ONIONS, EGG, FLOUR, CORNMEAL, CILANTRO,
SUGAR, HOT PEPPER SAUCE, SALT AND PEPPER; PULSE A
FEW TIMES TO BLEND. TRANSFER TO A LARGE BOWL AND
STIR IN THE REMAINING CORN. COVER AND REFRIGERATE
FOR 20 MINUTES TO ALLOW BATTER TO THICKEN
SLIGHTLY.

IN A LARGE SKILLET, HEAT 2 TBSP (25 ML) OIL OVER
MEDIUM-HIGH HEAT. WORKING IN BATCHES, DROP IN
BATTER IN 1/4-CUP (50 ML) SCOOPS AND COOK FOR 3 TO
4 MINUTES PER SIDE, PRESSING DOWN GENTLY WITH A

SPATULA, UNTIL GOLDEN BROWN ON BOTH SIDES AND SET ON THE INSIDE. TRANSFER FRITTERS TO A PLATE LINED WITH PAPER TOWELS AND KEEP WARM. REPEAT WITH THE REMAINING BATTER, ADDING AND HEATING OIL AS NEEDED BETWEEN BATCHES. MAKES ABOUT 6 LARGE FRITTERS.

MAKE AHEAD: LET FRITTERS COOL, COVER AND REFRIGERATE FOR UP TO 1 DAY OR LAYER BETWEEN WAXED PAPER IN AN AIRTIGHT CONTAINER AND FREEZE FOR UP TO 2 WEEKS. REHEAT ON BAKING SHEETS IN A 375°F (190°C) OVEN FOR 15 MINUTES.

TIP: FOR APPETIZER-SIZE FRITTERS, DROP TABLESPOONFULS (15 ML) OF BATTER INTO PAN. THEY WILL ONLY NEED ABOUT 2 MINUTES PER SIDE TO BROWN.

YOU KNOW YOU'RE GETTING OLDER WHEN YOUR BODY MAKES MORE NOISE THAN YOUR CAR.

CREAMY PARSNIP AND TOMATO BAKE

THIS IS SUCH AN UNUSUAL COMBINATION — AND IT TASTES GREAT! IT GOES WELL WITH ROAST MEATS AND BAKED HAM.

3 TBSP	VEGETABLE OIL	45 ML
2 LBS	PARSNIPS (ABOUT 5), PEELED AND THINLY SLICED	1 KG
	SALT AND FRESHLY GROUND BLACK PEPPER	
1 CUP	WHIPPING (35%) CREAM	250 ML
4 TO 5	TOMATOES, PEELED (SEE TIP, PAGE 267), SEEDED AND SLICED	4 TO 5
1 CUP	SHREDDED SWISS CHEESE	250 ML
1/4 CUP	DRY BREAD CRUMBS	50 ML
1 TBSP	BUTTER	15 ML

PREHEAT OVEN TO 325°F (160°C). GREASE AN 8-CUP (2 L) CASSEROLE DISH. IN A LARGE SKILLET, HEAT OIL OVER MEDIUM HEAT. SAUTÉ PARSNIPS FOR 4 TO 5 MINUTES OR UNTIL SLIGHTLY SOFTENED AND STARTING TO BROWN. PLACE ONE-THIRD OF THE PARSNIPS IN PREPARED DISH. SEASON TO TASTE WITH SALT AND PEPPER AND POUR IN 1/3 CUP (75 ML) CREAM. PLACE ONE-THIRD OF THE TOMATO SLICES ON TOP. SPRINKLE WITH 1/3 CUP (75 ML) CHEESE. REPEAT LAYERS TWO MORE TIMES. SPRINKLE WITH BREAD CRUMBS AND DOT WITH BUTTER. BAKE, UNCOVERED, FOR ABOUT 40 MINUTES OR UNTIL PARSNIPS ARE FORK-TENDER AND CASSEROLE IS BUBBLING AND BROWN. SERVES 6.

MAKE AHEAD: AFTER ASSEMBLING THE CASSEROLE, COVER AND REFRIGERATE FOR UP TO 6 HOURS. BAKE FOR 45 TO 50 MINUTES.

STIR-FRIED SPINACH

STIR-FRYING IS AN APPEALING WAY TO COOK LEAFY GREENS SUCH AS SPINACH, SWISS CHARD AND BOK CHOY. SERVE THIS AS A "BED" UNDER GRILLED OR PAN-FRIED FISH OR AS AN EASY SIDE DISH.

1½ LBS	SPINACH (8 TO 10 CUPS/2 TO 2.5 L PACKED)	750 G
1 TBSP	BUTTER	15 ML
2 TBSP	TOASTED PINE NUTS (SEE TIP, PAGE 165)	25 ML
2	CLOVES GARLIC, MINCED	2
	SALT AND FRESHLY GROUND BLACK PEPPER	

REMOVE ANY TOUGH STEMS FROM SPINACH. WASH THOROUGHLY IN COLD WATER AND DRY IN A SALAD SPINNER. IN A LARGE SKILLET, MELT BUTTER OVER MEDIUM-HIGH HEAT. ADD A FEW HANDFULS OF SPINACH AND, AS IT STARTS TO COOK DOWN, GRADUALLY ADD MORE UNTIL IT IS ALL IN THE PAN. SAUTÉ FOR ABOUT 3 MINUTES OR UNTIL WILTED. USING A SPATULA, PUSH THE SPINACH TO ONE SIDE OF THE PAN. ADD PINE NUTS AND GARLIC TO THE JUICES IN THE CLEARED SPACE AND SAUTÉ FOR ABOUT 2 MINUTES OR UNTIL FRAGRANT AND PINE NUTS ARE LIGHTLY BROWNED. STIR TO COMBINE WITH THE SPINACH AND SEASON TO TASTE WITH SALT AND PEPPER. SERVES 4.

TIP: MAKE A DOUBLE BATCH OF STIR-FRIED SPINACH AND SERVE HALF FOR DINNER. THE NEXT DAY, TOSS THE REMAINING PORTION WITH FRESHLY COOKED PASTA OR STIR INTO STEAMED RICE FOR ANOTHER DELICIOUS AND HEALTHY SIDE DISH.

SCALLOPED POTATOES WITH FENNEL

FENNEL ADDS A MELLOW ANISEED FLAVOR TO THIS FAMILY FAVORITE.

I	FENNEL BULB	I
4 TBSP	BUTTER, DIVIDED	60 ML
I	ONION, THINLY SLICED	I
2	CLOVES GARLIC, MINCED	2
4	BAKING POTATOES, PEELED AND THINLY SLICED	4
	SALT AND FRESHLY GROUND BLACK PEPPER	
I½ CUPS	WHIPPING (35%) CREAM	375 ML
I CUP	CHICKEN BROTH	250 ML

PREHEAT OVEN TO 375°F (190°C). GREASE AN 8-INCH (20 CM) SQUARE BAKING DISH. IF THE FENNEL HAS THE FEATHERY STALKS ATTACHED, TRIM THEM OFF ABOUT I INCH (2.5 CM) ABOVE THE BULB. CUT IN HALF VERTICALLY AND REMOVE THE WOODY CORE, THEN SLICE EACH HALF VERY THINLY. IN A LARGE SKILLET, MELT 2 TBSP (25 ML) OF THE BUTTER OVER MEDIUM-HIGH HEAT. SAUTÉ FENNEL, ONION AND GARLIC FOR 5 TO 7 MINUTES OR UNTIL SOFTENED. LAYER HALF THE POTATOES IN PREPARED DISH. SEASON TO TASTE WITH SALT AND PEPPER. SPOON FENNEL AND ONIONS OVER TOP. LAYER WITH THE REMAINING POTATOES AND SEASON WITH SALT AND PEPPER. IN A BOWL, WHISK TOGETHER WHIPPING CREAM AND CHICKEN BROTH. POUR OVER POTATOES. PLACE DISH ON A BAKING SHEET (THE SAUCE SOMETIMES BUBBLES OVER THE EDGE). IN A SMALL MICROWAVE-SAFE BOWL,

MELT THE REMAINING BUTTER IN THE MICROWAVE. BRUSH TOPS OF POTATOES WITH MELTED BUTTER. COVER AND BAKE FOR 30 MINUTES. UNCOVER AND BAKE FOR 20 TO 30 MINUTES OR UNTIL TOP IS BROWN AND POTATOES ARE TENDER. SERVES 6.

HORSERADISH MASHED POTATOES

MAGNIFICENT WITH ANY BEEF DISH.

2 LBS	POTATOES, PEELED AND CUT INTO LARGE CHUNKS	1 KG
1 CUP	MILK	250 ML
3 TBSP	BUTTER	45 ML
2 TBSP	CREAMED HORSERADISH	25 ML
	SALT AND FRESHLY GROUND BLACK PEPPER	

IN A LARGE POT OF BOILING SALTED WATER, COOK POTATOES UNTIL TENDER, ABOUT 20 MINUTES. DRAIN AND TRANSFER TO A LARGE BOWL. IN A MICROWAVE-SAFE MEASURING CUP, COMBINE MILK AND BUTTER; MICROWAVE ON HIGH FOR 40 SECONDS TO WARM. ADD MILK MIXTURE AND HORSERADISH TO POTATOES AND MASH THOROUGHLY. SEASON TO TASTE WITH SALT AND PEPPER. SERVES 6 TO 8.

MAKE AHEAD: SPREAD MASHED POTATOES IN A BAKING DISH, LET COOL AND REFRIGERATE FOR UP TO 1 DAY. REHEAT IN THE MICROWAVE FOR ABOUT 3 MINUTES ON HIGH, STIRRING ONCE.

GOURMET STUFFED POTATOES, THREE WAYS

A MIDWEEK MEAL IN A PEEL. HERE ARE THREE IDEAS FOR THESE SUPER-SIZED SPUDS WITH CRISPY SHELLS AND FLUFFY FILLINGS. SERVE WITH A SALAD OR, FOR A LAZY WEEKEND SUPPER, WITH CRANBERRY BAKED BEANS (PAGE 257).

GARLICKY CHEESE AND HERB–STUFFED POTATOES

5	LARGE BAKING POTATOES	5
2 TBSP	OLIVE OIL	25 ML
1/3 CUP	WHIPPING (35%) CREAM	75 ML
4 TBSP	BUTTER	60 ML
1	PACKAGE (5 OZ/142 G) BOURSIN GARLIC-AND-HERB-FLAVORED FRESH SOFT CHEESE (SEE TIP, PAGE 39)	1
4	CLOVES ROASTED GARLIC (SEE TIP, OPPOSITE), MASHED	4
4 TBSP	CHOPPED FRESH CHIVES, DILL OR PARSLEY	60 ML
	SALT AND FRESHLY GROUND BLACK PEPPER	

PREHEAT OVEN TO 375°F (190°C). PRICK POTATOES ALL OVER WITH A FORK. RUB WITH OIL. PLACE DIRECTLY ON MIDDLE RACK OF OVEN AND BAKE FOR 1 1/4 TO 1 1/2 HOURS OR UNTIL TENDER. REMOVE FROM OVEN, LEAVING OVEN ON, AND LET COOL SLIGHTLY. SLICE OFF THE TOP QUARTER FROM EACH OF 4 POTATOES. SCRAPE THE FLESH FROM THESE TOPS INTO A LARGE BOWL AND DISCARD THE SKIN. USING A SPOON, SCOOP THE FLESH FROM THE LOWER PART OF THE 4 POTATOES INTO THE BOWL,

LEAVING A THIN LAYER OF POTATO INSIDE THE SKIN. CUT THE FIFTH POTATO IN HALF, SCRAPE THE FLESH INTO THE BOWL AND DISCARD THE SKIN. ADD CREAM, BUTTER, SOFT CHEESE AND ROASTED GARLIC TO THE BOWL AND MASH POTATOES UNTIL SMOOTH AND CREAMY. STIR IN CHIVES AND SEASON TO TASTE WITH SALT AND PEPPER. SPOON FILLING BACK INTO POTATO SHELLS. (THEY WILL BE HEAPING FULL!) PLACE ON A BAKING SHEET AND BAKE FOR ABOUT 30 MINUTES OR UNTIL TOPS ARE BROWNED. SERVES 4.

MAKE AHEAD: LET COOL, PLACE STUFFED POTATOES IN A SHALLOW AIRTIGHT CONTAINER AND REFRIGERATE FOR UP TO I DAY. OR WRAP EACH STUFFED POTATO IN PLASTIC WRAP, PLACE IN AN AIRTIGHT CONTAINER AND FREEZE FOR UP TO 2 WEEKS. REHEAT FROM FROZEN IN A 350°F (180°C) OVEN FOR 50 TO 60 MINUTES.

TIP: ROASTED GARLIC HAS A MORE MELLOW FLAVOR THAN RAW GARLIC, AND IT'S EASY TO DO. SLICE THE TOP QUARTER OFF A BULB OF GARLIC. DRIZZLE WITH A LITTLE OLIVE OIL, WRAP IN FOIL AND PLACE ON A BAKING SHEET. ROAST IN A 375°F (190°C) OVEN FOR ABOUT 30 MINUTES. LET COOL AND SQUEEZE THE CLOVES OUT OF THEIR SKINS. YOU CAN ROAST SEVERAL BULBS OF GARLIC AT A TIME SO YOU'LL ALWAYS HAVE THEM ON HAND. TO FREEZE ROASTED GARLIC, PLACE THE SKINNED CLOVES ON A BAKING SHEET, FREEZE UNTIL HARD, THEN WRAP IN PLASTIC WRAP AND STORE IN AN AIRTIGHT CONTAINER FOR UP TO 2 MONTHS.

HAM AND MUSHROOM-STUFFED POTATOES

5	LARGE BAKING POTATOES	5
3 TBSP	OLIVE OIL, DIVIDED	45 ML
2 CUPS	SLICED WHITE MUSHROOMS	500 ML
I CUP	CHOPPED BOILED HAM	250 ML
4	GREEN ONIONS, CHOPPED	4
$1/3$ CUP	WHIPPING (35%) CREAM	75 ML
4 TBSP	BUTTER	60 ML
I TBSP	DIJON MUSTARD	15 ML
	SALT AND FRESHLY GROUND BLACK PEPPER	
$1^1/4$ CUPS	SHREDDED SHARP (OLD) CHEDDAR CHEESE	300 ML

PREHEAT OVEN TO 375°F (190°C). PRICK POTATOES ALL OVER WITH A FORK. RUB WITH 2 TBSP (25 ML) OF THE OIL. PLACE DIRECTLY ON MIDDLE RACK OF OVEN AND BAKE FOR $1^1/4$ TO $1^1/2$ HOURS OR UNTIL TENDER. REMOVE FROM OVEN, LEAVING OVEN ON, AND LET COOL SLIGHTLY.

MEANWHILE, IN A LARGE SKILLET, HEAT THE REMAINING OIL OVER MEDIUM HEAT. SAUTÉ MUSHROOMS FOR ABOUT 5 MINUTES OR UNTIL SOFTENED AND BROWNED. REMOVE FROM HEAT AND STIR IN HAM AND GREEN ONIONS; SET ASIDE. SLICE OFF THE TOP QUARTER FROM EACH OF 4 POTATOES. SCRAPE THE FLESH FROM THESE TOPS INTO A LARGE BOWL AND DISCARD THE SKIN. USING A SPOON, SCOOP THE FLESH FROM THE LOWER PART OF THE 4 POTATOES INTO THE BOWL, LEAVING A THIN LAYER OF POTATO INSIDE THE SKIN. CUT THE FIFTH POTATO IN

HALF, SCRAPE THE FLESH INTO THE BOWL AND DISCARD THE SKIN. ADD CREAM, BUTTER AND MUSTARD TO THE BOWL AND MASH POTATOES UNTIL SMOOTH AND CREAMY. SEASON TO TASTE WITH SALT AND PEPPER. STIR IN MUSHROOM MIXTURE AND 1 CUP (250 ML) OF THE CHEESE. SPOON FILLING BACK INTO POTATO SHELLS. (THEY WILL BE HEAPING FULL!) SPRINKLE THE REMAINING CHEESE OVER TOP. PLACE ON A BAKING SHEET AND BAKE FOR ABOUT 30 MINUTES OR UNTIL CHEESE IS MELTED. SERVES 4.

MAKE AHEAD: LET COOL, PLACE STUFFED POTATOES IN A SHALLOW AIRTIGHT CONTAINER AND REFRIGERATE FOR UP TO 1 DAY. OR WRAP EACH STUFFED POTATO IN PLASTIC WRAP, PLACE IN AN AIRTIGHT CONTAINER AND FREEZE FOR UP TO 2 WEEKS. REHEAT FROM FROZEN IN A 350°F (180°C) OVEN FOR 50 TO 60 MINUTES.

"BE YOURSELF — EVERYONE ELSE IS TAKEN."
— OSCAR WILDE

GREEK-STYLE STUFFED POTATOES

5	LARGE BAKING POTATOES	5
2 TBSP	OLIVE OIL	25 ML
$1/2$ CUP	SOUR CREAM	125 ML
4 TBSP	BUTTER	60 ML
4	GREEN ONIONS, CHOPPED	4
2	ROASTED RED BELL PEPPERS (SEE TIP, OPPOSITE), DRAINED AND CHOPPED	2
2	TOMATOES, SEEDED AND CHOPPED	2
2	CLOVES GARLIC, MINCED	2
1 CUP	CRUMBLED FETA CHEESE	250 ML
	SALT AND FRESHLY GROUND BLACK PEPPER	

PREHEAT OVEN TO 375°F (190°C). PRICK POTATOES ALL OVER WITH A FORK. RUB WITH OIL. PLACE DIRECTLY ON MIDDLE RACK OF OVEN AND BAKE FOR $1 1/4$ TO $1 1/2$ HOURS OR UNTIL TENDER. REMOVE FROM OVEN, LEAVING OVEN ON, AND LET COOL SLIGHTLY. SLICE OFF THE TOP QUARTER FROM EACH OF 4 POTATOES. SCRAPE THE FLESH FROM THESE TOPS INTO A LARGE BOWL AND DISCARD THE SKIN. USING A SPOON, SCOOP THE FLESH FROM THE LOWER PART OF THE 4 POTATOES INTO THE BOWL, LEAVING A THIN LAYER OF POTATO INSIDE THE SKIN. CUT THE FIFTH POTATO IN HALF, SCRAPE THE FLESH INTO THE BOWL AND DISCARD THE SKIN. ADD SOUR CREAM AND BUTTER TO THE BOWL AND MASH POTATOES UNTIL SMOOTH AND CREAMY. STIR IN GREEN ONIONS, ROASTED PEPPERS, TOMATOES, GARLIC AND FETA. SEASON TO TASTE WITH SALT AND PEPPER (REMEMBERING THAT

FETA IS VERY SALTY). SPOON FILLING BACK INTO POTATO SHELLS. (THEY WILL BE HEAPING FULL!) PLACE ON A BAKING SHEET AND BAKE FOR ABOUT 30 MINUTES OR UNTIL TOPS ARE BROWNED. SERVES 4.

MAKE AHEAD: LET COOL, PLACE STUFFED POTATOES IN A SHALLOW AIRTIGHT CONTAINER AND REFRIGERATE FOR UP TO 1 DAY. OR WRAP EACH STUFFED POTATO IN PLASTIC WRAP, PLACE IN AN AIRTIGHT CONTAINER AND FREEZE FOR UP TO 2 WEEKS. REHEAT FROM FROZEN IN A 350°F (180°C) OVEN FOR 50 TO 60 MINUTES.

TIP: ROASTED RED BELL PEPPERS ARE SOLD IN JARS OR IN THE DELI SECTION OF YOUR SUPERMARKET, BUT IT'S EASY TO ROAST YOUR OWN. PREHEAT OVEN TO 425°F (220°C). CUT PEPPERS INTO QUARTERS, REMOVE SEEDS AND BRUSH WITH OLIVE OIL. PLACE SKIN SIDE DOWN ON A BAKING SHEET LINED WITH PARCHMENT PAPER AND ROAST FOR ABOUT 30 MINUTES OR UNTIL SKINS ARE BLACKENED AND PUFFED. TRANSFER PEPPERS TO A BOWL, COVER AND LET STAND FOR 15 MINUTES TO STEAM, THEN PEEL OFF SKINS. STORE IN AN AIRTIGHT CONTAINER IN THE REFRIGERATOR FOR UP TO 5 DAYS. OR CUT INTO STRIPS, SPREAD IN A SINGLE LAYER ON A BAKING SHEET AND FREEZE. PACK FROZEN PEPPER PIECES INTO FREEZER BAGS AND STORE FOR UP TO 3 MONTHS.

SWEET POTATO LATKES

THESE LITTLE PANCAKES ARE USUALLY MADE WITH REGULAR POTATOES. THIS VERSION IS SWEET AND COLORFUL, AND GOES WELL WITH GRILLED MEATS.

1 LB	SWEET POTATOES	500 G
1	SMALL ONION	1
2 TBSP	FRESHLY SQUEEZED LEMON JUICE	25 ML
3	GREEN ONIONS, THINLY SLICED	3
2	EGGS, LIGHTLY BEATEN	2
1/3 CUP	ALL-PURPOSE FLOUR	75 ML
1 TSP	SALT	5 ML
1/2 TSP	CAYENNE PEPPER	2 ML
1/4 TSP	FRESHLY GROUND BLACK PEPPER	1 ML
1/4 CUP	VEGETABLE OIL	50 ML

PEEL SWEET POTATOES AND GRATE INTO A LARGE BOWL. GRATE ONION INTO THE SAME BOWL. STIR IN LEMON JUICE. PLACE VEGETABLES IN A CLEAN TEA TOWEL AND WRING OUT EXCESS LIQUID. RETURN TO THE BOWL AND ADD GREEN ONIONS, EGGS, FLOUR, SALT, CAYENNE AND BLACK PEPPER. IN A LARGE SKILLET, HEAT OIL OVER MEDIUM-HIGH HEAT. WORKING IN BATCHES, SPOON HEAPING TABLESPOONFULS (15 ML) OF SWEET POTATO MIXTURE INTO THE PAN, FLATTENING SLIGHTLY WITH A SPATULA. (DON'T BE TEMPTED TO MAKE THEM BIGGER OR THEY WON'T COOK PROPERLY IN THE MIDDLE.) FRY LATKES FOR 2 TO 3 MINUTES PER SIDE OR UNTIL GOLDEN BROWN ON BOTH SIDES. THE EDGES WILL BE UNEVEN AND CRISPY. TRANSFER TO A PLATE LINED WITH PAPER TOWELS AND KEEP WARM. REPEAT WITH THE REMAINING SWEET

POTATO MIXTURE, ADDING AND HEATING OIL AS NEEDED BETWEEN BATCHES. MAKES ABOUT 20 LATKES.

MAKE AHEAD: LET LATKES COOL, COVER AND REFRIGERATE FOR UP TO 1 DAY OR LAYER BETWEEN WAXED PAPER IN AN AIRTIGHT CONTAINER AND FREEZE FOR UP TO 2 WEEKS. REHEAT IN A 375°F (190°C) OVEN FOR 15 TO 20 MINUTES.

MASHED MAPLE GINGER SQUASH

PERFECT AS A SIDE DISH FOR CHICKEN OR HAM.

1	SMALL BUTTERNUT SQUASH, PEELED AND FINELY CHOPPED (ABOUT 3 CUPS/750 ML)	1
1/3 CUP	WATER	75 ML
1 TBSP	CHOPPED GINGERROOT	15 ML
2 TSP	BUTTER	10 ML
2 TBSP	PURE MAPLE SYRUP (OR TO TASTE)	25 ML
	SALT AND FRESHLY GROUND BLACK PEPPER	

IN A LARGE SKILLET, COMBINE SQUASH AND WATER; BRING TO A BOIL OVER MEDIUM-HIGH HEAT. REDUCE HEAT, COVER AND SIMMER FOR 12 TO 15 MINUTES OR UNTIL SQUASH IS TENDER AND WATER HAS ALMOST EVAPORATED. (LIFT THE LID A COUPLE OF TIMES TO MAKE SURE IT'S NOT DRYING OUT AND ADD A SPOONFUL OR TWO MORE WATER IF NECESSARY.) ADD GINGER, BUTTER, MAPLE SYRUP AND SALT AND PEPPER TO TASTE; INCREASE HEAT TO MEDIUM-HIGH AND COOK, STIRRING, FOR 2 MINUTES OR UNTIL SQUASH IS COATED AND GLOSSY. TRANSFER TO A LARGE BOWL AND ROUGHLY MASH, LEAVING SOME SMALL CHUNKS. SERVE IMMEDIATELY. SERVES 4.

ROASTED SWEET POTATO AND PARSNIP PURÉE

AN IDEAL MAKE-AHEAD SIDE DISH FOR THANKSGIVING DINNER OR ANY TIME YOU'RE SERVING A ROAST.

1 LB	SWEET POTATOES	500 G
1 LB	PARSNIPS	500 G
2 TBSP	OLIVE OIL	25 ML
1/2 CUP	WHIPPING (35%) CREAM	125 ML
3 TBSP	PACKED BROWN SUGAR	45 ML
3 TBSP	BUTTER, MELTED	45 ML
	SALT AND FRESHLY GROUND BLACK PEPPER	
2 TBSP	THINLY SLICED FRESH BASIL	25 ML

PREHEAT OVEN TO 375°F (190°C). PEEL AND CHOP SWEET POTATOES AND PARSNIPS. IN A LARGE BOWL, TOSS VEGETABLES WITH OIL. SPREAD IN A SINGLE LAYER ON A RIMMED BAKING SHEET. BAKE FOR ABOUT 45 MINUTES OR UNTIL GOLDEN BROWN AND SOFTENED. LET COOL SLIGHTLY. TRANSFER TO A FOOD PROCESSOR AND ADD CREAM, BROWN SUGAR AND BUTTER; PURÉE UNTIL SMOOTH. TRANSFER TO A SERVING BOWL AND SEASON TO TASTE WITH SALT AND PEPPER. STIR IN BASIL. SERVES 4 TO 6.

MAKE AHEAD: SPREAD PURÉE IN A BAKING DISH, LET COOL AND REFRIGERATE FOR UP TO 1 DAY. REHEAT IN THE MICROWAVE FOR ABOUT 3 MINUTES ON HIGH, STIRRING ONCE.

BEANS, PASTA AND RICE

CHICKPEA CURRY

CHICKPEAS ARE ALSO KNOWN AS GARBANZO BEANS. THE VISITING VEGETARIAN WILL BE IMPRESSED WITH THIS QUICK AND MILDLY SPICY DISH, WHICH TASTES EVEN BETTER THE NEXT DAY. SERVE OVER STEAMED BASMATI RICE WITH A DOLLOP OF MANGO CHUTNEY AND WARM NAAN — AND GRILLED CHICKEN BREASTS TO KEEP THE REST OF THE FAMILY HAPPY.

1 TBSP	VEGETABLE OIL	15 ML
1	ONION, CHOPPED	1
2	CLOVES GARLIC, MINCED	2
1 TBSP	MADRAS CURRY POWDER	15 ML
2 TSP	CHOPPED GINGERROOT	10 ML
1/2 TSP	SALT	2 ML
1	CAN (14 OZ/398 ML) WHOLE TOMATOES WITH JUICE (SEE TIP, PAGE 173), CHOPPED	1
1	CAN (14 TO 19 OZ/398 TO 540 ML) CHICKPEAS, DRAINED AND RINSED	1
3/4 CUP	WATER (APPROX.)	175 ML
1 TBSP	FRESHLY SQUEEZED LIME JUICE	15 ML
1 1/2 TSP	LIQUID HONEY	7 ML
2 TBSP	CHOPPED FRESH CILANTRO	25 ML

IN A LARGE SAUCEPAN, HEAT OIL OVER MEDIUM HEAT. SAUTÉ ONION FOR 5 TO 7 MINUTES OR UNTIL SOFTENED. ADD GARLIC, CURRY POWDER, GINGER AND SALT; SAUTÉ FOR 15 SECONDS OR UNTIL FRAGRANT (BE CAREFUL NOT TO SCORCH THE CURRY POWDER). ADD TOMATOES AND BRING TO A BOIL. REDUCE HEAT AND SIMMER FOR ABOUT 5 MINUTES OR UNTIL SAUCE THICKENS. ADD CHICKPEAS, WATER, LIME JUICE AND HONEY; SIMMER FOR 10 MINUTES

CONTINUED ON PAGE 257...

Corn Fritters (page 240)

Gourmet Stuffed Potatoes,
Three Ways (pages 246–250)

Swiss Chard and Tomato Pasta (page 261)

Aromatic Cashew Rice Pilaf (page 276)

OR UNTIL CHICKPEAS ARE HEATED THROUGH AND SAUCE IS SLIGHTLY THICKENED, ADDING MORE WATER IF IT LOOKS TOO THICK. STIR IN CILANTRO. SERVES 3 TO 4.

MAKE AHEAD: LET COOL, TRANSFER TO AN AIRTIGHT CONTAINER AND REFRIGERATE FOR UP TO 2 DAYS OR FREEZE FOR UP TO 1 MONTH.

— CRANBERRY BAKED BEANS —

A SURE-FIRE HIT AT YOUR NEXT FAMILY BARBECUE.

2	CANS (EACH 14 OZ/398 ML) BAKED BEANS IN TOMATO SAUCE	2
1	CAN (14 TO 19 OZ/398 TO 540 ML) KIDNEY BEANS, DRAINED AND RINSED	1
1	CAN (14 OZ/398 ML) CRANBERRY JELLY	1
1	CAN (10 OZ/284 ML) TOMATO SOUP	1
1	CLOVE GARLIC, MINCED	1
1/2	SMALL ONION, CHOPPED	1/2
1 TSP	PREPARED MUSTARD	5 ML
10	SLICES BACON OR TURKEY BACON	10
1/4 CUP	PACKED BROWN SUGAR	50 ML

PREHEAT OVEN TO 350°F (180°C). GREASE A 13- BY 9-INCH (33 BY 23 CM) BAKING DISH. IN A LARGE BOWL, COMBINE BAKED BEANS, KIDNEY BEANS, CRANBERRY JELLY, TOMATO SOUP, GARLIC, ONION AND MUSTARD. TRANSFER TO PREPARED BAKING DISH. ARRANGE BACON ACROSS THE TOP IN A CRISSCROSS PATTERN. SPRINKLE WITH BROWN SUGAR. BAKE FOR 1 HOUR OR UNTIL BACON IS CRISP AND BEANS ARE BUBBLING. SERVES 12.

ASIAN NOODLES WITH VEGETABLES

THE PERFECT PARTNER FOR CHINESE BARBECUE
PORK (PAGE 220). LEFTOVER ASIAN NOODLES WITH
VEGETABLES ARE GOOD COLD AS A LUNCHBOX SALAD. OR
TURN THEM INTO A QUICK AND SATISFYING WRAP: JUST
REHEAT THE NOODLES IN THE MICROWAVE AND TUCK
THEM INTO A WARMED FLOUR TORTILLA WITH SOME
COOKED CHICKEN OR PORK AND A BIG SPOONFUL OF
SWEET CHILI SAUCE. FANTASTIC!

I	PACKAGE (I LB/450 G) STEAMED CHINESE NOODLES	I

SAUCE

1/3 CUP	CHICKEN BROTH (APPROX.)	75 ML
3 TBSP	SOY SAUCE	45 ML
3 TBSP	OYSTER SAUCE	45 ML
I TBSP	GRANULATED SUGAR	15 ML
I TSP	CORNSTARCH	5 ML
I TSP	ASIAN CHILI PASTE (SEE TIP, PAGE 231)	5 ML
1/2 TSP	SESAME OIL	2 ML

I TBSP	VEGETABLE OIL	15 ML
I	ONION, THINLY SLICED	I
I	RED BELL PEPPER, THINLY SLICED	I
2	CLOVES GARLIC, MINCED	2
I TBSP	CHOPPED GINGERROOT	15 ML
I	PACKAGE (IO OZ/284 G) PREWASHED SPINACH (ABOUT 6 CUPS/1.5 L PACKED)	I
I	PACKAGE (IO OZ/284 G) BEAN SPROUTS (ABOUT 4 CUPS/I L)	I
2 TBSP	TOASTED SESAME SEEDS (SEE TIP, PAGE 93)	25 ML

IN A LARGE POT OF BOILING WATER, COOK NOODLES FOR ABOUT 30 SECONDS. DRAIN INTO A COLANDER AND PLACE UNDER COLD RUNNING WATER TO COOL. DRAIN AGAIN AND SET ASIDE.

SAUCE: IN A MEDIUM BOWL, WHISK TOGETHER CHICKEN BROTH, SOY SAUCE, OYSTER SAUCE, SUGAR, CORNSTARCH, CHILI PASTE AND SESAME OIL; SET ASIDE.

IN A LARGE SKILLET OR WOK, HEAT OIL OVER MEDIUM-HIGH HEAT. SAUTÉ ONION AND RED PEPPER FOR 5 TO 7 MINUTES OR UNTIL SOFTENED. ADD GARLIC AND GINGER; SAUTÉ FOR 15 SECONDS OR UNTIL FRAGRANT. ADD SPINACH AND SAUTÉ UNTIL WILTED, ABOUT 2 MINUTES. ADD BEAN SPROUTS, RESERVED NOODLES, SAUCE AND SESAME SEEDS; COOK, STIRRING, FOR 3 TO 4 MINUTES OR UNTIL INGREDIENTS ARE COATED WITH SAUCE. IF NOODLES ARE TOO DRY, ADD MORE BROTH. SERVES 4.

TIP: THE BAGS OF STEAMED NOODLES, PREWASHED SPINACH AND BEAN SPROUTS YOU FIND IN YOUR GROCERY STORE MAY VARY SLIGHTLY IN SIZE FROM THOSE GIVEN IN THE RECIPE. IF THE BAGS YOU BUY ARE 1 OR 2 OZ (28 TO 56 G) MORE OR LESS, IT WON'T AFFECT THE RECIPE. BUT IF THE BAGS ARE SIGNIFICANTLY LARGER, USE ONLY THE AMOUNT REQUIRED BY THE RECIPE AND SAVE THE REST FOR ANOTHER MEAL.

QUICK BAKED MACARONI AND CHEESE

SIMPLE AND DELICIOUS. DINNER'S READY IN 40 MINUTES, AND THERE'S ONLY ONE DISH TO WASH. DON'T TURN UP YOUR NOSE AT THE EVAPORATED MILK — IT WORKS.

1	CAN (12 OZ OR 370 ML) EVAPORATED MILK (NO SUBSTITUTES)	1
2 CUPS	WATER	500 ML
2 TBSP	BUTTER	25 ML
1 TBSP	DIJON MUSTARD	15 ML
1/2 TSP	SALT	2 ML
1/4 TSP	HOT PEPPER SAUCE	1 ML
	FRESHLY GROUND BLACK PEPPER	
2 CUPS	MACARONI	500 ML
2 CUPS	SHREDDED SHARP (OLD) CHEDDAR CHEESE	500 ML
1/4 CUP	DRY BREAD CRUMBS OR SODA CRACKER CRUMBS	50 ML
1/4 CUP	FRESHLY GRATED PARMESAN CHEESE	50 ML

PREHEAT OVEN TO 350°F (180°C). GREASE AN 8-INCH (20 CM) SQUARE BAKING DISH. IN A SAUCEPAN, COMBINE EVAPORATED MILK, WATER, BUTTER, MUSTARD, SALT, HOT PEPPER SAUCE AND BLACK PEPPER TO TASTE; BRING ALMOST TO A BOIL OVER MEDIUM-HIGH HEAT. STIR IN MACARONI, TRANSFER TO PREPARED BAKING DISH AND COVER TIGHTLY WITH FOIL. BAKE FOR 30 MINUTES, STIRRING HALFWAY THROUGH. ADD CHEESE, STIRRING UNTIL MELTED AND THE SAUCE STARTS TO THICKEN. COMBINE BREAD CRUMBS AND PARMESAN; SPRINKLE OVER MACARONI. BAKE, UNCOVERED, FOR 10 MINUTES OR UNTIL LIGHTLY BROWNED. *SERVES 3 TO 4.*

SWISS CHARD AND TOMATO PASTA

THIS COLORFUL AND SATISFYING VEGETARIAN PASTA DISH IS BEST MADE WITH FRESH LOCAL TOMATOES WHEN THEY'RE IN SEASON.

1 LB	FUSILLI OR OTHER CHUNKY PASTA	500 G
3 TBSP	OLIVE OIL	45 ML
2	RED BELL PEPPERS, CHOPPED	2
4	CLOVES GARLIC, MINCED	4
4 TO 5	TOMATOES, PEELED (SEE TIP, PAGE 267), SEEDED AND CHOPPED	4 TO 5
4 CUPS	PACKED SWISS CHARD OR SPINACH, CHOPPED	1 L
1/4 CUP	FRESHLY GRATED PARMESAN CHEESE	50 ML
2 TBSP	BUTTER	25 ML
2 TBSP	BALSAMIC VINEGAR	25 ML
	SALT AND FRESHLY GROUND BLACK PEPPER	

IN A LARGE POT OF BOILING WATER, COOK PASTA ACCORDING TO PACKAGE DIRECTIONS. DRAIN AND RETURN TO POT.

MEANWHILE, IN A LARGE SKILLET, HEAT OIL OVER MEDIUM-HIGH HEAT. SAUTÉ RED PEPPERS FOR 5 MINUTES OR UNTIL SOFTENED. ADD GARLIC AND SAUTÉ FOR 15 SECONDS OR UNTIL FRAGRANT. ADD TOMATOES AND SWISS CHARD; SAUTÉ FOR 4 TO 5 MINUTES OR UNTIL TOMATOES ARE SQUISHY AND SWISS CHARD IS WILTED. STIR IN PARMESAN, BUTTER AND VINEGAR. SEASON TO TASTE WITH SALT AND PEPPER. TOSS WITH PASTA. SERVES 4.

PASTA WITH BROCCOLI AND BACON

DINNER IN A HURRY.

3 CUPS	BOWTIE OR FUSILLI PASTA	750 ML
4 CUPS	BROCCOLI FLORETS AND PEELED STEMS, FINELY CHOPPED	1 L
2 TBSP	OLIVE OIL	25 ML
1/2 CUP	PINE NUTS	125 ML
2	CLOVES GARLIC, SLICED	2
1/3 CUP	CHICKEN BROTH, DIVIDED	75 ML
4	SLICES BACON, COOKED CRISP AND CRUMBLED	4
1/2 CUP	FRESHLY GRATED PARMESAN CHEESE	125 ML

IN A LARGE POT OF BOILING WATER, COOK PASTA ACCORDING TO PACKAGE DIRECTIONS. TWO MINUTES BEFORE PASTA IS READY, ADD BROCCOLI AND COOK FOR 2 MINUTES. DRAIN AND SET ASIDE. IN A LARGE SKILLET, HEAT OIL OVER MEDIUM HEAT. SAUTÉ PINE NUTS FOR 1 MINUTE OR UNTIL LIGHTLY BROWNED. COMBINE GARLIC AND 2 TBSP (25 ML) CHICKEN STOCK; ADD TO PAN AND SAUTÉ FOR 15 SECONDS OR UNTIL FRAGRANT (BE CAREFUL NOT TO BURN THE GARLIC). STIR IN PASTA MIXTURE AND THE REMAINING BROTH; COOK UNTIL HEATED THROUGH. SERVE SPRINKLED WITH BACON AND PARMESAN. SERVES 4.

"WHATEVER YOU DO WILL BE INSIGNIFICANT AND IT IS VERY IMPORTANT THAT YOU DO IT."
— MOHANDAS GHANDI

ANGEL HAIR PASTA WITH SHRIMP

A NICE LIGHT PASTA DISH THAT IS QUICK AND EASY.

4 TBSP	OLIVE OIL	60 ML
1	SHALLOT, MINCED	1
4	CLOVES GARLIC, MINCED	4
1/2 CUP	CHOPPED FRESH PARSLEY	125 ML
3/4 CUP	DRY WHITE WINE	175 ML
3	TOMATOES, PEELED (SEE TIP, PAGE 267), SEEDED AND CHOPPED	3
1 LB	LARGE SHRIMP, PEELED AND DEVEINED (ABOUT 30)	500 G
	SALT AND FRESHLY GROUND BLACK PEPPER	
1 LB	ANGEL HAIR PASTA	500 G
	CHOPPED FRESH PARSLEY (OPTIONAL)	
	FRESHLY GRATED PARMESAN CHEESE (OPTIONAL)	

IN A LARGE SKILLET, HEAT OIL OVER MEDIUM-HIGH HEAT. REDUCE HEAT TO MEDIUM, ADD SHALLOT AND SAUTÉ FOR 2 TO 3 MINUTES OR UNTIL LIGHTLY BROWNED. ADD GARLIC AND PARSLEY; SAUTÉ FOR 15 SECONDS OR UNTIL FRAGRANT. ADD WINE AND COOK UNTIL LIQUID IS REDUCED BY HALF, ABOUT 5 MINUTES. ADD TOMATOES, SHRIMP AND SALT AND PEPPER TO TASTE; REDUCE HEAT AND SIMMER, STIRRING OCCASIONALLY, FOR ABOUT 5 MINUTES OR UNTIL SHRIMP ARE PINK AND OPAQUE AND TOMATOES ARE SOFTENED.

MEANWHILE, IN A LARGE POT OF BOILING WATER, COOK PASTA ACCORDING TO PACKAGE DIRECTIONS. DRAIN AND TOSS WITH SHRIMP MIXTURE. SERVE SPRINKLED WITH PARSLEY AND PARMESAN, IF DESIRED. SERVES 4.

SPAGHETTI WITH TOMATO VODKA SAUCE

RUMOR HAS IT THAT AN ITALIAN VODKA COMPANY CREATED THIS POPULAR RECIPE AS AN ADVERTISING STUNT. MOLTO BENE! YOU CAN LEAVE IT CHUNKY OR PURÉE IT FOR A SMOOTH SAUCE, AS YOU PLEASE.

I TBSP	OLIVE OIL	15 ML
I	ONION, FINELY CHOPPED	I
2	CLOVES GARLIC, MINCED	2
1/4 CUP	VODKA	50 ML
I	CAN (28 OZ/796 ML) WHOLE TOMATOES WITH JUICE (SEE TIP, PAGE 173), CHOPPED	I
I TSP	SALT (OR TO TASTE)	5 ML
1/4 TSP	FRESHLY GROUND BLACK PEPPER	I ML
PINCH	HOT PEPPER FLAKES	PINCH
I LB	SPAGHETTI	500 G
1/2 CUP	WHIPPING (35%) CREAM, WARMED	125 ML
1/2 CUP	FRESHLY GRATED PARMESAN CHEESE	125 ML

IN A LARGE SAUCEPAN, HEAT OIL OVER MEDIUM HEAT. SAUTÉ ONION FOR ABOUT 5 MINUTES OR UNTIL SOFTENED. COMBINE GARLIC AND VODKA; ADD TO PAN AND SAUTÉ FOR 2 TO 3 MINUTES OR UNTIL LIQUID HAS ALMOST EVAPORATED AND GARLIC IS FRAGRANT. ADD TOMATOES, SALT, BLACK PEPPER AND HOT PEPPER FLAKES; BRING TO A SIMMER. REDUCE HEAT AND SIMMER FOR 15 MINUTES OR UNTIL SLIGHTLY THICKENED.

MEANWHILE, IN A LARGE POT OF BOILING WATER, COOK SPAGHETTI ACCORDING TO PACKAGE DIRECTIONS. DRAIN AND RETURN TO POT.

IF DESIRED, USING AN IMMERSION BLENDER, OR IN A FOOD PROCESSOR OR BLENDER IN BATCHES, PURÉE SAUCE UNTIL SMOOTH. RETURN TO PAN, IF NECESSARY, STIR IN CREAM AND REHEAT OVER MEDIUM HEAT, STIRRING OFTEN, UNTIL STEAMING. DO NOT LET BOIL OR CREAM MAY CURDLE. TOSS WITH SPAGHETTI. SERVE SPRINKLED WITH PARMESAN. SERVES 4.

MAKE AHEAD: BEFORE ADDING THE CREAM, LET SAUCE COOL, TRANSFER TO AN AIRTIGHT CONTAINER AND REFRIGERATE FOR UP TO 2 DAYS OR FREEZE FOR UP TO 1 MONTH. THAW AND REHEAT, THEN CONTINUE WITH THE RECIPE.

TIP: COMBINING MINCED GARLIC WITH A SMALL AMOUNT OF LIQUID — IN THIS CASE, VODKA — HELPS PREVENTS IT FROM BURNING WHEN YOU'RE SAUTÉING IT. IF YOU FIND YOUR GARLIC DARKENS TOO QUICKLY IN OTHER RECIPES, COMBINE IT WITH 1 TBSP (15 ML) WATER BEFORE ADDING IT TO THE PAN.

VARIATION: AFTER HEATING THE OIL, SAUTÉ 2 CHOPPED SLICES PANCETTA OR BACON UNTIL CRISP. USING A SLOTTED SPOON, TRANSFER TO A PLATE LINED WITH PAPER TOWELS. POUR OFF ALL BUT 1 TBSP (15 ML) FAT AND CONTINUE WITH RECIPE. STIR THE PANCETTA INTO THE SAUCE JUST BEFORE ADDING THE CREAM.

SPAGHETTI WITH CHICKEN, SPINACH AND FRESH TOMATOES

A MIDWEEK DINNER DISH FOR YOUR CREW.

4	BONELESS SKINLESS CHICKEN BREASTS, CUT INTO BITE-SIZE PIECES	4
4	CLOVES GARLIC, MINCED	4
2 TBSP	OLIVE OIL	25 ML
1/2 TSP	DRIED OREGANO	2 ML
1/2 TSP	DRIED ROSEMARY	2 ML
	SALT AND FRESHLY GROUND BLACK PEPPER	
1 LB	SPAGHETTI	500 G
1/2 CUP	CHICKEN BROTH	125 ML
1/4 CUP	DRY WHITE WINE	50 ML
5	TOMATOES, PEELED (SEE TIP, OPPOSITE), SEEDED AND CHOPPED	5
1	PACKAGE (10 OZ/284 G) PREWASHED SPINACH (ABOUT 6 CUPS/1.5 L PACKED)	1
1/2 CUP	FRESHLY GRATED PARMESAN CHEESE	125 ML

IN A LARGE BOWL, TOSS CHICKEN WITH GARLIC, OIL, OREGANO, ROSEMARY AND SALT AND PEPPER TO TASTE. COVER AND REFRIGERATE FOR 30 MINUTES.

IN A LARGE POT OF BOILING WATER, COOK SPAGHETTI ACCORDING TO PACKAGE DIRECTIONS.

MEANWHILE, HEAT A LARGE NONSTICK SKILLET OVER MEDIUM-HIGH HEAT. ADD CHICKEN, USING A SPATULA TO SCRAPE IN ANY OIL AND HERBS CLINGING TO THE SIDES OF THE BOWL. SAUTÉ CHICKEN FOR ABOUT 5 MINUTES OR UNTIL BROWNED AND NO LONGER PINK INSIDE. TRANSFER TO A PLATE AND KEEP WARM. ADD BROTH AND WINE TO

SKILLET, REDUCE HEAT AND SIMMER, SCRAPING UP BROWN BITS FROM BOTTOM OF PAN, FOR 4 TO 5 MINUTES OR UNTIL REDUCED BY HALF. ADD TOMATOES AND SPINACH (THE PAN WILL LOOK VERY FULL, BUT THE SPINACH SOON SHRINKS); SIMMER FOR 5 TO 6 MINUTES, TURNING THE VEGETABLES OCCASIONALLY WITH A SPATULA, UNTIL TOMATOES ARE JUST SOFTENED AND SPINACH IS WILTED.

DRAIN PASTA, RESERVING $\frac{1}{2}$ CUP (125 ML) WATER. RETURN CHICKEN TO PAN AND REHEAT. TASTE AND ADJUST SEASONING WITH SALT AND PEPPER, IF DESIRED. TOSS WITH SPAGHETTI, ADDING A LITTLE OF THE RESERVED WATER IF IT'S TOO DRY. SERVE SPRINKLED GENEROUSLY WITH PARMESAN. SERVES 4.

TIP: TO PEEL FRESH TOMATOES, CUT AN X IN THE SKIN AT THE BOTTOM OF EACH TOMATO. PLUNGE INTO BOILING WATER FOR ABOUT 15 SECONDS. USING A SLOTTED SPOON, TRANSFER TOMATOES TO A BOWL OF ICE WATER TO STOP THE COOKING PROCESS. PEEL OFF SKINS, STARTING FROM THE X. A PARING KNIFE MAKES THIS EASIER.

WHEN YOU WISH YOU COULD RETURN TO YOUR YOUTH, REMEMBER ALGEBRA CLASS.

FUSILLI WITH CREAMY SMOKED SALMON SAUCE

IF YOU CAN'T GET THIS DISH ON THE TABLE IN 20 MINUTES, WE'LL EAT OUR OVEN MITTS!

6 CUPS	FUSILLI PASTA (ABOUT ONE 12-OZ/375 G BOX)	1.5 L
1 TBSP	BUTTER	15 ML
2	RED OR YELLOW BELL PEPPERS, CHOPPED	2
1	SHALLOT, FINELY CHOPPED	1
2	CLOVES GARLIC, MINCED	2
10 TO 12 OZ	SMOKED SALMON FILLETS (SEE TIP, OPPOSITE)	300 TO 375 G
1 1/2 CUPS	WHIPPING (35%) CREAM	375 ML
	SALT AND FRESHLY GROUND BLACK PEPPER (OPTIONAL)	
1 TBSP	LEMON JUICE (OR TO TASTE)	15 ML
1/4 CUP	CHOPPED FRESH PARSLEY	50 ML

IN A LARGE POT OF BOILING WATER, COOK PASTA ACCORDING TO PACKAGE DIRECTIONS.

MEANWHILE, IN A LARGE SKILLET, MELT BUTTER OVER MEDIUM-HIGH HEAT. SAUTÉ RED PEPPERS AND SHALLOT FOR 2 TO 3 MINUTES OR UNTIL JUST SOFTENED. ADD GARLIC AND SAUTÉ FOR 15 SECONDS OR UNTIL FRAGRANT. ADD SMOKED SALMON AND CREAM; REDUCE HEAT AND SIMMER FOR ABOUT 3 MINUTES OR UNTIL SAUCE IS SLIGHTLY THICKENED. IF DESIRED, SEASON TO TASTE WITH SALT AND PEPPER (BUT REMEMBER THAT THE SALMON ADDS LOTS OF FLAVOR). DRAIN PASTA AND TOSS WITH SAUCE AND LEMON JUICE. SERVE SPRINKLED WITH PARSLEY. SERVES 4.

TIP: YOU NEED TO BUY SMOKED SALMON FILLETS, SOMETIMES CALLED BBQ TIPS. THEY'RE THE KIND THAT CAN BE FLAKED, NOT LOX. YOU CAN ALSO MAKE THIS DISH WITH SMOKED TROUT OR SMOKED MACKEREL FILLETS.

HOW DID I GET OVER THE HILL WITHOUT GETTING TO THE TOP?

TORTELLINI WITH BROCCOLI AND CREAMY TOMATO SAUCE

HERE'S A FASTA PASTA DISH FOR YOUR BUSY FAMILY.

4 CUPS	CHEESE OR MEAT TORTELLINI	1 L
4 CUPS	BROCCOLI FLORETS	1 L
2 CUPS	SPAGHETTI SAUCE	500 ML
4 OZ	LIGHT CREAM CHEESE, AT ROOM TEMPERATURE	125 G
2	TOMATOES, COARSELY CHOPPED	2
	FRESHLY GROUND BLACK PEPPER	
	FRESHLY GRATED PARMESAN CHEESE	

IN A LARGE POT OF BOILING WATER, COOK TORTELLINI ACCORDING TO PACKAGE DIRECTIONS. TWO MINUTES BEFORE PASTA IS READY, ADD BROCCOLI AND COOK FOR 2 MINUTES. DRAIN AND SET ASIDE. IN A LARGE SAUCEPAN, HEAT SPAGHETTI SAUCE OVER MEDIUM HEAT. ADD CREAM CHEESE AND STIR UNTIL MELTED. STIR IN TORTELLINI MIXTURE, TOMATOES AND PEPPER TO TASTE. SERVE IN INDIVIDUAL BOWLS AND PASS THE PARMESAN SEPARATELY. SERVES 4.

CHICKEN RAVIOLI WITH SAGE CREAM SAUCE

THIS SAUCE IS ALSO DELICIOUS TOSSED WITH COOKED FETTUCCINE. SERVE WITH A SALAD AND GARLIC BREAD.

2 TBSP	BUTTER	25 ML
I	SHALLOT, MINCED	I
4 TBSP	FINELY CHOPPED FRESH SAGE (SEE TIP, BELOW)	60 ML
2 TO 3	CLOVES GARLIC, MINCED	2 TO 3
2 CUPS	WHIPPING (35%) CREAM	500 ML
	SALT AND FRESHLY GROUND BLACK PEPPER	
4 CUPS	CHICKEN RAVIOLI OR TORTELLINI	I L
1/2 CUP	FRESHLY GRATED PARMESAN CHEESE	125 ML

IN A MEDIUM SAUCEPAN, MELT BUTTER OVER MEDIUM HEAT. SAUTÉ SHALLOT AND SAGE FOR 2 TO 3 MINUTES OR UNTIL SHALLOT IS TENDER. ADD GARLIC AND SAUTÉ FOR 15 SECONDS OR UNTIL FRAGRANT. ADD CREAM AND SIMMER, STIRRING OFTEN, FOR ABOUT 15 MINUTES OR UNTIL CREAM IS REDUCED BY HALF. DO NOT LET BOIL OR CREAM MAY CURDLE. SEASON TO TASTE WITH SALT AND PEPPER.

MEANWHILE, IN A LARGE POT OF BOILING WATER, COOK RAVIOLI ACCORDING TO PACKAGE DIRECTIONS. DRAIN, RESERVING 1/2 CUP (125 ML) WATER. TOSS RAVIOLI WITH SAUCE AND PARMESAN, ADDING A LITTLE OF THE RESERVED WATER IF IT'S TOO DRY. SERVES 3 TO 4.

TIP: YOU CAN USE I TBSP (15 ML) DRIED SAGE INSTEAD OF THE FRESH, BUT DON'T USE GROUND SAGE — IT'S TOO POWERFUL. FOR A SMOOTHER SAUCE, STRAIN BEFORE SERVING.

FETTUCCINE WITH HAM AND PEAS

MAKE THIS WITH A MIX OF PLAIN AND SPINACH-FLAVORED PASTA FOR A FUN AND SPEEDY DINNER THAT APPEALS TO KIDS.

1 LB	FETTUCCINE	500 G
2 TBSP	BUTTER	25 ML
6	GREEN ONIONS, CHOPPED	6
4 OZ	PROSCIUTTO OR HAM, CUT INTO THIN STRIPS	125 G
1 CUP	FROZEN PEAS, THAWED	250 ML
1 CUP	WHIPPING (35%) CREAM	250 ML
1/2 CUP	FRESHLY GRATED PARMESAN CHEESE	250 ML
	SALT AND FRESHLY GROUND BLACK PEPPER (OPTIONAL)	
	CHOPPED FRESH PARSLEY	

IN A LARGE POT OF BOILING WATER, COOK FETTUCCINE ACCORDING TO PACKAGE DIRECTIONS. DRAIN AND RETURN TO POT.

MEANWHILE, IN A LARGE SKILLET, MELT BUTTER OVER MEDIUM HEAT. SAUTÉ GREEN ONIONS FOR ABOUT 1 MINUTE OR UNTIL SOFTENED. ADD PROSCIUTTO AND SAUTÉ FOR 2 MINUTES OR UNTIL LIGHTLY BROWNED. ADD PEAS AND SAUTÉ FOR 2 MINUTES OR UNTIL HEATED THROUGH. ADD CREAM AND SIMMER, STIRRING OFTEN, FOR 2 MINUTES OR UNTIL STEAMING. DO NOT LET BOIL OR CREAM MAY CURDLE. STIR IN PARMESAN. IF DESIRED, SEASON TO TASTE WITH SALT AND PEPPER (BUT REMEMBER THAT PROSCIUTTO AND PARMESAN ARE BOTH QUITE SALTY). TOSS WITH FETTUCCINE. SERVE SPRINKLED WITH PARSLEY. SERVES 4.

SHRIMP-STUFFED JUMBO SHELLS

THIS ELEGANT MAKE-AHEAD LUNCH OR SUPPER FOR COMPANY ALSO WORKS WELL FOR BUFFETS. SERVE WITH A GREEN SALAD AND CRUSTY BREAD.

24 TO 30	JUMBO PASTA SHELLS	24 TO 30
2	EGGS, LIGHTLY BEATEN	2
2	CLOVES GARLIC, MINCED	2
1	TOMATO, PEELED (SEE TIP, PAGE 267), SEEDED AND CHOPPED	1
1 LB	LIGHT RICOTTA CHEESE	500 G
1 CUP	SHREDDED MOZZARELLA CHEESE	250 ML
1/2 CUP	FRESHLY GRATED PARMESAN CHEESE	125 ML
1/2 CUP	PACKED FRESH BASIL LEAVES, SHREDDED (OR 1 TSP/5 ML DRIED BASIL)	125 ML
1 TBSP	FRESHLY SQUEEZED LEMON JUICE	15 ML
1 TSP	SALT	5 ML
1/4 TSP	FRESHLY GROUND BLACK PEPPER	1 ML
1 LB	LARGE SHRIMP, PEELED, DEVEINED AND EACH SHRIMP CUT INTO 3 PIECES	500 G
1	JAR (24 OZ/700 ML) SPAGHETTI SAUCE	1
1 CUP	DRY BREAD CRUMBS OR SODA CRACKER CRUMBS	250 ML

PREHEAT OVEN TO 375°F (190°C). GREASE A 13- BY 9-INCH (33 BY 23 CM) BAKING DISH. IN A LARGE POT OF BOILING WATER, COOK PASTA ACCORDING TO PACKAGE DIRECTIONS (COOK A FEW EXTRA IN CASE SOME BREAK). DRAIN AND PLUNGE INTO ICE WATER. DRAIN AGAIN AND SPREAD OUT ON A CLEAN KITCHEN TOWEL. IN A LARGE BOWL, COMBINE EGGS, GARLIC, TOMATO, RICOTTA, MOZZARELLA, PARMESAN, BASIL, LEMON JUICE, SALT AND PEPPER. STIR IN SHRIMP. SPOON SHRIMP MIXTURE INTO PASTA SHELLS, DIVIDING

EVENLY AND BEING CAREFUL NOT TO TEAR THE SHELLS. POUR SPAGHETTI SAUCE INTO PREPARED BAKING DISH. NESTLE FILLED SHELLS IN THE BAKING DISH, PUSHING THEM DOWN GENTLY TO SIT IN THE SAUCE. SPRINKLE WITH BREAD CRUMBS. BAKE FOR ABOUT 20 MINUTES OR UNTIL SAUCE IS BUBBLING AND TOP IS GOLDEN BROWN. SERVES 8.

MAKE AHEAD: BEFORE BAKING, COVER AND REFRIGERATE FOR UP TO 4 HOURS. INCREASE BAKING TIME TO ABOUT 30 MINUTES.

TIP: SHRIMP ARE SOLD BY COUNT, WHICH MEANS THE APPROXIMATE NUMBER OF SHRIMP YOU GET TO THE POUND. FOR EXAMPLE, JUMBO SHRIMP ARE 21 TO 25 COUNT, LARGE SHRIMP ARE 26 TO 30 COUNT OR 31 TO 40 COUNT AND MEDIUM SHRIMP ARE 41 TO 50 COUNT. FOR THIS RECIPE, GO FOR THE 31 TO 40 COUNT LARGE SHRIMP.

COCONUT MANGO RICE

THE EXCITING TROPICAL TASTES OF THIS RICE
DISH COMPLEMENT GRILLED CHICKEN AND FISH.
IT'S THE PERFECT ACCOMPANIMENT FOR MADRAS
CHICKEN SKEWERS (PAGE 176).

1½ CUPS	BASMATI OR JASMINE RICE	375 ML
2 TBSP	BUTTER	25 ML
1	SMALL ONION, FINELY CHOPPED	1
1	RED BELL PEPPER, CHOPPED	1
2	CLOVES GARLIC, MINCED	2
2 TBSP	MINCED GINGERROOT	25 ML
1 TBSP	MADRAS CURRY POWDER	15 ML
1	CAN (14 OZ/400 ML) COCONUT MILK (SEE TIP, OPPOSITE)	1
2½ CUPS	WATER	625 ML
4	GREEN ONIONS, CHOPPED	4
1	MANGO, PEELED AND CHOPPED (SEE TIP, PAGE 66)	1
½ CUP	PACKED FRESH CILANTRO, CHOPPED	125 ML
¼ CUP	SLICED ALMONDS, TOASTED (SEE TIP, PAGE 277)	50 ML

RINSE RICE IN SEVERAL CHANGES OF COLD WATER AND
DRAIN THOROUGHLY; SET ASIDE. IN A LARGE SAUCEPAN,
MELT BUTTER OVER MEDIUM HEAT. SAUTÉ ONION AND RED
PEPPER FOR ABOUT 5 MINUTES OR UNTIL SOFTENED. ADD
GARLIC AND GINGER; SAUTÉ FOR 15 SECONDS OR UNTIL
FRAGRANT. ADD RICE AND CURRY POWDER, STIRRING TO
COAT RICE. ADD COCONUT MILK AND WATER; BRING TO A
SIMMER. REDUCE HEAT, COVER AND SIMMER FOR ABOUT
20 MINUTES OR UNTIL LIQUID IS ABSORBED AND RICE IS

TENDER. REMOVE FROM HEAT AND FLUFF WITH A FORK, STIRRING IN GREEN ONIONS, MANGO, CILANTRO AND ALMONDS. SERVES 4.

TIP: IN CASE YOU'RE WONDERING, LIGHT COCONUT MILK WORKS FINE IN THIS RECIPE.

ALWAYS FLUFFY BASMATI RICE

MORE AND MORE HOME COOKS ARE DISCOVERING BASMATI RICE – AND WITH GOOD REASON. IT HAS AN APPEALING AROMA AND NUTTY TASTE THAT GOES WELL WITH INDIAN AND ASIAN DISHES, AND IT TURNS OUT NICE AND FLUFFY ALMOST EVERY TIME. THE SECRET IS TO SOAK THE RICE IN COLD WATER BEFORE COOKING. BROWN BASMATI RICE IS READILY AVAILABLE BUT TAKES LONGER TO COOK. THE METHOD GIVEN HERE WORKS BEST FOR WHITE BASMATI RICE.

2 CUPS	WHITE BASMATI RICE	500 ML
4 CUPS	BOILING WATER	1 L
1/2 TSP	SALT	2 ML

PLACE RICE IN A LARGE BOWL AND COVER WITH COLD WATER; LET STAND FOR 30 MINUTES. DRAIN AND RINSE WELL UNDER COLD RUNNING WATER. PLACE RICE IN A LARGE SAUCEPAN AND ADD BOILING WATER AND SALT; BRING TO A BOIL OVER HIGH HEAT. REDUCE HEAT TO MEDIUM, COVER AND COOK FOR 3 MINUTES, THEN REMOVE FROM HEAT. KEEP COVERED AND LET RICE STEAM FOR 10 MINUTES OR UNTIL WATER IS ABSORBED AND RICE IS TENDER. FLUFF WITH A FORK. SERVES 6.

AROMATIC CASHEW RICE PILAF

THIS COLORFUL, FRAGRANT AND MILDLY SPICY
RICE IS THE IDEAL ACCOMPANIMENT FOR BUTTER
CHICKEN (PAGE 178) OR ANY OTHER INDIAN-STYLE
CURRY WITH A RICH-FLAVORED SAUCE.

1 1/2 CUPS	WHITE BASMATI RICE	375 ML
1 TBSP	VEGETABLE OIL	15 ML
1/2 TSP	CUMIN SEEDS	2 ML
4	WHOLE CLOVES	4
1	PIECE (2 INCHES/5 CM) CINNAMON STICK	1
1 TSP	SALT	5 ML
1/2 TSP	GROUND CARDAMOM	2 ML
1	ONION, FINELY CHOPPED	1
3 CUPS	BOILING WATER	750 ML
1	CARROT, FINELY CHOPPED	1
1/2 CUP	FROZEN PEAS	125 ML
1/2 CUP	FROZEN CORN KERNELS	125 ML
1/4 CUP	UNSALTED ROASTED CASHEWS OR SLICED ALMONDS, TOASTED (SEE TIP, OPPOSITE)	50 ML
2 TBSP	CHOPPED FRESH CILANTRO (OPTIONAL)	25 ML

PLACE RICE IN A LARGE BOWL AND COVER WITH COLD
WATER; LET STAND FOR 30 MINUTES. DRAIN AND RINSE
WELL UNDER COLD RUNNING WATER.

IN A LARGE SAUCEPAN, HEAT OIL OVER MEDIUM-HIGH HEAT.
SAUTÉ CUMIN SEEDS FOR ABOUT 40 SECONDS OR UNTIL
BROWNED AND FRAGRANT. ADD CLOVES, CINNAMON STICK,
SALT AND CARDAMOM; SAUTÉ FOR 15 SECONDS OR UNTIL
FRAGRANT. ADD ONION AND SAUTÉ FOR 3 TO 4 MINUTES
OR UNTIL GOLDEN BROWN. ADD RICE, STIRRING TO COAT

WITH SPICES. ADD BOILING WATER, CARROT, PEAS AND CORN; BRING TO A BOIL. REDUCE HEAT, COVER AND SIMMER FOR 10 TO 12 MINUTES OR UNTIL WATER IS ABSORBED. REMOVE FROM HEAT, STIR IN CASHEWS, COVER AND LET RICE STEAM FOR 10 MINUTES OR UNTIL TENDER. DISCARD CLOVES AND CINNAMON STICK. FLUFF WITH A FORK, STIRRING IN CILANTRO (IF USING). SERVES 4 TO 6.

TIP: TOASTING NUTS HELPS BRING OUT THEIR FLAVOR. THE QUICKEST METHOD IS ON THE STOVETOP. SPREAD NUTS OUT IN AN UNGREASED NONSTICK SKILLET AND PLACE OVER MEDIUM HEAT. SHAKE OR STIR FREQUENTLY, TO PREVENT BURNING, FOR 4 TO 5 MINUTES OR UNTIL FRAGRANT AND STARTING TO BROWN. TIP ONTO A COLD PLATE TO STOP THE COOKING PROCESS AND LET COOL COMPLETELY.

TWO AGING BATHING BEAUTIES COMMISERATING: "AT OUR AGE SWIMMING CAN BE DANGEROUS — LIFEGUARDS DON"T TRY AS HARD!"

SUPER SIMPLE COUSCOUS

MOMS ARE ETERNALLY GRATEFUL FOR THIS TINY, PERFECT PASTA FROM NORTH AFRICA. IT COOKS IN A FLASH, AND CHILDREN LOVE IT. HERE'S A BASIC RECIPE AND THREE VARIATIONS.

2 CUPS	CHICKEN OR VEGETABLE BROTH OR WATER	500 ML
1 TBSP	BUTTER	15 ML
1/2 TSP	SALT	2 ML
1 CUP	COUSCOUS	250 ML

IN A MEDIUM SAUCEPAN, COMBINE CHICKEN BROTH, BUTTER AND SALT; BRING TO A BOIL. STIR IN COUSCOUS, REMOVE FROM HEAT, COVER AND LET STAND FOR 6 TO 8 MINUTES OR UNTIL LIQUID IS ABSORBED. FLUFF WITH A FORK. SERVES 4.

VARIATIONS

COUSCOUS WITH CRANBERRIES AND PECANS: STIR IN 1/2 CUP (125 ML) EACH DRIED CRANBERRIES AND CHOPPED TOASTED PECANS WHILE FLUFFING.

ALMOND TOMATO COUSCOUS: STIR IN 2 SMALL TOMATOES, DICED, 1/4 CUP (50 ML) TOASTED SLICED ALMONDS, 2 TBSP (25 ML) FINELY SHREDDED FRESH MINT AND 2 TBSP (25 ML) FRESHLY SQUEEZED LEMON JUICE WHILE FLUFFING.

PARMESAN PARSLEY COUSCOUS: STIR IN 1/4 CUP (50 ML) EACH FRESHLY GRATED PARMESAN CHEESE AND CHOPPED FRESH PARSLEY WHILE FLUFFING.

COOKIES, BARS AND SQUARES

FOUR GENERATIONS
ICEBOX COOKIES

SINCE HER GRANDMOTHER'S DAY, JEAN COULTON'S FAMILY ACROSS THE PRAIRIES HAVE ENJOYED THESE FANTASTIC CHRISTMAS COOKIES. ANOTHER WINNER FOR YOUR HOLIDAY BAKING LIST.

3 2/3 CUPS	ALL-PURPOSE FLOUR	900 ML
2 TSP	GROUND CINNAMON	10 ML
1 TSP	BAKING SODA	5 ML
1 TSP	GROUND CLOVES	5 ML
1 CUP	GRANULATED SUGAR	250 ML
1 CUP	PACKED BROWN SUGAR	250 ML
1 CUP	BUTTER, AT ROOM TEMPERATURE	250 ML
3	EGGS	3
1 CUP	MIXED GLACÉ (CANDIED) FRUIT OR DATES, CHOPPED	250 ML
1/2 CUP	WALNUTS OR HAZELNUTS, CHOPPED	125 ML

IN A LARGE BOWL, SIFT TOGETHER FLOUR, CINNAMON, BAKING SODA AND CLOVES; SET ASIDE. IN ANOTHER LARGE BOWL, CREAM GRANULATED SUGAR, BROWN SUGAR AND BUTTER UNTIL LIGHT AND FLUFFY. BEAT IN EGGS, ONE AT A TIME. STIR IN FLOUR MIXTURE. STIR IN FRUIT AND NUTS. FORM DOUGH INTO FOUR 12-INCH (30 CM) LONG LOGS. WRAP IN PLASTIC WRAP AND FREEZE FOR 2 HOURS TO FIRM UP.

PREHEAT OVEN TO 350°F (180°C). USING A SHARP KNIFE, SLICE DOUGH INTO 1/4-INCH (0.5 CM) THICK ROUNDS. PLACE ABOUT 2 INCHES (5 CM) APART ON UNGREASED BAKING SHEETS. BAKE FOR 6 TO 10 MINUTES OR UNTIL LIGHTLY

BROWNED. LET COOL ON BAKING SHEETS ON RACKS FOR 2 MINUTES. TRANSFER TO RACKS TO COOL COMPLETELY. MAKES ABOUT 70 COOKIES.

MAKE AHEAD: PLACE COOKIES BETWEEN LAYERS OF WAXED PAPER IN AN AIRTIGHT CONTAINER AND STORE AT ROOM TEMPERATURE FOR UP TO 5 DAYS. WRAP LOGS OF UNCOOKED DOUGH IN A DOUBLE LAYER OF PLASTIC WRAP AND REFRIGERATE FOR UP TO I WEEK, OR OVERWRAP WITH HEAVY-DUTY FOIL AND FREEZE FOR UP TO I MONTH.

TIP: TO KEEP NUTS FRESH-TASTING, STORE THEM IN AN AIRTIGHT CONTAINER IN THE FREEZER. AT ROOM TEMPERATURE, THE NATURAL OILS IN NUTS (ESPECIALLY WALNUTS) MAY TURN RANCID, MAKING THEM TASTE BITTER.

VARIATION: OMIT THE FRUIT AND NUTS AND MIX IN $1/2$ CUP (125 ML) CRUSHED CANDY CANES.

WHEN IT COMES TO DIETING, REMEMBER ONE SIMPLE RULE: IF YOU CAN'T LOSE IT, DECORATE IT.

SNEAKY LEMON COOKIES

ZESTY AND VERY PRETTY. THESE COOKIES APPEAR TO BE MADE FROM SCRATCH, BUT THE SNEAKY PART IS THAT THEY'RE BASED ON A PACKAGE OF CAKE MIX. PERFECT WHEN YOU'RE FACING A TIME CRUNCH IN THE KITCHEN.

1	PACKAGE (18 OZ/515 G) WHITE CAKE MIX	1
2	EGGS	2
1/3 CUP	VEGETABLE OIL	75 ML
2 TBSP	GRATED LEMON ZEST	25 ML
1/4 CUP	FRESHLY SQUEEZED LEMON JUICE	50 ML
1/3 CUP	CONFECTIONER'S (ICING) SUGAR	75 ML

PREHEAT OVEN TO 375°F (190°C). PLACE CAKE MIX IN A LARGE BOWL. ADD EGGS, OIL, LEMON ZEST AND LEMON JUICE; STIR UNTIL BLENDED. PLACE CONFECTIONER'S SUGAR IN A SHALLOW BOWL. DROP TEASPOONFULS (5 ML) OF BATTER INTO THE SUGAR AND ROLL UNTIL COVERED WITH SUGAR AND ROUNDED. PLACE 2 INCHES (5 CM) APART ON AN UNGREASED BAKING SHEET AND SET ON TOP OF ANOTHER BAKING SHEET (THIS WILL PREVENT THE COOKIES FROM BURNING ON THE BOTTOM). BAKE FOR 7 TO 9 MINUTES OR UNTIL TOPS ARE LIGHTLY BROWNED AND CRACKED. LET COOL ON BAKING SHEET ON A RACK FOR 2 MINUTES. TRANSFER TO RACK TO COOL COMPLETELY. MAKES ABOUT 30 COOKIES.

MAKE AHEAD: TRANSFER TO AN AIRTIGHT CONTAINER AND STORE AT ROOM TEMPERATURE FOR UP TO 5 DAYS, OR PLACE BETWEEN LAYERS OF WAXED PAPER IN AN AIRTIGHT CONTAINER AND FREEZE FOR UP TO 2 WEEKS.

GINGER SPARKLES

THIS CLASSY COOKIE NEVER GOES OUT OF STYLE.

2¼ CUPS	ALL-PURPOSE FLOUR	550 ML
1/4 CUP	FINELY CHOPPED CANDIED GINGER	50 ML
2 TSP	BAKING SODA	10 ML
1 TSP	GROUND CINNAMON	5 ML
1 TSP	GROUND GINGER	5 ML
1 TBSP	MINCED GINGERROOT	15 ML
1/2 TSP	GROUND CLOVES	2 ML
1 CUP	PACKED BROWN SUGAR	250 ML
3/4 CUP	BUTTER, AT ROOM TEMPERATURE	175 ML
1/4 CUP	LIGHT (FANCY) MOLASSES	50 ML
1	EGG	1
	GRANULATED SUGAR	

PREHEAT OVEN TO 350°F (180°C). GREASE A BAKING SHEET. IN A LARGE BOWL, COMBINE FLOUR, CANDIED GINGER, BAKING SODA, CINNAMON, GROUND GINGER, GINGERROOT AND CLOVES; SET ASIDE. IN ANOTHER LARGE BOWL, CREAM BROWN SUGAR AND BUTTER UNTIL LIGHT AND FLUFFY. BEAT IN MOLASSES AND EGG. STIR IN FLOUR MIXTURE. FORM DOUGH INTO 1-INCH (2.5 CM) BALLS AND DIP TOPS IN GRANULATED SUGAR. PLACE 3 INCHES (7.5 CM) APART ON PREPARED BAKING SHEET. BAKE FOR 10 TO 12 MINUTES OR UNTIL SET. LET COOL FOR 3 TO 4 MINUTES. TRANSFER TO A RACK TO COOL COMPLETELY. MAKES ABOUT 50 COOKIES.

MAKE AHEAD: TRANSFER TO AN AIRTIGHT CONTAINER AND STORE AT ROOM TEMPERATURE FOR UP TO 5 DAYS, OR PLACE BETWEEN LAYERS OF WAXED PAPER IN AN AIRTIGHT CONTAINER AND FREEZE FOR UP TO 2 WEEKS.

ALMOND BITES

THESE DELICATE BITE-SIZE COOKIES ARE
THE IDEAL TREAT WITH AN AFTERNOON CUP OF TEA
OR AN AFTER-DINNER COFFEE.

1 CUP	ALL-PURPOSE FLOUR	250 ML
1 CUP	GROUND ALMONDS	250 ML
1/4 TSP	BAKING POWDER	1 ML
PINCH	SALT	PINCH
3/4 CUP	GRANULATED SUGAR	175 ML
1/2 CUP	BUTTER, AT ROOM TEMPERATURE	125 ML
1	EGG WHITE	1
1 TSP	PURE ALMOND EXTRACT	5 ML
	WHOLE BLANCHED ALMONDS (OPTIONAL)	

IN A BOWL, COMBINE FLOUR, GROUND ALMONDS, BAKING
POWDER AND SALT; SET ASIDE. IN A LARGE BOWL, CREAM
SUGAR AND BUTTER UNTIL LIGHT AND FLUFFY. BEAT IN EGG
WHITE AND ALMOND EXTRACT. STIR IN FLOUR MIXTURE
UNTIL DOUGH FORMS A BALL. WRAP DOUGH IN PLASTIC
WRAP AND REFRIGERATE FOR 2 HOURS TO FIRM UP.

PREHEAT OVEN TO 350°F (180°C). GREASE A LARGE BAKING
SHEET. SHAPE TEASPOONFULS (5 ML) OF DOUGH INTO
SMALL BALLS. PLACE 2 INCHES (5 CM) APART ON PREPARED
BAKING SHEET. USING THE BOTTOM OF A GLASS, FLATTEN
COOKIES SLIGHTLY. IF DESIRED, PLACE A WHOLE ALMOND
IN THE CENTER OF EACH COOKIE. BAKE FOR 10 TO
12 MINUTES OR UNTIL SET AND VERY LIGHTLY BROWNED.
LET COOL ON BAKING SHEET ON A RACK FOR 2 MINUTES.
TRANSFER TO RACK TO COOL COMPLETELY. MAKES ABOUT
36 COOKIES.

MAKE AHEAD: TRANSFER TO AN AIRTIGHT CONTAINER AND STORE AT ROOM TEMPERATURE FOR UP TO 5 DAYS, OR PLACE BETWEEN LAYERS OF WAXED PAPER IN AN AIRTIGHT CONTAINER AND FREEZE FOR UP TO 2 WEEKS.

TIP: CHECKING COOKIE DONENESS IS IMPORTANT TO SUCCESS. EVEN A MINUTE OR TWO CAN MAKE A BIG DIFFERENCE TO THE RESULTS. ALWAYS CHECK FOR DONENESS A MINUTE OR TWO BEFORE THE END OF THE STATED BAKING TIME.

NEVER PUT OFF TO TODAY WHAT YOU CAN PUT OFF TILL TOMORROW.

DRESSED-UP PEANUT BUTTER COOKIES

HEAVENLY AND UNBELIEVABLY EASY TO MAKE. JUST REMEMBER TO LET THESE COOKIES COOL LONG ENOUGH FOR THE CHOCOLATE ROSETTES TO SET.

1 3/4 CUPS	ALL-PURPOSE FLOUR	425 ML
1/2 CUP	GRANULATED SUGAR	125 ML
1/2 CUP	PACKED BROWN SUGAR	125 ML
1/2 CUP	PEANUT BUTTER	125 ML
1/2 CUP	BUTTER, AT ROOM TEMPERATURE	125 ML
1	EGG	1
1 TSP	BAKING SODA	5 ML
1 TSP	VANILLA EXTRACT	5 ML
	ADDITIONAL GRANULATED SUGAR	
30	CHOCOLATE ROSETTES	30

PREHEAT OVEN TO 375°F (190°C). GREASE A BAKING SHEET. IN A LARGE BOWL, BEAT FLOUR, GRANULATED SUGAR, BROWN SUGAR, PEANUT BUTTER, BUTTER, EGG, BAKING SODA AND VANILLA UNTIL WELL COMBINED. ROLL INTO THIRTY 1-INCH (2.5 CM) BALLS. ROLL IN GRANULATED SUGAR. PLACE 2 INCHES (5 CM) APART ON PREPARED BAKING SHEET AND, USING A FORK, FLATTEN SLIGHTLY. BAKE FOR ABOUT 8 MINUTES OR UNTIL PUFFY AND LIGHTLY BROWNED. REMOVE FROM OVEN AND IMMEDIATELY PLACE A CHOCOLATE ROSETTE IN THE CENTER OF EACH COOKIE. LET COOL FOR 5 MINUTES. TRANSFER TO A RACK TO COOL COMPLETELY. *MAKES 30 COOKIES.*

MAKE AHEAD: LAYER WITH WAXED PAPER IN AN AIRTIGHT CONTAINER AND STORE AT ROOM TEMPERATURE FOR UP TO 5 DAYS OR FREEZE FOR UP TO 2 WEEKS.

WINNIE THE POOH
CHOCOLATE CHIP COOKIES

A FOREVER FAVORITE. WE DON'T KNOW WHY THEY ARE CALLED THIS, THEY JUST ARE. DO NOT OVERCOOK — POOH AND PIGLET LIKE THEM CHEWY!

5 1/2 CUPS	ALL-PURPOSE FLOUR	1.375 L
1 1/2 TSP	BAKING SODA	7 ML
1 1/2 TSP	SALT	7 ML
1 1/2 CUPS	GRANULATED SUGAR	375 ML
1 1/2 CUPS	PACKED BROWN SUGAR	375 ML
2 CUPS	BUTTER, AT ROOM TEMPERATURE	500 ML
3	EGGS	3
1 TBSP	VANILLA EXTRACT	15 ML
2 CUPS	SEMISWEET OR MILK CHOCOLATE CHIPS	500 ML

PREHEAT OVEN TO 350°F (180°C). GREASE 2 BAKING SHEETS. IN A BOWL, COMBINE FLOUR, BAKING SODA AND SALT; SET ASIDE. IN A LARGE BOWL, CREAM GRANULATED SUGAR, BROWN SUGAR AND BUTTER. BEAT IN EGGS, ONE AT A TIME, AND VANILLA. STIR IN FLOUR MIXTURE. STIR IN CHOCOLATE CHIPS. DROP BY TABLESPOONFULS (15 ML) ONTO PREPARED BAKING SHEETS, SPACING THEM 3 INCHES (7.5 CM) APART. BAKE FOR ABOUT 10 MINUTES OR UNTIL COOKIES ARE LIGHTLY BROWNED. LET COOL ON BAKING SHEETS ON RACKS FOR 5 MINUTES. TRANSFER TO RACKS TO COOL COMPLETELY. MAKES ABOUT 84 COOKIES.

MAKE AHEAD: TRANSFER TO AN AIRTIGHT CONTAINER AND STORE AT ROOM TEMPERATURE FOR UP TO 5 DAYS, OR PLACE BETWEEN LAYERS OF WAXED PAPER IN AN AIRTIGHT CONTAINER AND FREEZE FOR UP TO 2 WEEKS.

CHOCOLATE MINT COOKIES

1 CUP	GRANULATED SUGAR	250 ML
1/2 CUP	BUTTER, AT ROOM TEMPERATURE	125 ML
1 TSP	PURE PEPPERMINT EXTRACT	5 ML
1	EGG	1
2 OZ	SEMISWEET CHOCOLATE, MELTED (SEE TIP, BELOW) AND COOLED	60 G
1 CUP	ALL-PURPOSE FLOUR	250 ML
1/2 TSP	SALT	2 ML
1 1/2 CUPS	MINT-FLAVORED SEMISWEET CHOCOLATE CHIPS	375 ML

PREHEAT OVEN TO 350°F (180°C). IN A LARGE BOWL, BEAT SUGAR, BUTTER, PEPPERMINT EXTRACT, EGG AND MELTED CHOCOLATE UNTIL LIGHT AND FLUFFY. STIR IN FLOUR AND SALT. STIR IN CHOCOLATE CHIPS. DROP BY HEAPING TEASPOONFULS (5 ML) ONTO UNGREASED BAKING SHEETS, SPACING THEM 3 INCHES (7.5 CM) APART. USING THE BOTTOM OF A GLASS, FLATTEN COOKIES SLIGHTLY. BAKE FOR 7 TO 8 MINUTES OR UNTIL SET. LET COOL ON BAKING SHEETS ON RACKS FOR 2 MINUTES. TRANSFER TO RACKS TO COOL COMPLETELY. MAKES ABOUT 30 COOKIES.

MAKE AHEAD: TRANSFER TO AN AIRTIGHT CONTAINER AND STORE AT ROOM TEMPERATURE FOR UP TO 5 DAYS, OR PLACE BETWEEN LAYERS OF WAXED PAPER IN AN AIRTIGHT CONTAINER AND FREEZE FOR UP TO 2 WEEKS.

TIP: TO MELT CHOCOLATE, PLACE CHOPPED CHOCOLATE IN A DRY MICROWAVE-SAFE BOWL. HEAT ON MEDIUM (50%) FOR 30 SECONDS. STIR AND HEAT IN ADDITIONAL 30-SECOND INCREMENTS UNTIL ALMOST MELTED. STIR UNTIL SMOOTH AND FULLY MELTED.

CHOCOLATE TOFFEE COOKIES

THESE WON'T LAST LONG.

1 1/4 CUPS	ALL-PURPOSE FLOUR	300 ML
1/2 TSP	BAKING SODA	2 ML
1/4 TSP	SALT	1 ML
3/4 CUP	FIRMLY PACKED BROWN SUGAR	175 ML
1/2 CUP	BUTTER, AT ROOM TEMPERATURE	125 ML
1 TSP	VANILLA EXTRACT	5 ML
1	EGG, LIGHTLY BEATEN	1
3 OZ	SEMISWEET CHOCOLATE, CUT INTO CHUNKS (ABOUT 1/2 CUP/125 ML)	90 G
2	CHOCOLATE-COVERED TOFFEE BARS, CHOPPED (ABOUT 1/2 CUP/125 ML)	2

PREHEAT OVEN TO 350°F (180°C). IN A BOWL, SIFT TOGETHER FLOUR, BAKING SODA AND SALT; SET ASIDE. IN A LARGE BOWL, CREAM BROWN SUGAR, BUTTER AND VANILLA UNTIL LIGHT AND FLUFFY. BEAT IN EGG. STIR IN FLOUR MIXTURE UNTIL JUST COMBINED. GENTLY STIR IN CHOCOLATE AND CHOCOLATE-COVERED TOFFEE. DROP BY HEAPING TEASPOONFULS (5 ML) ONTO UNGREASED BAKING SHEETS, SPACING THEM 2 INCHES (5 CM) APART. BAKE FOR ABOUT 10 MINUTES OR UNTIL GOLDEN BROWN. LET COOL ON BAKING SHEETS ON RACKS FOR 5 MINUTES. TRANSFER TO RACKS TO COOL COMPLETELY. MAKES ABOUT 30 COOKIES.

MAKE AHEAD: PLACE BETWEEN LAYERS OF WAXED PAPER IN AN AIRTIGHT CONTAINER AND STORE AT ROOM TEMPERATURE FOR UP TO 5 DAYS OR FREEZE FOR UP TO 2 WEEKS.

CRANBERRY PISTACHIO BISCOTTI

BISCOTTI, WHICH MEANS "TWICE-COOKED," ARE CRUNCHY
ITALIAN COOKIES THAT ARE VERY POPULAR WITH
COFFEE LOVERS. THEY ARE EXTREMELY EASY TO MAKE
AT HOME. THIS RECIPE IS A VARIATION OF ONE CREATED
BY CHEF SONNY SUNG OF EDMONTON, ALBERTA.

2½ CUPS	ALL-PURPOSE FLOUR	625 ML
2½ TSP	BAKING POWDER	12 ML
4	EGGS	4
1¼ CUPS	GRANULATED SUGAR	300 ML
½ CUP	BUTTER, MELTED AND COOLED	125 ML
	GRATED ZEST OF 2 ORANGES	
½ CUP	FRESHLY SQUEEZED ORANGE JUICE	125 ML
2½ TBSP	WHITE OR CIDER VINEGAR	32 ML
1 TBSP	VANILLA EXTRACT	15 ML
¾ CUP	DRIED CRANBERRIES	175 ML
½ CUP	PISTACHIOS, CHOPPED	125 ML

PREHEAT OVEN TO 300°F (150°C). GREASE A 13- BY 9-INCH
(33 BY 23 CM) METAL BAKING PAN AND LINE WITH
PARCHMENT PAPER. IN A BOWL, SIFT TOGETHER FLOUR
AND BAKING POWDER; SET ASIDE. IN A LARGE BOWL, BEAT
EGGS AND SUGAR UNTIL VERY LIGHT, FOAMY AND TRIPLED
IN VOLUME. BEAT IN BUTTER. STIR IN ORANGE ZEST,
ORANGE JUICE, VINEGAR AND VANILLA. STIR IN FLOUR
MIXTURE. STIR IN CRANBERRIES AND PISTACHIOS. POUR
INTO PREPARED PAN AND SMOOTH TOP. BAKE FOR 30 TO
35 MINUTES OR UNTIL GOLDEN AND A TESTER INSERTED
IN THE CENTER COMES OUT CLEAN. REMOVE FROM OVEN,
LEAVING OVEN ON, AND LET COOL IN PAN ON A RACK FOR
15 MINUTES.

TURN OUT ONTO A CUTTING BOARD AND, USING A SHARP KNIFE, TRIM OFF EDGES. (YOU'LL HAVE NO SHORTAGE OF VOLUNTEERS TO NIBBLE ON THE TRIM!) CUT DOUGH INTO 24 PIECES. PLACE CUT SIDE DOWN ON A LARGE BAKING SHEET LINED WITH PARCHMENT PAPER. BAKE FOR 20 TO 25 MINUTES, TURNING ONCE, UNTIL GOLDEN BROWN. TURN OFF OVEN BUT LEAVE BISCOTTI IN OVEN FOR AT LEAST I HOUR OR UNTIL VERY DRY AND CRISP. MAKES 24 BISCOTTI.

MAKE AHEAD: TRANSFER TO AN AIRTIGHT CONTAINER AND STORE AT ROOM TEMPERATURE FOR UP TO I WEEK, OR PLACE BETWEEN LAYERS OF WAXED PAPER IN AN AIRTIGHT CONTAINER AND FREEZE FOR UP TO I MONTH.

TIP: WRAP IN DECORATIVE CELLOPHANE BAGS AND TIE WITH RIBBON FOR A PERFECT CHRISTMAS OR HOSTESS GIFT.

I ALWAYS WANTED TO BE SOMEONE; NOW I REALIZE I SHOULD HAVE BEEN MORE SPECIFIC.

CARDAMOM SHORTBREAD

CARDAMOM IS A FRAGRANT SPICE THAT'S RELATED TO GINGER. WE MOST COMMONLY ASSOCIATE CARDAMOM WITH CURRIES, BUT IN SCANDINAVIA, IT IS A POPULAR INGREDIENT IN BAKING. THIS SHORTBREAD DOUGH IS PATTED INTO BAKING PANS RATHER THAN ROLLED — IT'S A BREEZE TO PUT TOGETHER.

1½ TO 1¾ CUPS	ALL-PURPOSE FLOUR, DIVIDED	375 TO 425 ML
¼ CUP	RICE FLOUR (SEE TIP, OPPOSITE)	50 ML
2 TSP	GROUND CARDAMOM	10 ML
¼ TSP	SALT	1 ML
1 CUP	BUTTER, AT ROOM TEMPERATURE	250 ML
¾ CUP	CONFECTIONER'S (ICING) SUGAR	175 ML
2 TBSP	GRANULATED SUGAR	25 ML

PREHEAT OVEN TO 325°F (160°C). IN A BOWL, WHISK TOGETHER 1¼ CUPS (300 ML) OF THE ALL-PURPOSE FLOUR, RICE FLOUR, CARDAMOM AND SALT; SET ASIDE. IN A LARGE BOWL, BEAT BUTTER UNTIL SOFT. BEAT IN CONFECTIONER'S SUGAR UNTIL LIGHT AND FLUFFY. BEAT IN FLOUR MIXTURE. TURN DOUGH OUT ONTO A FLOURED WORK SURFACE AND KNEAD, WORKING IN THE REMAINING FLOUR UNTIL DOUGH BEGINS TO CRACK. (THERE MIGHT BE A SMALL AMOUNT OF FLOUR LEFT OVER). DIVIDE DOUGH IN HALF AND PAT INTO 2 UNGREASED 8-INCH (20 CM) ROUND CAKE PANS. USING A FORK, SCORE EACH INTO 12 OR 16 WEDGES AND MAKE A DECORATIVE BORDER AROUND THE EDGE. SPRINKLE WITH GRANULATED SUGAR. BAKE FOR ABOUT 25 MINUTES OR UNTIL CENTERS ARE GOLDEN BROWN AND EDGES ARE SLIGHTLY DARKER.

LET COOL IN PANS ON A RACK FOR 5 MINUTES, THEN USE A SHARP KNIFE TO CUT EACH SHORTBREAD INTO WEDGES. LET COOL COMPLETELY IN PANS. MAKES 24 TO 32 WEDGES.

MAKE AHEAD: TRANSFER TO AN AIRTIGHT CONTAINER AND STORE AT ROOM TEMPERATURE FOR UP TO 5 DAYS, OR PLACE BETWEEN LAYERS OF WAXED PAPER IN AN AIRTIGHT CONTAINER AND FREEZE FOR UP TO 2 WEEKS.

TIP: RICE FLOUR IS COMMONLY USED IN SCOTTISH SHORTBREAD RECIPES, AS IT LENDS A DELICIOUS CRUMBLY TEXTURE. LOOK FOR IT IN THE BAKING AISLE.

VARIATION: OMIT THE CARDAMOM AND ADD I TSP (5 ML) VANILLA EXTRACT AND/OR 2 TSP (IO ML) GRATED LEMON ZEST.

THE BEST YEARS OF HER LIFE WERE THE TEN BETWEEN 29 AND 30.

CHOIR BARS

THESE CHERRY COCONUT BARS ARE SO POPULAR WITH A FRIEND'S CHURCH GROUP THAT SHE DUBBED THEM "CHOIR BARS." YOU'LL BE SINGING THEIR PRAISES TOO!

BASE

I CUP	ALL-PURPOSE FLOUR	250 ML
1/4 CUP	GRANULATED SUGAR	50 ML
1/2 CUP	BUTTER	125 ML

FILLING

1/3 CUP	ALL-PURPOSE FLOUR	75 ML
I TSP	BAKING POWDER	5 ML
2	EGGS	2
I	CAN (14 OZ OR 300 ML) SWEETENED CONDENSED MILK	I
I TSP	ALMOND OR VANILLA EXTRACT	5 ML
1 1/4 CUPS	SWEETENED SHREDDED COCONUT	300 ML
3/4 CUP	DRAINED MARASCHINO CHERRIES, CHOPPED	175 ML

BASE: PREHEAT OVEN TO 350°F (180°C). GREASE A 9-INCH (23 CM) SQUARE METAL BAKING PAN AND LINE WITH PARCHMENT PAPER. IN A LARGE BOWL, COMBINE FLOUR AND SUGAR. USING YOUR FINGERS OR A PASTRY BLENDER, BLEND IN BUTTER UNTIL MIXTURE RESEMBLES COARSE BREAD CRUMBS. PAT INTO BOTTOM OF PREPARED PAN. BAKE FOR ABOUT 10 MINUTES OR UNTIL SET AND LIGHTLY BROWNED. REMOVE FROM OVEN, LEAVING OVEN ON, AND LET COOL.

FILLING: IN A SMALL BOWL, SIFT TOGETHER FLOUR AND BAKING POWDER; SET ASIDE. IN A LARGE BOWL, BEAT

EGGS, CONDENSED MILK AND ALMOND EXTRACT. STIR IN FLOUR MIXTURE. STIR IN COCONUT AND CHERRIES.

SPREAD FILLING OVER BASE. BAKE FOR 25 TO 30 MINUTES OR UNTIL TOP IS GOLDEN AND A TESTER INSERTED IN THE CENTER COMES OUT CLEAN. (IF EDGES START TO BROWN TOO QUICKLY, REDUCE TEMPERATURE TO 325°F/160°C AND COVER PAN LOOSELY WITH FOIL.) LET COOL COMPLETELY IN PAN ON A RACK. CUT INTO BARS. MAKES 16 BARS.

MAKE AHEAD: TRANSFER TO AN AIRTIGHT CONTAINER AND STORE AT ROOM TEMPERATURE FOR UP TO 2 DAYS.

TIP: SUBSTITUTE CHOPPED GLACÉ (CANDIED) CHERRIES FOR THE MARASCHINO CHERRIES.

MIDDLE AGE IS WHEN YOUR HAIR TURNS FROM GRAY TO BLACK.

PALM BEACH BARS

AS HARRY NILSSON WOULD SING, "YOU PUT DE LIME IN DE COCONUT." AND EAT IT ALL UP.

BASE

I CUP	GRAHAM CRACKER CRUMBS	250 ML
1/4 CUP	UNSWEETENED SHREDDED COCONUT	50 ML
1/4 CUP	GRANULATED SUGAR	50 ML
1/3 CUP	BUTTER, MELTED	75 ML

FILLING

I	CAN (14 OZ OR 300 ML) SWEETENED CONDENSED MILK	I
	GRATED ZEST OF I LIME	
1/3 CUP	FRESHLY SQUEEZED LIME JUICE (2 TO 3 LIMES)	75 ML
3 TBSP	GRANULATED SUGAR	45 ML
2 TBSP	CORNSTARCH	25 ML
I	EGG	I
1/4 CUP	UNSWEETENED SHREDDED COCONUT, TOASTED (SEE TIP, PAGE 327)	50 ML

BASE: PREHEAT OVEN TO 325°F (160°C). GREASE A 9-INCH (23 CM) SQUARE METAL BAKING PAN AND LINE WITH PARCHMENT PAPER. IN A MEDIUM BOWL, COMBINE CRACKER CRUMBS, COCONUT, SUGAR AND BUTTER. PRESS INTO BOTTOM OF PREPARED PAN. BAKE FOR ABOUT 8 MINUTES OR UNTIL SET AND LIGHTLY BROWNED. REMOVE FROM OVEN, LEAVING OVEN ON, AND LET COOL.

FILLING: IN A BOWL, WHISK TOGETHER CONDENSED MILK, LIME ZEST, LIME JUICE, SUGAR, CORNSTARCH AND EGG.

POUR FILLING OVER BASE. BAKE FOR ABOUT 25 MINUTES OR UNTIL EDGES ARE SET AND NOT STICKY BUT CENTER IS STILL SLIGHTLY SOFT. SPRINKLE WITH TOASTED COCONUT. LET COOL COMPLETELY IN PAN ON A RACK, THEN REFRIGERATE FOR 2 HOURS, UNTIL CHILLED. CUT INTO BARS. MAKES 16 BARS.

MAKE AHEAD: TRANSFER TO AN AIRTIGHT CONTAINER AND REFRIGERATE FOR UP TO 3 DAYS.

TIP: BEFORE SQUEEZING JUICE FROM LEMONS AND LIMES, PRICK THEM WITH A FORK AND MICROWAVE THEM ON HIGH FOR ABOUT 20 SECONDS. THE SLIGHTLY WARMED CITRUS FRUIT WILL GIVE UP NOTICEABLY MORE JUICE THAN IF SQUEEZED WHEN COLD.

"WHAT I DON'T LIKE ABOUT OFFICE CHRISTMAS PARTIES IS LOOKING FOR A JOB THE NEXT DAY."
— PHYLLIS DILLER

BIRD SEED BARS

THESE WILL FLY!

I CUP	SESAME SEEDS, TOASTED (SEE TIP, PAGE 93)	250 ML
I CUP	UNSALTED SUNFLOWER SEEDS	250 ML
I CUP	UNSALTED RAW OR ROASTED PEANUTS	250 ML
I CUP	UNSWEETENED SHREDDED COCONUT	250 ML
I CUP	PUMPKIN SEEDS	250 ML
1/2 CUP	BUTTER	125 ML
1/2 CUP	PACKED BROWN SUGAR	125 ML
1/4 CUP	LIQUID HONEY	50 ML

LINE A 13- BY 9-INCH (33 BY 23 CM) BAKING PAN WITH WAXED PAPER. IN A LARGE BOWL, COMBINE SESAME SEEDS, SUNFLOWER SEEDS, PEANUTS, COCONUT AND PUMPKIN SEEDS; SET ASIDE. IN A MEDIUM SAUCEPAN, MELT BUTTER, SUGAR AND HONEY OVER MEDIUM HEAT, STIRRING; BRING TO A BOIL. REDUCE HEAT AND SIMMER, STIRRING OCCASIONALLY, FOR ABOUT 3 MINUTES OR UNTIL SLIGHTLY THICKENED. POUR OVER SEED MIXTURE AND STIR WELL. SPREAD IN PREPARED PAN. REFRIGERATE FOR 2 HOURS, UNTIL CHILLED. CUT INTO BARS. MAKES 25 TO 36 BARS.

MAKE AHEAD: PLACE BETWEEN LAYERS OF WAXED PAPER IN AN AIRTIGHT CONTAINER AND REFRIGERATE FOR UP TO 5 DAYS OR FREEZE FOR UP TO I MONTH.

CHEWY TRAIL MIX BARS

THESE CHEWY, NO-BAKE BARS ARE BEST ENJOYED STRAIGHT FROM THE FRIDGE. TO TOTE IN A LUNCH BAG, WRAP THE BARS IN PLASTIC WRAP AND TUCK BESIDE THE COOL PACK OR A FROZEN JUICE BOX. THIS WILL KEEP THEM NICE AND FIRM.

1 CUP	PEANUT BUTTER (SMOOTH OR CRUNCHY)	250 ML
1 CUP	LIQUID HONEY	250 ML
1/2 CUP	HOT CHOCOLATE MIX	125 ML
1/4 CUP	UNSWEETENED COCOA POWDER, SIFTED	50 ML
3/4 CUP	CHOPPED WALNUTS, PECANS OR PISTACHIOS	175 ML
3/4 CUP	RAISINS OR DRIED CRANBERRIES	175 ML
1/2 CUP	UNSALTED SUNFLOWER SEEDS	125 ML
1/2 CUP	UNSWEETENED SHREDDED COCONUT	125 ML
1/4 CUP	SESAME SEEDS	50 ML

GREASE A 13- BY 9-INCH (33 BY 23 CM) BAKING PAN AND LINE WITH PARCHMENT PAPER. IN A LARGE SAUCEPAN, GENTLY HEAT PEANUT BUTTER AND HONEY OVER LOW HEAT, WHISKING TO BLEND WELL. DO NOT LET BOIL. WHISK IN HOT CHOCOLATE MIX AND COCOA. STIR IN WALNUTS, RAISINS, SUNFLOWER SEEDS, COCONUT AND SESAME SEEDS. SPREAD IN PREPARED PAN, SMOOTHING TOP. REFRIGERATE FOR 2 HOURS, UNTIL CHILLED. CUT INTO BARS. MAKES 25 TO 36 BARS.

MAKE AHEAD: PLACE BETWEEN LAYERS OF WAXED PAPER IN AN AIRTIGHT CONTAINER AND REFRIGERATE FOR UP TO 5 DAYS.

CHOCOLATE PECAN CARAMEL BARS

A-MMM-AZING!

BASE

2 CUPS	ALL-PURPOSE FLOUR	500 ML
1 CUP	PACKED BROWN SUGAR	250 ML
1/2 CUP	BUTTER	125 ML
1 1/2 CUPS	PECAN HALVES	375 ML

FILLING

1 CUP	BUTTER	250 ML
3/4 CUP	PACKED BROWN SUGAR	175 ML
3 TBSP	WHIPPING (35%) CREAM	45 ML

1 CUP	SEMISWEET CHOCOLATE CHIPS	250 ML

BASE: PREHEAT OVEN TO 350°F (180°C). GREASE A 13- BY 9-INCH (33 BY 23 CM) METAL BAKING PAN AND LINE WITH PARCHMENT PAPER, LEAVING A 1-INCH (2.5 CM) OVERHANG. IN A FOOD PROCESSOR, PULSE FLOUR, BROWN SUGAR AND BUTTER TO FINE CRUMBS. (YOU CAN ALSO DO THIS IN A LARGE BOWL BY RUBBING THE MIXTURE THROUGH YOUR FINGERS UNTIL IT RESEMBLES COARSE BREAD CRUMBS). PAT INTO BOTTOM OF PREPARED PAN AND SPRINKLE WITH PECANS. BAKE FOR 10 MINUTES OR UNTIL PECANS START TO TOAST AND CRUST IS PARTIALLY COOKED. REMOVE FROM OVEN, LEAVING OVEN ON.

FILLING: IN A SAUCEPAN, MELT BUTTER AND BROWN SUGAR OVER MEDIUM HEAT; BRING TO A BOIL, STIRRING CONSTANTLY FOR 1 MINUTE. REMOVE FROM HEAT AND WHISK IN CREAM.

CAREFULLY POUR FILLING OVER PECANS. BAKE FOR 12 TO 15 MINUTES, CHECKING PERIODICALLY TO MAKE SURE IT'S NOT BURNING, UNTIL SET. REMOVE FROM OVEN, IMMEDIATELY SPREAD CHOCOLATE CHIPS OVER TOP AND LET STAND UNTIL SLIGHTLY MELTED. RUN A FORK THROUGH CHOCOLATE TO GIVE IT A SWIRLY EFFECT. REFRIGERATE FOR 2 HOURS, UNTIL CHILLED. USING THE EDGES OF THE PARCHMENT PAPER AS HANDLES, REMOVE FROM PAN AND TRANSFER TO A CUTTING BOARD. USING A SHARP KNIFE, CUT INTO BARS. MAKES 25 TO 36 BARS.

MAKE AHEAD: PLACE BETWEEN LAYERS OF WAXED PAPER IN AN AIRTIGHT CONTAINER AND REFRIGERATE FOR UP TO 5 DAYS OR FREEZE FOR UP TO 2 WEEKS.

TIP: THE CRUST IS VERY FIRM, SO YOU'LL NEED TO USE A VERY SHARP KNIFE AND SOME ELBOW GREASE TO SLICE IT INTO BARS.

YOU CAN'T SCARE ME; I HAVE CHILDREN.

CRANBERRY NUT CHOCOLATE SQUARES

THESE SINFULLY DELICIOUS SQUARES MUST BE MADE WITH GOOD-QUALITY DARK CHOCOLATE — NO BAKER'S CHOCOLATE, PLEASE! SERVE THEM WITH COFFEE AS AN AFTER-DINNER TREAT OR ANYTIME YOU FEEL THE NEED TO INDULGE.

20	DIGESTIVE COOKIES	20
$3/4$ CUP	PECANS, TOASTED (SEE TIP, OPPOSITE) AND CHOPPED	175 ML
$1/2$ CUP	DRIED CRANBERRIES	125 ML
$1/3$ CUP	BUTTER, AT ROOM TEMPERATURE	75 ML
$3 1/2$ OZ	GOOD-QUALITY DARK CHOCOLATE (ABOUT 1 BAR)	100 G
3 TBSP	CORN SYRUP	45 ML

LINE AN 8-INCH (20 CM) SQUARE BAKING PAN WITH FOIL. PLACE COOKIES IN A PLASTIC BAG AND SQUEEZE OR THUMP THEM INTO COARSE CRUMBS, LEAVING A FEW PEA-SIZE PIECES. POUR INTO A MEDIUM BOWL AND ADD PECANS AND CRANBERRIES; SET ASIDE. IN A SAUCEPAN, GENTLY MELT BUTTER, CHOCOLATE AND CORN SYRUP OVER LOW HEAT, STIRRING TO COMBINE. DO NOT LET BOIL. POUR OVER COOKIE MIXTURE AND STIR WELL. SPREAD IN PREPARED PAN. REFRIGERATE FOR 2 HOURS, UNTIL CHILLED. CUT INTO SQUARES. MAKES 16 SQUARES.

MAKE AHEAD: PLACE BETWEEN LAYERS OF WAXED PAPER IN AN AIRTIGHT CONTAINER AND REFRIGERATE FOR UP TO 5 DAYS OR FREEZE FOR UP TO 2 WEEKS.

TIP: TOASTING NUTS HELPS BRING OUT THEIR FLAVOR. THE QUICKEST METHOD IS ON THE STOVETOP. SPREAD NUTS OUT IN AN UNGREASED NONSTICK SKILLET AND PLACE OVER MEDIUM HEAT. SHAKE OR STIR FREQUENTLY, TO PREVENT BURNING, FOR 4 TO 5 MINUTES OR UNTIL FRAGRANT AND STARTING TO BROWN. TIP ONTO A COLD PLATE TO STOP THE COOKING PROCESS AND LET COOL COMPLETELY.

VARIATION: USE GOOD-QUALITY WHITE CHOCOLATE AND PISTACHIOS IN PLACE OF THE DARK CHOCOLATE AND PECANS.

"THE PRACTICE OF PUTTING WOMEN ON A PEDESTAL BEGAN TO DIE OUT WHEN IT WAS DISCOVERED THAT THEY COULD GIVE ORDERS BETTER FROM THERE."
— BETTY GRABLE

OATS TO GO

QUICK AND EASY. PERFECT FOR TUCKING INTO KIDS' LUNCH BAGS OR AS AN AFTER-SCHOOL SNACK.

1/2 CUP	BUTTER	125 ML
1/2 CUP	GRANULATED SUGAR	125 ML
1/3 CUP	CORN SYRUP	75 ML
2 CUPS	QUICK-COOKING ROLLED OR FLAKED OATS (NOT INSTANT)	500 ML

PREHEAT OVEN TO 350°F (180°C). GREASE A 9-INCH (23 CM) SQUARE METAL BAKING PAN AND LINE WITH PARCHMENT PAPER, LEAVING A 1-INCH (2.5 CM) OVERHANG. (IF YOU DON'T USE PARCHMENT PAPER, YOU'LL NEVER GET THESE CHEWY LITTLE DEVILS OUT OF THE PAN). IN A LARGE SAUCEPAN, MELT BUTTER, SUGAR AND CORN SYRUP OVER MEDIUM HEAT, STIRRING OFTEN. STIR IN ROLLED OATS. SPREAD IN PREPARED PAN AND LET COOL UNTIL FIRM. USING THE EDGES OF THE PARCHMENT PAPER AS HANDLES, REMOVE FROM PAN AND TRANSFER TO A CUTTING BOARD. CUT INTO SQUARES. MAKES 16 SQUARES.

MAKE AHEAD: PLACE BETWEEN LAYERS OF WAXED PAPER IN AN AIRTIGHT CONTAINER AND STORE AT ROOM TEMPERATURE FOR UP TO 5 DAYS OR FREEZE FOR UP TO 2 WEEKS.

TIP: LINING A BAKING PAN WITH PARCHMENT PAPER PREVENTS STICKING. IT ALSO REDUCES THE CHANCES OF BURNING THE BOTTOM OF CAKES AND COOKIES AND SAVES ON CLEANUP. IF YOU DON'T HAVE PARCHMENT PAPER, YOU CAN USE A SILICONE BAKING MAT (WHICH CAN BE WASHED AND REUSED) OR FOIL.

DESSERTS

YOGURT FRUIT DIP

SERVE THIS BRIGHT, SIMPLE DESSERT IN INDIVIDUAL BOWLS AND SET OUT A PLATE OF FRUIT SKEWERS FOR GUESTS TO DIP INTO THE SAUCE. TRY IT WITH CHOPPED MELON, PINEAPPLE CHUNKS, HULLED STRAWBERRIES, GRAPES, SLICED KIWIFRUIT AND SLICED BANANAS.

1/2 CUP	PLAIN YOGURT	125 ML
1/2 CUP	SOUR CREAM	125 ML
1 TBSP	LIQUID HONEY	15 ML
	GRATED ZEST OF 1 LEMON	
1 TBSP	FRESHLY SQUEEZED LEMON JUICE	15 ML
1 TSP	VANILLA EXTRACT	5 ML
2 TBSP	SWEETENED SHREDDED COCONUT, TOASTED (OPTIONAL)	25 ML

IN A SMALL BOWL, WHISK TOGETHER YOGURT, SOUR CREAM, HONEY, LEMON ZEST, LEMON JUICE AND VANILLA. COVER AND REFRIGERATE FOR AT LEAST 1 HOUR, UNTIL CHILLED, OR FOR UP TO 4 HOURS. SPOON INTO INDIVIDUAL DIPPING BOWLS AND GARNISH WITH COCONUT, IF DESIRED. MAKES 1 1/4 CUPS (300 ML).

GIVE A MAN A FISH AND YOU CAN FEED HIM FOR A DAY. TEACH A MAN TO FISH AND YOU'RE RID OF HIM FOR THE WEEKEND.

CHOCOLATE-DIPPED STRAWBERRIES

SIMPLE AND ELEGANT. CHOOSE PERFECT BERRIES AND QUALITY CHOCOLATE — BAKER'S CHOCOLATE IS A NO-NO! SERVE WITH ALMOND BITES (PAGE 284) OR CARDAMOM SHORTBREAD (PAGE 292).

| 15 | FIRM STRAWBERRIES (WITH HULLS) | 15 |
| 7 OZ | GOOD-QUALITY DARK CHOCOLATE (ABOUT 2 BARS), CHOPPED | 200 G |

LINE A BAKING SHEET WITH WAXED PAPER. WIPE STRAWBERRIES CLEAN WITH A CLEAN DAMP TEA TOWEL OR PAPER TOWEL, THEN GENTLY BLOT DRY. (THEY MUST BE COMPLETELY DRY OR THE CHOCOLATE WILL SEIZE AND BECOME LUMPY.) PLACE CHOCOLATE IN A SMALL, DEEP, COMPLETELY DRY MICROWAVE-SAFE BOWL. MICROWAVE ON LOW (10%) IN 15-SECOND INCREMENTS UNTIL GLOSSY BUT NOT COMPLETELY MELTED. (THIS PREVENTS THE CHOCOLATE FROM SCORCHING.) REMOVE FROM MICROWAVE AND STIR GENTLY UNTIL FULLY MELTED. HOLDING STRAWBERRIES BY THEIR HULLS, DIP THEM IN CHOCOLATE, THEN PLACE ON PREPARED BAKING SHEET. REFRIGERATE FOR AT LEAST 30 MINUTES, UNTIL SET, OR FOR UP TO 3 HOURS. MAKES 15.

TIP: IF THESE ARE MADE TOO FAR IN ADVANCE, THE STRAWBERRY JUICES START TO SEEP THROUGH THE CHOCOLATE.

BAKED APPLES WITH FRUIT-PORT STUFFING

THESE ARE SOME APPLES!

1/4 CUP	DRIED APRICOTS, CHOPPED	50 ML
1/4 CUP	DRIED CHERRIES, BLUEBERRIES OR CRANBERRIES	50 ML
3/4 CUP	ORANGE JUICE OR UNSWEETENED APPLE JUICE, DIVIDED	175 ML
1/2 CUP	PORT	125 ML
2 TBSP	PACKED BROWN SUGAR	25 ML
1/4 CUP	WALNUTS OR PECANS, CHOPPED	50 ML
4	GOLDEN DELICIOUS APPLES	4
4 TSP	BUTTER	20 ML
	WHIPPED CREAM OR VANILLA ICE CREAM	

IN A MEDIUM SAUCEPAN, COMBINE APRICOTS, CHERRIES, 1/2 CUP (125 ML) OF THE ORANGE JUICE, PORT AND BROWN SUGAR; BRING TO A BOIL. REDUCE HEAT AND SIMMER FOR 15 TO 20 MINUTES OR UNTIL FRUIT IS PLUMP AND JUICE IS SYRUPY. REMOVE FROM HEAT AND STIR IN WALNUTS.

PREHEAT OVEN TO 350°F (180°C). GREASE AN 8-INCH (20 CM) SQUARE GLASS BAKING DISH. WASH AND DRY APPLES AND REMOVE CORES, USING AN APPLE CORER OR A PARING KNIFE. CUT A THIN SLICE FROM THE BOTTOM OF APPLES TO HELP THEM STAND UPRIGHT. PLACE APPLES IN PREPARED BAKING DISH. PACK FRUIT MIXTURE INTO APPLES, DIVIDING EVENLY. SPOON LEFTOVER SYRUP FROM FRUIT MIXTURE OVER AND AROUND APPLES. POUR THE REMAINING ORANGE JUICE INTO THE DISH. PLACE 1 TSP (5 ML) BUTTER ON TOP OF EACH APPLE. COVER LOOSELY WITH FOIL AND BAKE FOR ABOUT 1 HOUR, BASTING TWO OR THREE TIMES

WITH THE SYRUPY JUICES IN DISH, UNTIL APPLES ARE TENDER AND SKINS START TO CRINKLE. SERVE WITH SOME OF THE JUICES SPOONED OVER EACH APPLE AND A DOLLOP OF WHIPPED CREAM OR A SCOOP OF ICE CREAM. SERVES 4.

BRANDIED CARAMEL BANANAS

WHEN YOU NEED A LAST-MINUTE DESSERT, THIS ONE IS ALWAYS A HIT.

3 TBSP	BUTTER	45 ML
2 TBSP	PACKED BROWN SUGAR	25 ML
4	FIRM RIPE BANANAS, CUT INTO I-INCH (2.5 CM) SLICES	4
3 TBSP	BRANDY	45 ML
I TBSP	ORANGE-FLAVORED LIQUEUR	15 ML
	VANILLA BEAN ICE CREAM	

IN A LARGE NONSTICK SKILLET, MELT BUTTER OVER MEDIUM-HIGH HEAT. ADD BROWN SUGAR, REDUCE HEAT AND SIMMER UNTIL SUGAR DISSOLVES AND IS THE COLOR OF CARAMEL, ABOUT 4 MINUTES. (DO NOT STIR THE CARAMEL, BUT KEEP AN EYE ON IT BECAUSE IT COULD BURN.) ADD BANANAS AND SIMMER FOR 2 MINUTES OR UNTIL SOFTENED BUT NOT MUSHY. REMOVE FROM HEAT AND ADD BRANDY AND LIQUEUR. RETURN TO HEAT AND RETURN TO A SIMMER. SERVE BANANAS IMMEDIATELY OVER VANILLA BEAN ICE CREAM, WITH SAUCE DRIZZLED OVER TOP. SERVES 4.

STRAWBERRY FOOL

FOOL CAN BE MADE WITH ALMOST ANY FRUIT,
INCLUDING MANGOS AND PEACHES, BUT IS
BEST WITH BERRIES. IT LOOKS BEE-YOU-TEE-FUL
SERVED IN STEMMED WINE GLASSES!
SERVE WITH ALMOND BITES (PAGE 284).

2 CUPS	FRESH OR UNSWEETENED FROZEN STRAWBERRIES	500 ML
1/2 CUP	GRANULATED SUGAR (OR TO TASTE), DIVIDED	125 ML
1 CUP	WHIPPING (35%) CREAM	250 ML
1 TSP	VANILLA EXTRACT (OPTIONAL)	5 ML
	FRESH STRAWBERRIES	
	FRESH MINT LEAVES, TOASTED ALMOND SLICES OR SHAVED CHOCOLATE (OPTIONAL)	

IF STRAWBERRIES ARE FRESH, HULL AND WASH THEM
AND PAT DRY. CUT INTO QUARTERS. IF STRAWBERRIES
ARE FROZEN, THAW COMPLETELY AND PAT DRY. PLACE
STRAWBERRIES IN A FOOD PROCESSOR AND PURÉE.
TRANSFER TO A BOWL AND STIR IN 1/4 CUP (50 ML) OF
THE SUGAR. TASTE AND ADD MORE SUGAR, IF DESIRED
(SWEET SEASONAL BERRIES MIGHT NEED LESS SUGAR,
WHILE FROZEN BERRIES MIGHT NEED MORE). IN ANOTHER
BOWL, WHIP CREAM UNTIL SOFT PEAKS FORM. ADD THE
REMAINING 1/4 CUP (50 ML) SUGAR AND WHIP UNTIL STIFF
PEAKS FORM. FOLD IN STRAWBERRY PURÉE, CREATING A
SWIRLED PATTERN. SPOON INTO SERVING GLASSES AND
GARNISH WITH FRESH STRAWBERRIES AND, IF DESIRED,
MINT, ALMONDS OR CHOCOLATE SHAVINGS. SERVE
IMMEDIATELY OR REFRIGERATE FOR UP TO 2 HOURS.
SERVES 4.

"MASSACRED" BERRIES

THE KIDS NAMED THIS ONE, BUT THE RIGHT WORD IS "MACERATED" — JUST A FANCY TERM FOR MIXING FRUIT WITH SUGAR (AND SOMETIMES BOOZE) AND LETTING IT SIT UNTIL IT IS VERY SWEET AND JUICY. STIR IT INTO VANILLA YOGURT, SPOON IT OVER POUND CAKE OR VANILLA BEAN ICE CREAM OR — OUR FAVORITE — TOP BERRIES WITH A BIG DOLLOP OF SYLLABUB (PAGE 336) AND A WEDGE OF CARDAMOM SHORTBREAD (PAGE 292).

2 CUPS	STRAWBERRIES, HULLED AND HALVED	500 ML
1/4 CUP	ORANGE- OR LEMON-FLAVORED LIQUEUR	50 ML
2 TBSP	GRANULATED SUGAR	25 ML
1 TSP	GRATED LEMON ZEST	5 ML
2 CUPS	BLUEBERRIES	500 ML
2 TBSP	CHOPPED FRESH MINT (OPTIONAL)	25 ML

IN A LARGE BOWL, COMBINE STRAWBERRIES, LIQUEUR, SUGAR AND LEMON ZEST, STIRRING VERY GENTLY. LET STAND FOR AT LEAST 30 MINUTES OR FOR UP TO 2 HOURS TO ALLOW STRAWBERRIES TO GIVE OFF THEIR JUICE. STIR IN BLUEBERRIES AND MINT (IF USING). SERVES 6 TO 8.

VARIATIONS: USE ANOTHER LIQUEUR, SUCH AS ALMOND- OR RASPBERRY-FLAVORED. IF SERVING TO CHILDREN, SIMPLY OMIT THE LIQUEUR OR SUBSTITUTE AN EQUAL AMOUNT OF FRESHLY SQUEEZED ORANGE JUICE.

UPSIDE-DOWN RHUBARB AND GINGER PUDDING

THE TANG OF RHUBARB AND THE ZING OF GINGER MAKE THIS ONE OF OUR FAVORITE DESSERTS. SERVE WITH WHIPPED CREAM OR A SCOOP OF VANILLA ICE CREAM.

BASE

2 TBSP	BUTTER, MELTED	25 ML
1/2 CUP	PACKED BROWN SUGAR	125 ML
3 CUPS	CHOPPED RHUBARB (SEE TIP, OPPOSITE)	750 ML
1/3 CUP	CHOPPED CANDIED GINGER	75 ML

TOPPING

1 1/2 CUPS	ALL-PURPOSE FLOUR	375 ML
2 TSP	BAKING POWDER	10 ML
1 TSP	GROUND GINGER	5 ML
1/4 TSP	SALT	1 ML
PINCH	GROUND NUTMEG	PINCH
3/4 CUP	GRANULATED SUGAR	175 ML
1/2 CUP	BUTTER, AT ROOM TEMPERATURE	125 ML
2	EGGS	2
1 TSP	VANILLA EXTRACT	5 ML
1 CUP	SOUR CREAM OR PLAIN YOGURT	250 ML

PREHEAT OVEN TO 350°F (180°C). GREASE AN 8-INCH (20 CM) SQUARE GLASS OR CERAMIC BAKING DISH.

BASE: POUR BUTTER INTO BAKING DISH AND SWIRL TO COVER BOTTOM. SPRINKLE WITH BROWN SUGAR. SPREAD RHUBARB EVENLY IN DISH AND SPRINKLE WITH CANDIED GINGER. SET ASIDE.

TOPPING: IN A BOWL, COMBINE FLOUR, BAKING POWDER, GROUND GINGER, SALT AND NUTMEG; SET ASIDE. IN A LARGE BOWL, CREAM GRANULATED SUGAR AND BUTTER UNTIL LIGHT AND FLUFFY. BEAT IN EGGS, ONE AT A TIME, AND VANILLA. STIR IN FLOUR MIXTURE ALTERNATELY WITH SOUR CREAM, MAKING TWO ADDITIONS OF EACH.

SPREAD TOPPING OVER BASE. BAKE FOR ABOUT 45 MINUTES OR UNTIL TOP IS GOLDEN AND A TESTER INSERTED IN THE CENTER COMES OUT CLEAN. LET COOL IN DISH ON A RACK FOR 20 MINUTES. GENTLY RUN A KNIFE AROUND THE EDGE OF THE DISH AND INVERT PUDDING ONTO A SERVING PLATE. SERVES 6.

TIP: IF USING FROZEN RHUBARB, IT'S IMPORTANT TO THAW IT AND SQUEEZE OUT EXCESS MOISTURE *BEFORE* MEASURING.

THE KITCHEN WAS PERFECTLY CLEAN YESTERDAY — SORRY YOU MISSED IT.

OLD-FASHIONED RICE PUDDING

A SIMPLE METHOD AND A SATISFYING RESULT. POP IT IN THE OVEN BEFORE YOU START DINNER, AND A CREAMY, COMFORTING DESSERT IS READY WHEN YOU ARE.

1/3 CUP	SHORT-GRAIN WHITE RICE (SUCH AS ARBORIO)	75 ML
1/4 TO 1/2 CUP	RAISINS	50 TO 125 ML
3 TBSP	GRANULATED SUGAR	45 ML
1 TBSP	BUTTER	15 ML
1 TSP	FRESHLY GRATED ORANGE ZEST	5 ML
1 TSP	VANILLA EXTRACT	5 ML
1/2 TSP	GROUND CINNAMON	2 ML
1	EGG	1
3 CUPS	WHOLE MILK (SEE TIP, BELOW)	750 ML
PINCH	GROUND NUTMEG	PINCH

PREHEAT OVEN TO 325°F (160°C). GREASE A 6-CUP (1.5 L) BAKING DISH OR CASSEROLE DISH. SPRINKLE RICE IN BOTTOM OF DISH. ADD RAISINS, SUGAR, BUTTER, ORANGE ZEST, VANILLA AND CINNAMON. IN A SMALL BOWL, BEAT EGG AND MILK. POUR OVER RICE AND STIR. SPRINKLE EVENLY WITH NUTMEG. BAKE, UNCOVERED, FOR ABOUT 1 1/4 HOURS OR UNTIL RICE IS TENDER AND CREAMY. SERVES 4.

TIP: USE WHOLE MILK TO GET A RICH, CREAMY, DELICIOUS RICE PUDDING. REDUCED-FAT OR SKIM MILK WON'T BE AS FLAVORFUL.

STRAWBERRY TIRAMISU

A FRESH, SUMMERY TWIST ON AN ITALIAN CLASSIC.

8 CUPS	STRAWBERRIES, HULLED AND SLICED, DIVIDED	2 L
1/2 CUP	ORANGE JUICE	125 ML
1/2 CUP	ORANGE-FLAVORED LIQUEUR	125 ML
1/4 CUP	CONFECTIONER'S (ICING) SUGAR	50 ML
1 CUP	WHIPPING (35%) CREAM	250 ML
1 CUP	MASCARPONE CHEESE (SEE TIP, BELOW)	250 ML
24	LADYFINGER SPONGES	24
	TOASTED SLICED ALMONDS	
	SHAVED CHOCOLATE	

RESERVE 2 CUPS (500 ML) OF THE STRAWBERRIES FOR DECORATING THE TIRAMISU. PLACE THE REMAINING STRAWBERRIES IN A LARGE BOWL AND GENTLY STIR IN ORANGE JUICE, LIQUEUR AND SUGAR. LET STAND AT ROOM TEMPERATURE FOR ABOUT 1 HOUR TO BLEND THE FLAVORS.

IN A LARGE BOWL, WHIP CREAM UNTIL SOFT PEAKS FORM. GENTLY FOLD IN MASCARPONE. ARRANGE HALF THE LADYFINGERS IN A 9-INCH (23 CM) SQUARE GLASS DISH. SPOON IN HALF THE STRAWBERRIES AND THEIR JUICE. SPREAD HALF THE CREAM MIXTURE OVER THE STRAWBERRIES. REPEAT LAYERS. COVER AND REFRIGERATE FOR AT LEAST 6 HOURS OR FOR UP TO 1 DAY. JUST BEFORE SERVING, SPRINKLE WITH ALMONDS AND DECORATE WITH RESERVED STRAWBERRIES AND CHOCOLATE SHAVINGS. *SERVES 6 TO 8.*

TIP: MASCARPONE IS AN ITALIAN CREAM CHEESE. LOOK FOR IT IN THE DELI SECTION OF THE SUPERMARKET.

BLUEBERRY CRISP

YOU CAN NEVER HAVE ENOUGH FRUIT CRISP RECIPES.
SERVE WITH ICE CREAM OR WHIPPED CREAM.

FILLING

4 CUPS	FRESH OR FROZEN BLUEBERRIES	1 L
2 TBSP	GRANULATED SUGAR	25 ML
1 TBSP	ALL-PURPOSE FLOUR	15 ML
1 TSP	GROUND CINNAMON	5 ML
1 TSP	GRATED LEMON ZEST	5 ML

TOPPING

1/2 CUP	ALL-PURPOSE FLOUR	125 ML
1/2 CUP	PACKED BROWN SUGAR	125 ML
1/4 CUP	COLD BUTTER, CUT INTO PIECES	50 ML
1/4 CUP	QUICK-COOKING ROLLED OR FLAKED OATS (NOT INSTANT)	50 ML
1/2 CUP	WALNUTS, HAZELNUTS OR ALMONDS, CHOPPED	125 ML

PREHEAT OVEN TO 375°F (190°C). GREASE AN 8-INCH (20 CM) SQUARE GLASS BAKING DISH.

FILLING: IN A LARGE BOWL, TOSS BLUEBERRIES WITH SUGAR, FLOUR, CINNAMON AND LEMON ZEST. TRANSFER TO BAKING DISH.

TOPPING: IN ANOTHER LARGE BOWL, COMBINE FLOUR AND BROWN SUGAR. USING YOUR FINGERS OR A PASTRY BLENDER, BLEND IN BUTTER UNTIL MIXTURE RESEMBLES COARSE BREAD CRUMBS (YOU CAN ALSO DO THIS IN A FOOD PROCESSOR). STIR IN OATS AND NUTS. SPRINKLE EVENLY OVER BLUEBERRIES (SOME BERRIES MIGHT POKE THROUGH, WHICH IS FINE).

BAKE FOR 30 TO 40 MINUTES OR UNTIL FRUIT IS BUBBLING AND TOP IS BROWNED. IF TOPPING BROWNS TOO QUICKLY, COVER LOOSELY WITH FOIL. LET COOL FOR 10 MINUTES BEFORE SERVING. SERVES 6 TO 8.

VENETIAN SORBET

THE PERFECT LIGHT DESSERT FOR A LADIES' LUNCH OR A DINNER PARTY FINALE. IN VENICE, YOUR WAITER WOULD PREPARE THIS COOL CONFECTION AT THE TABLE, BUT YOU CAN WHIP IT UP (LITERALLY) IN THE KITCHEN WHILE YOUR GUESTS CONTINUE TO VISIT.

2 CUPS	LEMON SORBET OR LEMON ICE CREAM	500 ML
1/2 CUP	PROSECCO (DRY ITALIAN SPARKLING WINE)	125 ML
	GRATED ZEST OF 1 LEMON	
	SLICED STRAWBERRIES	

CHILL 4 CHAMPAGNE FLUTES. SPOON SORBET INTO A LARGE BOWL AND BREAK IT UP WITH A SPOON. ADD WINE, WHIPPING WITH A WHISK (NO MACHINES — THEY MELT THE ICE) TO FORM A SOFT, FOAMY MIXTURE. DON'T WHIP TOO MUCH, OR IT'LL BECOME TOO LIQUID. POUR INTO A PITCHER AND SERVE IMMEDIATELY IN CHAMPAGNE FLUTES, GARNISHED WITH LEMON ZEST AND A STRAWBERRY SLICE. SERVES 4.

TIP: THE DRINKS WILL SEPARATE IF LEFT STANDING, SO DRINK UP AND ENJOY!

CRANBERRY PIE

THIS PIE TAKES ONLY MINUTES TO WHIP TOGETHER,
BUT IT WILL REALLY IMPRESS YOUR GUESTS.
SERVE WITH A DOLLOP OF WHIPPED CREAM, A
SCOOP OF ICE CREAM OR SIMPLY SPRINKLED WITH
CONFECTIONER'S (ICING) SUGAR.

3 CUPS	FRESH OR FROZEN CRANBERRIES	750 ML
3/4 CUP	PECANS, TOASTED (SEE TIP, PAGE 327) AND CHOPPED	175 ML
1 ~~1/2~~ CUPS	GRANULATED SUGAR, DIVIDED	375 ML
1 CUP	ALL-PURPOSE FLOUR	250 ML
2	EGGS, LIGHTLY BEATEN	2
~~1/2 & 4~~ CUP 3/4	BUTTER, MELTED	175 ML
2 TBSP	ORANGE-FLAVORED LIQUEUR	25 ML
2 TSP	GRATED ORANGE ZEST	10 ML
3/4 TSP	BAKING POWDER	3 ML

PREHEAT OVEN TO 325°F (160°C). GREASE AND LIGHTLY
FLOUR A 10-INCH (25 CM) PIE PLATE. PLACE CRANBERRIES
IN PIE PLATE AND SPRINKLE WITH PECANS AND 1/2 CUP
(125 ML) OF THE SUGAR. IN A BOWL, WHISK TOGETHER
THE REMAINING SUGAR, FLOUR, EGGS, BUTTER, LIQUEUR,
ORANGE ZEST AND BAKING POWDER UNTIL SMOOTH.
POUR OVER CRANBERRIES. BAKE FOR ABOUT ~~45~~ 45 MINUTES
OR UNTIL TOP IS GOLDEN AND A TESTER INSERTED IN
THE CENTER COMES OUT CLEAN. LET COOL SLIGHTLY
ON A RACK. SERVE WARM OR AT ROOM TEMPERATURE.
SERVES 8.

LITTLE CHERRY TARTS

SO TEMPTING. SO TASTY. SO EASY. YOU'LL BE VOTED THE QUEEN OF TARTS.

24	FROZEN MINI TART SHELLS	24
1	EGG WHITE, BEATEN	1
2 CUPS	FRESH CHERRIES, HALVED (SEE TIP, BELOW)	500 ML
3/4 CUP	SOUR CREAM	175 ML
1/2 CUP	GRANULATED SUGAR	125 ML
2	WHOLE EGGS	2
1	EGG YOLK	1

PREHEAT OVEN TO 350°F (180°C). PLACE TART SHELLS ON A LARGE BAKING SHEET. BRUSH THE INSIDE OF TART SHELLS WITH EGG WHITE. DIVIDE CHERRIES AMONG TART SHELLS, PLACING 3 OR 4 CHERRIES IN EACH. IN A MEDIUM BOWL, WHISK TOGETHER SOUR CREAM, SUGAR, EGGS AND EGG YOLK. POUR OVER CHERRIES. BAKE FOR 15 TO 17 MINUTES, ROTATING THE TRAY ONCE, UNTIL FILLING IS SET. MAKES 24 MINI TARTS.

TIP: IF FRESH CHERRIES ARE NOT AVAILABLE, YOU CAN SUBSTITUTE A 14-OZ (398 ML) CAN OF CHERRIES IN LIGHT SYRUP, DRAINED AND PITS REMOVED.

LEMON CURD TART

THIS LIGHT, LEMONY TART IS THE PERFECT SWEET ENDING TO A RICH MEAL. SERVE IT BY ITSELF OR DRESS IT UP WITH A GENEROUS SPRINKLING OF FRESH BLUEBERRIES OR RASPBERRIES.

LEMON CURD

3	EGGS	3
1 CUP	GRANULATED SUGAR	250 ML
1/2 CUP	BUTTER	125 ML
1 TBSP	GRATED LEMON ZEST	15 ML
1/2 CUP	FRESHLY SQUEEZED LEMON JUICE (2 TO 3 LEMONS)	125 ML

CRUST

1 CUP	ALL-PURPOSE FLOUR	250 ML
1/2 CUP	CONFECTIONER'S (ICING) SUGAR	125 ML
2 TBSP	GRATED LEMON ZEST	25 ML
1/2 CUP	COLD BUTTER, CUT INTO PIECES	125 ML
2 TBSP	FRESHLY SQUEEZED LEMON JUICE	25 ML
1 1/2 CUPS	BLUEBERRIES OR RASPBERRIES (OPTIONAL)	375 ML

LEMON CURD: IN A MEDIUM SAUCEPAN, WHISK EGGS AND SUGAR UNTIL FOAMY AND LIGHT-COLORED. ADD BUTTER, LEMON ZEST AND LEMON JUICE. COOK OVER MEDIUM HEAT, WHISKING, UNTIL THE MIXTURE THICKENS AND FORMS A RIBBON ON THE SURFACE WHEN DRIZZLED FROM A SPOON. TRANSFER TO A BOWL AND REFRIGERATE FOR AT LEAST 1 HOUR, UNTIL CHILLED, OR FOR UP TO 3 DAYS.

CONTINUED ON PAGE 321...

Cranberry Pistachio Biscotti (page 290) and Cardamom Shortbread (page 292)

Chewy Trail Mix Bars (page 299)

Brandied Caramel Bananas (page 309)

Lemon Cheesecake (page 328)

CRUST: IN A LARGE BOWL, COMBINE FLOUR, CONFECTIONER'S SUGAR AND LEMON ZEST. USING YOUR FINGERS OR A PASTRY BLENDER, BLEND IN BUTTER UNTIL MIXTURE RESEMBLES COARSE BREAD CRUMBS (YOU CAN ALSO DO THIS IN A FOOD PROCESSOR). GRADUALLY ADD LEMON JUICE, STIRRING WITH A FORK UNTIL DOUGH FORMS A BALL. WRAP DOUGH IN PLASTIC WRAP AND REFRIGERATE FOR 30 MINUTES (SEE TIP, BELOW).

IF DOUGH IS STIFF, LET IT STAND AT ROOM TEMPERATURE FOR 10 MINUTES, UNTIL IT IS MORE PLIABLE. ON A FLOURED WORK SURFACE, ROLL OUT DOUGH TO AN 11-INCH (28 CM) CIRCLE. LIFT DOUGH INTO A 9-INCH (23 CM) TART OR FLAN PAN WITH A REMOVABLE BOTTOM AND PRESS TO FIT THE BOTTOM AND SIDES. (IF THE PASTRY TEARS, GENTLY PAT IT IN THE PAN; IT'LL BE FINE ONCE IT BAKES.) TRIM THE EDGES. REFRIGERATE FOR 30 MINUTES.

MEANWHILE, PREHEAT OVEN TO 425°F (220°C). PRICK BOTTOM AND SIDES OF CRUST TO PREVENT SHRINKAGE. BAKE FOR 10 MINUTES. REDUCE OVEN TEMPERATURE TO 350°F (180°C) AND BAKE FOR 8 TO 10 MINUTES OR UNTIL GOLDEN. LET COOL COMPLETELY.

REMOVE CRUST FROM PAN AND PLACE ON A SERVING PLATE. SPREAD LEMON CURD INSIDE. IF USING, SPRINKLE BLUEBERRIES OVER TOP. SERVES 6 TO 8.

TIP: LETTING PIE DOUGH REST IN THE REFRIGERATOR AFTER MIXING, AND AGAIN AFTER ROLLING, ALLOWS THE GLUTEN IN THE FLOUR TO RELAX. THIS HELPS PREVENT YOUR PIE CRUST FROM SHRINKING DURING BAKING.

RASPBERRY APPLE TART

THIS LOVELY JAMMY TART IS ESPECIALLY POPULAR WITH KIDS.

CRUST

1 CUP + 2 TBSP	ALL-PURPOSE FLOUR	275 ML
1 TSP	CONFECTIONER'S (ICING) SUGAR	5 ML
1 TSP	GROUND CINNAMON	5 ML
PINCH	SALT	PINCH
1/2 CUP	COLD BUTTER, CUT INTO PIECES	125 ML
1	EGG YOLK	1
2 TBSP	COLD WATER	25 ML

FILLING

1 TBSP	BUTTER	15 ML
2	LARGE APPLES, PEELED AND CHOPPED	2
4 CUPS	FRESH OR FROZEN RASPBERRIES	1 L
1 CUP	PACKED BROWN SUGAR	250 ML
1 TSP	FRESHLY SQUEEZED LEMON JUICE	5 ML
1 TSP	CORNSTARCH	5 ML

CRUST: IN A LARGE BOWL, COMBINE FLOUR, SUGAR, CINNAMON AND SALT. USING YOUR FINGERS OR A PASTRY BLENDER, BLEND IN BUTTER UNTIL MIXTURE RESEMBLES COARSE BREAD CRUMBS. (YOU CAN ALSO DO THIS IN A FOOD PROCESSOR). ADD EGG YOLK AND 1 TBSP (15 ML) COLD WATER, STIRRING WITH A FORK AND ADDING THE REMAINING COLD WATER, IF NEEDED, UNTIL DOUGH FORMS A BALL. WRAP DOUGH IN PLASTIC WRAP AND REFRIGERATE FOR 30 MINUTES (SEE TIP, PAGE 321).

FILLING: IN A LARGE SAUCEPAN, MELT BUTTER OVER MEDIUM HEAT. ADD APPLES, RASPBERRIES AND BROWN SUGAR; REDUCE HEAT TO LOW AND COOK, STIRRING OCCASIONALLY, UNTIL SUGAR IS DISSOLVED. INCREASE HEAT TO MEDIUM AND COOK, STIRRING OCCASIONALLY, FOR 10 TO 15 MINUTES OR UNTIL APPLES ARE SOFT AND MIXTURE THICKENS. IN SMALL BOWL, COMBINE LEMON JUICE AND CORNSTARCH. WHISK INTO HOT FRUIT MIXTURE AND COOK FOR 1 MINUTE OR UNTIL IT THICKENS A LITTLE MORE. TRANSFER TO A BOWL AND LET COOL COMPLETELY.

IF DOUGH IS STIFF, LET IT STAND AT ROOM TEMPERATURE FOR 10 MINUTES, UNTIL IT IS MORE PLIABLE. ON A FLOURED WORK SURFACE, ROLL DOUGH OUT TO AN 11-INCH (28 CM) CIRCLE. PLACE A 9-INCH (23 CM) TART OR FLAN PAN WITH A REMOVABLE BOTTOM ON A BAKING SHEET. LIFT DOUGH INTO THE PAN AND PRESS TO FIT THE BOTTOM AND SIDES. (IF THE PASTRY CRACKS OR BREAKS, JUST PATCH IT IN THE PAN — NO ONE WILL KNOW THE DIFFERENCE.) TRIM THE EDGES. REFRIGERATE FOR 30 MINUTES.

MEANWHILE, PREHEAT OVEN TO 375°F (190°C). SPOON COOLED FILLING INTO THE CRUST. BAKE FOR 25 TO 30 MINUTES OR UNTIL PASTRY IS LIGHTLY BROWNED. SERVE AT ROOM TEMPERATURE OR CHILLED. SERVES 8.

TIP: WHEN MAKING A TART OR PIE WITH A PRECOOKED FILLING, IT'S IMPORTANT TO COOL THE FILLING BEFORE PLACING IT IN AN UNCOOKED PASTRY SHELL. WARM FILLING MAKES THE CRUST SOGGY.

SHORTCUT APPLE STRUDEL

THIS DELICIOUS DESSERT USES FROZEN PUFF PASTRY, WHICH IS A LOT FASTER THAN FIDDLING WITH PHYLLO.

1/4 CUP	RAISINS	50 ML
2 TBSP	UNSWEETENED APPLE JUICE	25 ML
4	GOLDEN DELICIOUS APPLES	4
	JUICE OF 1/2 LEMON	
1/3 CUP	PACKED BROWN SUGAR	75 ML
1/4 CUP	PECANS, CHOPPED	50 ML
1/2 TSP	GROUND CINNAMON	2 ML
1/4 TSP	GROUND CLOVES	1 ML
1	PACKAGE (14 OZ/398 G) FROZEN PUFF PASTRY, THAWED	1
1/3 CUP	FRESH BREAD CRUMBS	75 ML
	COLD WATER	
	GRANULATED SUGAR	

PREHEAT OVEN TO 425°F (220°C). LINE A BAKING SHEET WITH PARCHMENT PAPER.

PLACE RAISINS AND APPLE JUICE IN A SMALL MICROWAVE-SAFE BOWL AND MICROWAVE ON HIGH FOR 20 SECONDS. LET STAND FOR 10 MINUTES TO PLUMP THE RAISINS.

MEANWHILE, PEEL, CORE AND THINLY SLICE APPLES AND PLACE IN A LARGE BOWL. DRAIN RAISINS, DISCARDING LIQUID, AND ADD TO APPLES. ADD LEMON JUICE, BROWN SUGAR, PECANS, CINNAMON AND CLOVES; TOSS TO COMBINE AND SET ASIDE.

ON A FLOURED WORK SURFACE, ROLL OUT PASTRY TO A 15- BY 12-INCH (38 BY 30 CM) RECTANGLE. WITH A LONG EDGE FACING YOU, GENTLY TRANSFER PASTRY

TO BAKING SHEET, LEAVING ABOUT ONE-THIRD OF THE PASTRY HANGING OVER THE LONG EDGE OF THE BAKING SHEET FARTHEST AWAY FROM YOU. SPRINKLE A 2- TO 3-INCH (5 TO 7.5 CM) BAND OF BREAD CRUMBS LENGTHWISE ALONG THE HALF OF THE PASTRY CLOSEST TO YOU, LEAVING A 1-INCH (2.5 CM) BORDER ALONG ALL EDGES. SPOON APPLES ON TOP OF THE BREAD CRUMBS, DISCARDING ANY LIQUID THAT HAS DRAINED FROM THEM. BRUSH ALL EDGES OF PASTRY WITH WATER. CAREFULLY PULL THE OTHER HALF OF THE PASTRY OVER THE APPLES, BRINGING THE TWO LONG EDGES TOGETHER AND MAKING A RECTANGULAR ENVELOPE. PRESS ALL EDGES TO SEAL, MARKING THEM DECORATIVELY WITH A FORK.

MAKE 4 SLITS IN THE TOP OF THE STRUDEL TO LET STEAM ESCAPE. BRUSH THE TOP WITH COLD WATER AND SPRINKLE LIGHTLY WITH GRANULATED SUGAR. BAKE FOR 10 MINUTES. REDUCE HEAT TO 375°F (190°C) AND BAKE FOR 20 TO 25 MINUTES OR UNTIL PUFFY AND GOLDEN BROWN. LET COOL ON BAKING SHEET FOR 15 MINUTES. TRANSFER TO A RACK UNTIL READY TO SLICE AND SERVE. SERVES 8.

TIP: BRUSHING THE TOP OF THE STRUDEL WITH COLD WATER, RATHER THAN BEATEN EGG, REDUCES THE CHANCE OF THE PASTRY BROWNING TOO MUCH BEFORE THE FILLING IS COOKED.

MY WIFE SAYS I NEVER LISTEN — AT LEAST, I THINK THAT'S WHAT SHE SAID.

PINEAPPLE PUFF

WHEN YOU'RE STUCK FOR A QUICK DESSERT, YOU CAN THROW THIS TOGETHER WITH INGREDIENTS ON HAND. SERVE WITH WHIPPED CREAM OR ICE CREAM.

1	CAN (19 OZ/540 ML) PINEAPPLE RINGS, DRAINED	1
2 TBSP	PACKED BROWN SUGAR	25 ML
1 TSP	GROUND CINNAMON	5 ML
1/2	PACKAGE (14 OZ/398 G) FROZEN PUFF PASTRY, THAWED	1/2
1	EGG WHITE, BEATEN	1
3 TBSP	SHREDDED COCONUT (SWEETENED OR UNSWEETENED), TOASTED (SEE TIP, OPPOSITE)	45 ML
3 TBSP	SLICED ALMONDS, TOASTED (SEE TIP, OPPOSITE)	45 ML
1 TBSP	BUTTER	15 ML
	GRANULATED SUGAR	

PREHEAT OVEN TO 375°F (190°C). LINE A BAKING SHEET WITH PARCHMENT PAPER. CUT PINEAPPLE RINGS IN HALF TO FORM SEMICIRCLES AND BLOT DRY WITH PAPER TOWELS. PLACE PINEAPPLE IN A BOWL AND GENTLY STIR IN BROWN SUGAR AND CINNAMON; SET ASIDE. ON A FLOURED WORK SURFACE, ROLL OUT PASTRY TO A 12- BY 10-INCH (30 BY 25 CM) RECTANGLE. PLACE PASTRY ON PREPARED BAKING SHEET AND BRUSH WITH EGG WHITE. SPRINKLE WITH COCONUT AND ALMONDS, LEAVING A 2-INCH (5 CM) BORDER ON ALL SIDES. ARRANGE PINEAPPLE ON TOP, PLACING PIECES CLOSELY TOGETHER LIKE A JIGSAW PUZZLE AND OVERLAPPING IF NECESSARY TO USE UP ALL THE FRUIT. DOT WITH BUTTER. BRING EDGES OF PASTRY

UP AND OVER THE PINEAPPLE, LEAVING THE FRUIT AT THE CENTER EXPOSED AND FOLDING THE PASTRY AS YOU GO. (DON'T WORRY IF IT LOOKS LESS THAN PERFECT; IT'S SUPPOSED TO BE RUSTIC.) BRUSH EDGES WITH EGG WHITE AND SPRINKLE WITH A LITTLE GRANULATED SUGAR. BAKE FOR ABOUT 30 MINUTES OR UNTIL GOLDEN BROWN AND PUFFY. SERVES 4 TO 6.

TIP: TOASTING COCONUT AND NUTS HELPS BRING OUT THEIR FLAVOR. THE QUICKEST METHOD IS ON THE STOVETOP. SPREAD COCONUT AND NUTS OUT IN AN UNGREASED NONSTICK SKILLET AND PLACE OVER MEDIUM HEAT. SHAKE OR STIR FREQUENTLY FOR 4 TO 5 MINUTES OR UNTIL FRAGRANT AND STARTING TO BROWN. TIP ONTO A COLD PLATE TO STOP THE COOKING PROCESS AND LET COOL COMPLETELY.

LEMON CHEESECAKE

LIGHT, LEMONY, LOVELY. SERVE WITH FRESH BERRIES AND/OR RASPBERRY SAUCE (SEE RECIPE, OPPOSITE).

CRUST

1½ ~~¾~~ CUP	GRAHAM CRACKER CRUMBS	175 ML
½ CUP	GRANULATED SUGAR	125 ML
½ CUP	MELTED BUTTER	125 ML

FILLING

1	ENVELOPE (¼ OZ/7 G) UNFLAVORED GELATIN	1
¼ CUP	COLD WATER	50 ML
¼ CUP	HOT WATER	50 ML
	FINELY GRATED ZEST OF 1 LEMON	
½ CUP	FRESHLY SQUEEZED LEMON JUICE	125 ML
1	PACKAGE (8 OZ/250 G) CREAM CHEESE, SOFTENED	1
1 CUP	GRANULATED SUGAR	250 ML
2 CUPS	WHIPPING (35%) CREAM	500 ML

CRUST: PREHEAT OVEN TO 350°F (180°C). IN A BOWL, COMBINE GRAHAM CRACKER CRUMBS, SUGAR AND BUTTER. PAT INTO A 9-INCH (23 CM) SPRINGFORM PAN. BAKE FOR 10 MINUTES OR UNTIL BROWNED.

FILLING: SPRINKLE GELATIN OVER COLD WATER, THEN ADD HOT WATER, STIRRING CONSTANTLY. STIR IN LEMON ZEST AND LEMON JUICE. LET COOL FOR A FEW MINUTES BUT DO NOT LET SET. IN A LARGE BOWL, BEAT CREAM CHEESE AND SUGAR UNTIL VERY SMOOTH. ADD GELATIN MIXTURE, STIRRING WELL. IN ANOTHER BOWL, WHIP CREAM UNTIL

STIFF PEAKS FORM. GENTLY FOLD WHIPPED CREAM INTO CHEESE MIXTURE.

POUR FILLING INTO CRUST. REFRIGERATE FOR AT LEAST 4 HOURS OR FOR UP TO 1 DAY. REMOVE FROM PAN AND SERVE. SERVES 8.

MAKE AHEAD: THIS CHEESECAKE ALSO FREEZES WELL. AFTER CHILLING AND REMOVING FROM PAN, PLACE ON A BAKING SHEET AND PLACE IN FREEZER, UNCOVERED, UNTIL FROZEN. WRAP IN A DOUBLE LAYER OF FOIL, PLACE IN A LARGE PLASTIC CONTAINER AND FREEZE FOR UP TO 2 WEEKS. TO SERVE, THAW OVERNIGHT IN THE REFRIGERATOR.

RASPBERRY SAUCE

1	PACKAGE (10 OZ/300 G) FROZEN RASPBERRIES, THAWED	1
1/4 CUP	GRANULATED SUGAR	50 ML
2 TSP	FRESHLY SQUEEZED LEMON JUICE	10 ML

IN A MEDIUM SAUCEPAN, COMBINE RASPBERRIES, SUGAR AND LEMON JUICE. COOK GENTLY OVER LOW HEAT, STIRRING OCCASIONALLY, UNTIL SUGAR IS DISSOLVED. STRAIN THROUGH A SIEVE AND LET COOL. MAKES ABOUT 2 CUPS (500 ML).

MAKE AHEAD: TRANSFER TO AN AIRTIGHT CONTAINER AND REFRIGERATE FOR UP TO 3 DAYS OR FREEZE FOR UP TO 2 MONTHS.

MARBLED SNACKING CAKE

SO GOOD IT DOESN'T NEED FROSTING.

2 CUPS	ALL-PURPOSE FLOUR	500 ML
I TSP	BAKING POWDER	5 ML
I TSP	BAKING SODA	5 ML
I CUP	GRANULATED SUGAR	250 ML
1/2 CUP	BUTTER, AT ROOM TEMPERATURE	125 ML
2	EGGS	2
I CUP	SOUR CREAM	250 ML
1/2 CUP	HAZELNUT COCOA SPREAD (SUCH AS NUTELLA)	125 ML
1/2 CUP	SEMISWEET CHOCOLATE CHIPS	125 ML
	CONFECTIONER'S (ICING) SUGAR	

PREHEAT OVEN TO 350°F (180°C). GREASE A 13- BY 9-INCH (33 BY 23 CM) METAL BAKING PAN AND LINE WITH PARCHMENT PAPER. IN A BOWL, COMBINE FLOUR, BAKING POWDER AND BAKING SODA; SET ASIDE. IN A LARGE BOWL, CREAM GRANULATED SUGAR AND BUTTER UNTIL LIGHT AND FLUFFY. BEAT IN EGGS, ONE AT A TIME. STIR IN FLOUR MIXTURE ALTERNATELY WITH SOUR CREAM, MAKING TWO ADDITIONS OF EACH. DIVIDE CAKE MIXTURE INTO TWO BOWLS. GENTLY STIR HAZELNUT COCOA SPREAD INTO ONE BOWL. STIR CHOCOLATE CHIPS INTO THE OTHER BOWL. DROP ALTERNATE SPOONFULS OF THE TWO MIXTURES INTO THE BAKING PAN. WITH THE TIP OF A KNIFE, GENTLY SWIRL THE MIXTURES TOGETHER FOR A MARBLED EFFECT. BAKE FOR 30 TO 35 MINUTES OR UNTIL A TESTER INSERTED IN THE CENTER COMES OUT CLEAN. LET COOL COMPLETELY IN PAN ON A RACK, THEN DUST WITH CONFECTIONER'S SUGAR. CUT INTO SQUARES. SERVES 16.

IF A DOG BARKS HIS HEAD OFF IN THE FOREST AND NO HUMAN HEARS HIM, IS HE STILL A BAD DOG?

CHOCOLATE WHIPPED CREAM ICING

A DELICIOUS TOPPING FOR YOUR FAVORITE SPONGE CAKE, POUND CAKE OR CUPCAKES.

2 CUPS	WHIPPING (35%) CREAM	500 ML
6 TBSP	UNSWEETENED COCOA POWDER	90 ML
6 TBSP	CONFECTIONER'S (ICING) SUGAR	90 ML
PINCH	SALT	PINCH

PLACE CREAM IN A LARGE BOWL AND SIFT IN COCOA, CONFECTIONER'S SUGAR AND SALT. REFRIGERATE FOR 1 HOUR. WHIP UNTIL STIFF PEAKS FORM AND CREAM IS THICK ENOUGH TO SPREAD. MAKES ABOUT $2\frac{3}{4}$ CUPS (675 ML).

TIP: FOR THE BEST RESULTS WHEN WHIPPING CREAM, MAKE SURE THE CREAM AND ALL UTENSILS ARE VERY COLD. POP A STAINLESS STEEL BOWL AND THE BEATERS INTO THE FREEZER FOR 15 MINUTES FIRST.

HAZELNUT BLUEBERRY CAKE

THAT JAR OF HAZELNUT COCOA SPREAD YOU
KEEP FOR THE KIDS IS THE SECRET INGREDIENT
IN THIS MOIST, LUSCIOUS CAKE.

CREAM CHEESE LAYER

1	PACKAGE (8 OZ/250 G) CREAM CHEESE, SOFTENED	1
1	EGG	1
1/4 CUP	GRANULATED SUGAR	50 ML
2 TSP	FINELY GRATED ORANGE ZEST	10 ML

TOPPING

1 1/2 CUPS	ALL-PURPOSE FLOUR	375 ML
2/3 CUP	PACKED BROWN SUGAR	150 ML
1/2 CUP	BUTTER	125 ML
3/4 CUP	HAZELNUTS, FINELY CHOPPED	175 ML

CAKE

2 CUPS	ALL-PURPOSE FLOUR	500 ML
1 TSP	BAKING POWDER	5 ML
1 TSP	BAKING SODA	5 ML
3/4 CUP	SOUR CREAM	175 ML
3/4 CUP	HAZELNUT COCOA SPREAD (SUCH AS NUTELLA)	175 ML
1 CUP	GRANULATED SUGAR	250 ML
1/2 CUP	BUTTER, AT ROOM TEMPERATURE	125 ML
2	EGGS	2
3 CUPS	FRESH OR FROZEN BLUEBERRIES	750 ML

PREHEAT OVEN TO 350°F (180°C). GREASE A 13- BY 9-INCH
(33 BY 23 CM) METAL BAKING PAN AND LINE WITH
PARCHMENT PAPER OR FOIL.

CREAM CHEESE LAYER: IN A SMALL BOWL, WHISK TOGETHER CREAM CHEESE, EGG, SUGAR AND ORANGE ZEST UNTIL SMOOTH. SET ASIDE.

TOPPING: IN A BOWL, COMBINE FLOUR AND BROWN SUGAR. USING YOUR FINGERS OR A PASTRY BLENDER, BLEND IN BUTTER UNTIL MIXTURE RESEMBLES COARSE BREAD CRUMBS. STIR IN HAZELNUTS. SET ASIDE.

CAKE: IN A BOWL, COMBINE FLOUR, BAKING POWDER AND BAKING SODA; SET ASIDE. IN ANOTHER BOWL, COMBINE SOUR CREAM AND HAZELNUT COCOA SPREAD; SET ASIDE. IN A LARGE BOWL, CREAM SUGAR AND BUTTER UNTIL LIGHT AND FLUFFY. BEAT IN EGGS, ONE AT A TIME. STIR IN FLOUR MIXTURE ALTERNATELY WITH SOUR CREAM MIXTURE, MAKING TWO ADDITIONS OF EACH. SPREAD IN PREPARED PAN AND SPRINKLE EVENLY WITH BLUEBERRIES. USING A SPATULA, SPREAD CREAM CHEESE LAYER OVER BLUEBERRIES. SPRINKLE WITH TOPPING. BAKE FOR 40 TO 50 MINUTES OR UNTIL A TESTER INSERTED IN THE CENTER COMES OUT CLEAN. SERVES 8 TO 10.

TIP: IF YOU USE FROZEN BERRIES, THE CAKE WILL TAKE LONGER TO COOK THAN IF YOU USE FRESH.

BUTTERFLY CUPCAKES

THESE PRETTY CUPCAKES, FLECKED WITH COLORED SPRINKLES AND TOPPED WITH PINK HONEY BUTTER FROSTING, ARE PERFECT FOR A LITTLE GIRL'S BIRTHDAY PARTY, A BABY SHOWER OR ANY OTHER GIRLIE GATHERING.

CUPCAKES

1 1/2 CUPS	ALL-PURPOSE FLOUR	375 ML
1 3/4 TSP	BAKING POWDER	8 ML
1/2 TSP	SALT	2 ML
1 CUP	GRANULATED SUGAR	250 ML
1/2 CUP	BUTTER, AT ROOM TEMPERATURE	125 ML
2	EGGS	2
2 TSP	VANILLA EXTRACT	10 ML
1/2 CUP	MILK	125 ML
2 TBSP	MULTI-COLORED SPRINKLES	25 ML

HONEY BUTTER FROSTING

3/4 CUP	BUTTER	175 ML
3 CUPS	CONFECTIONER'S (ICING SUGAR), SIFTED, DIVIDED	750 ML
2 TBSP	LIQUID HONEY	25 ML
2 TBSP	FRESHLY SQUEEZED LEMON JUICE	25 ML
	RED FOOD COLORING (OPTIONAL)	

CONFECTIONER'S (ICING SUGAR)

CUPCAKES: PREHEAT OVEN TO 350°F (180°C). LINE A 12-CUP MUFFIN PAN WITH PAPER LINERS. IN A BOWL, SIFT TOGETHER FLOUR, BAKING POWDER AND SALT; SET ASIDE. IN A LARGE BOWL, CREAM SUGAR AND BUTTER UNTIL

LIGHT AND VERY FLUFFY. BEAT IN EGGS, ONE AT A TIME, AND VANILLA. STIR IN FLOUR MIXTURE ALTERNATELY WITH MILK, MAKING TWO ADDITIONS OF EACH. FOLD IN SPRINKLES. SPOON INTO PREPARED MUFFIN CUPS, DIVIDING EVENLY. BAKE FOR ABOUT 20 MINUTES OR UNTIL RISEN AND GOLDEN BROWN AND A TESTER INSERTED IN THE CENTER OF A CUPCAKE COMES OUT CLEAN. TRANSFER CUPCAKES TO A RACK AND LET COOL COMPLETELY.

HONEY BUTTER FROSTING: IN A LARGE BOWL, BEAT BUTTER UNTIL LIGHT AND FLUFFY BUT NOT OILY. GRADUALLY BEAT IN HALF THE CONFECTIONER'S SUGAR. BEAT IN HONEY AND LEMON JUICE. BEAT IN THE REMAINING CONFECTIONER'S SUGAR UNTIL SMOOTH. IF DESIRED, STIR IN 1 OR 2 DROPS OF FOOD COLORING UNTIL FROSTING IS THE DESIRED SHADE OF PINK.

USING A SHARP KNIFE, CUT A SMALL SLICE OFF THE TOP OF EACH CUPCAKE. CUT EACH SLICE IN HALF. SPREAD FROSTING ON CUPCAKES. NESTLE THE HALVED SLICES AT ANGLES IN THE FROSTING TO LOOK LIKE WINGS. SIFT A LITTLE CONFECTIONER'S SUGAR OVER TOP. MAKES 12 CUPCAKES.

VARIATION: LEMON LOVER'S CUPCAKES: FOLLOW RECIPE ABOVE, BUT REPLACE THE SPRINKLES WITH 1 TBSP (15 ML) GRATED LEMON ZEST. WHEN CUPCAKES ARE COOLED, CUT A SMALL SLICE OFF THE TOP OF EACH. SPREAD CUPCAKES WITH LEMON CURD (SEE RECIPE, PAGE 320). LIGHTLY PLACE TOP BACK ON AND SIFT CONFECTIONER'S (ICING) SUGAR OVER TOP. SERVE AS A FUN DESSERT WITH A FEW FRESH RASPBERRIES OR BLUEBERRIES ALONGSIDE.

SYLLABUB

SYLLABUB ORIGINATED IN ENGLAND HUNDREDS OF YEARS AGO AND IS TRADITIONALLY MADE WITH MILK AND WINE. THERE HAVE BEEN MANY VARIATIONS OF THIS RECIPE. OURS IS MADE WITH CREAM AND SHERRY OR BRANDY. IT MAKES A LOVELY DESSERT PARFAIT OR CAN BE USED AS A TOPPING FOR "MASSACRED" BERRIES (PAGE 311).

2 CUPS	WHIPPING (35%) CREAM	500 ML
1 CUP	CONFECTIONER'S (ICING) SUGAR	250 ML
1/3 CUP	DRY SHERRY OR BRANDY	75 ML
	GRATED ZEST OF 1 LEMON	
1/4 CUP	FRESHLY SQUEEZED LEMON JUICE	50 ML
	GRATED NUTMEG	

IN A LARGE BOWL, WHIP CREAM AND SUGAR UNTIL SOFT PEAKS FORM. ADD SHERRY, LEMON ZEST AND LEMON JUICE; WHIP UNTIL THICK. SPOON INTO STEMMED WINE GLASSES AND GARNISH WITH NUTMEG. SERVES 4.

TIP: FOR THE BEST RESULTS WHEN WHIPPING CREAM, MAKE SURE THE CREAM AND ALL UTENSILS ARE VERY COLD. POP A STAINLESS STEEL BOWL AND THE BEATERS INTO THE FREEZER FOR 15 MINUTES FIRST.

Library and Archives Canada Cataloguing in Publication

Bravo!: Best of Bridge cookbook: brand-new volume, brand-new recipes.

Includes index.
ISBN 978-0-7788-0220-4

1. Cookery.

TX714.B72 2009   641.5   C2009-902270-2

INDEX